# THE WORLD'S MOST MYSTERIOUS PLACES

THE EARTH, ITS WONDERS, ITS SECRETS

# THE WORLD'S MOST
# MYSTERIOUS PLACES

Reader's
Digest

PUBLISHED BY

THE READER'S DIGEST ASSOCIATION LIMITED

LONDON NEW YORK MONTREAL SYDNEY CAPE TOWN

THE WORLD'S MOST MYSTERIOUS PLACES
Edited by Toucan Books Limited
Designed by Bradbury and Williams
Designer: Colin Woodman
Written by Tim Healey

Printing and binding: Printer Industria Gráfica. S. A., Barcelona.
Separations: Typongraph srl, Italy
Paper: Perigord-Condat, France

ISBN 0 276 42217 1

FRONT COVER *The Maya people of ancient Mexico played a
sophisticated ball game in the 'ball court' at Chichén Itzá. Inset: Stone
Age Polynesians carved and erected awe-inspiring stone figures on Easter
Island in the Pacific.*

BACK COVER *A dynasty of kings ruling central Java in the 9th century
AD built the magnificent Buddhist temple of Borobodur.*

PAGE 3 *Burial chambers burrowed into the cliffs at Tana Toraja on the
island of Sulawesi are among Indonesia's most remarkable holy places.*

# CONTENTS

# EXPLORING THE UNKNOWN

*Mysterious sites of all sorts, ancient and more modern, natural and man-made, with historical or supernatural associations, have stirred people's curiosity and exercised their powers of understanding throughout the centuries.*

Hiram Bingham, the American discoverer of Machu Picchu, wrote of his discovery: 'It seemed like an unbelievable dream. Dimly, I began to realise that this wall and its adjoining semi-circular temple over the cave were as fine as the finest stonework in the world. It fairly took my breath away. What could this place be?' The fantastic lost citadel of the Incas is among the great finds of 20th-century archaeology and, though Bingham made his discovery as far back as 1911, the extraordinary ruins, dramatically sited on a precipitous Andean ridge, continue to baffle the experts.

Machu Picchu is just one of the Earth's places of mystery, sites that stir the imagination and inspire wonder in mankind and the universe. From the painted caves of prehistoric Europe to the great pyramids of Egypt, from a Viking settlement in North America to the palace of Minos on Crete, the relics of past civilisations have furnished many tantalising conundrums. But by no means all sites belong to the province of archaeology. Lourdes in France is a place of holy apparitions and miraculous healings – 6 million pilgrims visit the town every year. Tunguska in Siberia was the location of an extraordinary cosmic disaster – a Hiroshima-like blast in June 1908 that laid waste an area the size of Leningrad. Transylvania is Dracula country, a region

UNKNOWN ARTISTS  *In 1995 a cave containing around 300 prehistoric paintings of animals was discovered in the Ardèche region of France.*

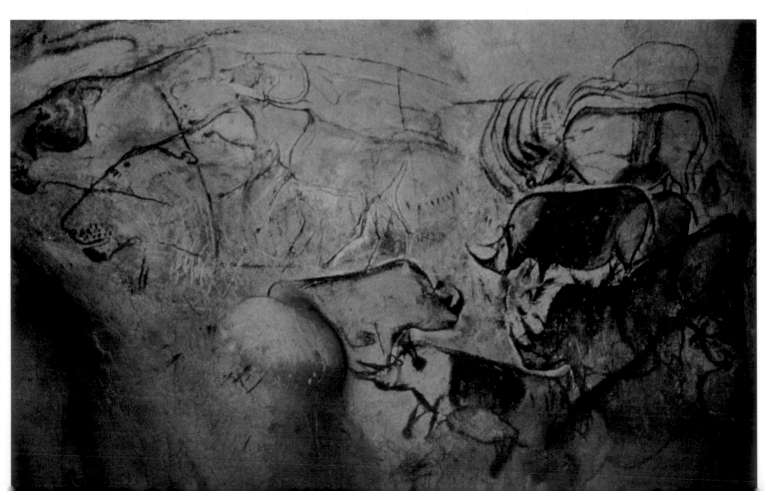

whose beautiful mountains and forests are steeped with the lore of vampires.

Sites come in such varied forms that they are hard to classify, and often the categories overlap, so a natural outcrop may be revered as a sacred site, and a prehistoric ring of stones may have paranormal associations. It is the nature of a mystery to lead into different realms of possibility.

### 'HERE BE MONSTERS . . .'

To people in past times, so much of the world was unknown that legends grew up around just about anywhere beyond the far horizon. Herodotus, the Greek historian of the 5th century BC, wrote that Arabia, the land from which his countrymen got their incense and aromatic gums, was infested with flying snakes. 'These snakes, the same which attempt to invade Egypt, are small in size and of various colours, and great numbers of them keep guard over all the trees which guard the frankincense.'

The Venetian traveller Marco Polo, in the 13th century, wrote that the men of Andaman Island in the Bay of Bengal had dogs' heads. 'I assure you that the whole aspect of their faces is that of big mastiffs. They are a very cruel race: whenever they can get hold of a man who is not one of their kind, they devour him.'

Piecing together reports from classical antiquity with more recent travellers' tales, medieval geographers imagined faraway places to be brimming with fabulous beasts and equally fantastic people. The Hereford Cathedral *Mappa Mundi*, a world map dating from about 1290, shows continents inhabited by the likes of unicorn, satyr and sphinx as well as a one-legged humanoid who uses his giant foot as an umbrella to shield himself from the sun. Other exotic humans are depicted in a 15th-century German manuscript that speaks of Indians with an eye in the centre of the forehead . . . headless Libyans with mouth and eyes in the middle of the chest . . . Sicilians with ears so large that they could fold them around their entire body . . . people with underlips so large that they could wrap them over their whole face. 'In the land of Ethiopia,' readers were assured, 'many

people walk bent down like cattle, and many live four hundred years. Many have horns, long noses and goats' feet.'

Some myths proved extraordinarily enduring. The seas, in medieval belief, were haunted by mermaids, typically possessing the head and torso of a lovely woman but fashioned below the waist like a fish. When Columbus returned from one of his voyages to America he solemnly noted in his log that he had sighted mermaids. It

**VAMPIRE HAUNTS** *Castle Bran in Transylvania presents a suitably sinister aspect. The 15th-century Transylvanian prince Vlad Dracul 'the Impaler' was an inspiration for Bram Stoker's* Dracula *(1897).*

is thought today that creatures of tropical waters, such as the dugong and manatee, which nurse their offspring in their flippers, could have been taken at a distance for mermaids cradling their young, and that in colder waters basking seals, which sometimes make an almost human wailing, might account for reports of sea maidens singing. The mythological tradition is certainly an ancient one: with or without fishtails, mermaids appear in Teutonic lore, in Greek and Roman stories of the sirens, and in even earlier Babylonian tales.

### MAULED BY LIONS, CHASED BY BEARS

Human explorers of the world have undertaken their odysseys in the name of God, conquest and commerce more than in the quest for knowledge. However, understanding has proved a greater prize than all the gold, slaves and spices that the adventurers brought home. Nothing more clearly displays the patient achievements of the truthseekers than the maps brought back by Captain Cook from his voyages to the southern seas during the 18th century.

Only a few hundred years after the medieval cartographers were sketching their unicorns and monstrous humanoids, Cook, an outstanding navigator, charted the coast of Australia with minutely exact

**MERMAID IN BORNEO** *This illustration, claimed to have been 'drawn from life', comes from an 18th-century Dutch volume. The creature depicted was said to have been caught off Borneo. 'It was 59 inches [150 cm] long . . . It lived on land for four days and uttered little cries like a mouse.'*

**MEDIEVAL WORLD VIEW** *Unicorns, dragons and other strange beings populate the Nile Delta, according to Hereford Cathedral's **Mappa Mundi**.*

delineations of bays and headlands. Where his knowledge was incomplete, he left his charts blank for others to complete in due course. The maps of Cook and contemporary cartographers survive as testaments to a new spirit of cool, scientific enquiry that would revolutionise society worldwide.

The explorers demonstrated astonishing bravery. Crossing unknown lands and seas involved every peril known to humanity: hunger and thirst; the extremities of heat and cold; fevers, diseases, wild animals and hostile peoples. Captain Cook was himself stabbed and bludgeoned to death in 1779 during a skirmish with Hawaiian islanders. Meriwether Lewis, exploring the Missouri River in the early 19th century, narrowly escaped slaughter by a rampaging brown bear. And in 1844, while travelling through the interior of southern Africa, David Livingstone was mauled by a lion who 'shook me as a terrier dog does a rat'.

The 17th-century French explorer Henri de Tonty, held prisoner by the Iroquois on the shore of Lake Michigan, listened while his captors debated whether he was to be burnt to death; one of the Indians plunged a knife into de Tonty's breast, damaging a rib near the heart, he reported after his escape. He also recalled 'a man behind me with a knife in his hand, who every now and then lifted up my hair'.

Mad with thirst in the desert east of Kashgar, Central Asia, the Swedish explorer Sven Hedin, who travelled extensively in Asia from the 1890s onwards, almost died from drinking the methylated spirits from

**GREAT EXPLORER** *In the 1770s Captain James Cook set new standards for map-making during three voyages of exploration in the south seas.*

his primus stove. Burke and Wills died of starvation in 1861 during a nightmarish attempt to cross unknown Australia. Their companion John King returned alive, but 'wasted to a shadow, and hardly to be distinguished as a civilised human being but by the remnants of the clothes upon him'.

### LOST CONTINENTS?

Jet-age communications have given tourists access to Patagonia in Argentina, land of giants, to the rose-red city of Petra in Jordan, and to once-fabled Timbuktu in Mali, West Africa. There are still a few blanks on the map – in the inaccessible rain forests of Irian Jaya and Papua New Guinea, for example,

**DOOMED JOURNEY** *Burke, Wills and King faced unknown perils when they attempted to cross Australia in 1861. Only King survived.*

where Stone Age peoples live existences barely touched by the 20th century. But in reality, Earth's last frontiers are found in the ocean depths, whose underwater mountains, canyons and abyssal plains have been revealed only very recently using echo-sounding apparatus, sonar scanning and satellite surveys. Using the latest techniques in undersea exploration, researchers have located the wrecks of the *Titanic* and the *Lusitania*, and found weird life forms flourishing beside underwater sulphur vents. They have also failed to discover places long reputed to have existed; there is no evidence in the Atlantic, for example, of the legendary lost continent of Atlantis.

The Greek philosopher Plato placed this marvellous land beyond the Strait of Gibraltar, claiming that it sank there amid violent earthquakes and floods. In fact, it is a geophysical impossibility for such a continent to have existed within the span of recorded history. Scans of the seabed reveal a great chain of underwater mountains in the mid-Atlantic, but they are rising – not sinking – as new material pours out of the Earth's interior.

Of course, land can disappear beneath the ocean. During the Ice Age a broad plain connected Asia with the part of North America where the waters of the Bering Strait now flow, and in wandering across the land bridge of 'Beringia', as it has been dubbed, the first humans colonised the

Americas. The possibility of other sunken continents absorbed many investigators. 'Lemuria', for example, was a huge, hypothetical landmass first named by the British zoologist Professor Philip Sclater in the 19th century. He and other scientists of his day had been struck by some remarkable similarities between forms of flora and fauna that flourished on both sides of the Indian Ocean although they were separated by thousands of miles of sea. The name of Lemuria was derived from the lemur and its relatives, found mainly on the island of Madagascar but also in India and on the Malay archipelago. Sclater proposed that the two areas had once been connected by a land bridge, and his notion was taken up by the German naturalist Ernst Haeckel, who used it to explain a gap in Darwin's theory of evolution. Lemuria was the cradle of humankind, the naturalist proposed. When it sank, it took with it the missing fossil link between man and the apes.

This idea also appealed to various occultists, who imagined the 'lost people of Lemuria' to be telepathic beings, or in contact with extraterrestrials. A colony of Lemurians was reported in 1932, on Mount Shasta, California, provoking excitement among enthusiasts for the paranormal.

Meanwhile, in the 20th century, between the two world wars, the notion of a lost Pacific continent called Mu also gained ground. It was proposed by an American, James Churchward, and explained the giant statues on Easter Island and the man-made islands of Nan Madol by the fact that they too had been linked by a land that sank, leaving behind the innumerable islands of Polynesia as relics of its existence.

Beringia was real enough, but the theories about Lemuria and Mu have been

**RAIN-FOREST SECRET** *In Irian Jaya, Indonesia, an ancient way of life still continues.*

**IRISH STEPPING STONES** *Contracting lava created the Giant's Causeway's uncannily symmetrical basalt columns.*

disproved by recent research into the undersea topography of both the Indian and the Pacific Ocean, made possible by 20th-century technology.

## EARTH'S UNSEEN ENERGIES

Mysteries do not need a supernatural dimension: the truth about the Earth's natural landforms, above and below sea level, can so amaze us that it needs no whiff of the occult to enhance its fascination. The forces that cause the continents to drift, mountains to rise and volcanoes to spit fire, are awesome enough. To gaze upon the coloured lakes of Keli Mutu in Indonesia, peer into the stalactite caverns of Mammoth

Cave in the United States or explore the weird coastline of the Giant's Causeway in Ireland is to experience nature's strangeness in supremely dramatic form.

However, the human instinct for the supernatural has not died, even in the age of science. Ancient and mystical associations still draw multitudes to Uluru (Ayers Rock) in Australia, Mount Fuji in Japan, the Delphi known to the Greeks and the Drachenfels of German legend. Ghosts, say believers in psychic phenomena, continue to walk the precincts of the White House and the Tower of London.

Should all supernatural lore connected with mysterious places be dismissed? Clairvoyants sometimes speak of 'emanations' – invisible imprints left behind by events at a particular place. Analogies are often quoted from the physical world: the air may stay warm in a room after the embers in the fireplace are cold, and a fragrance of roses may linger after the flowers are withdrawn. Is it impossible, then, to believe that the tormented psychic energy released by a murder might leave a disquieting aura to linger about the place of death? Or that an atmosphere of sanctity might survive in a church where people have hymned and prayed for generations?

Believers in paranormal phenomena have frequently likened psychic energies to the unseen currents that appear to guide dowsers to water and migrating birds to their breeding grounds. Birds are thought to navigate by the pattern of the Earth's magnetic field, and dowsers to react to it too, when their muscles cause a Y-shaped

twig to twitch as they pass over an underground stream.

Many people believe that the builders of Europe's prehistoric megaliths used dowsing skills when siting their giant monuments. In China, certainly, a sensitivity to invisible earth currents formed part of the art of *feng shui*, of key importance when sites for temples and palaces were chosen – it is still used in the siting and positioning of office blocks in Hong Kong. Some people remain sceptical of dowsers' claims, but their art – still little understood – has long and enduring traditions.

Scientists have their own limitations and, like other groups, cling to comfortable orthodoxies. The 18th-century French chemist Antoine Lavoisier denied in the face of all the evidence that meteors could fall from the heavens, because 'there are no stones in the sky'. A 29 lb (13 kg) meteorite which landed on a car in New York in 1992 proves him wrong. The history of science is littered with similarly dogmatic assertions, and the fact is that we do not know everything about the Earth's energies.

The phenomenon of ball lightning perfectly illustrates the point. UFOs, ghosts,

FIREBALL *The door of Blythburgh church bears the marks made, some say, by a devilish black dog. Equally mysterious ball lightning (inset) may have been the cause.*

fairies, will-o'-the-wisps and other similar curiosities have been attributed to floating balls of light that have often been reported by startled observers around the world. 'Ball lightning' appears not only outdoors but indoors, too: floating around farmers' barns, housewives' kitchens and once, as reported by the journal *Nature* in November 1969, down an airliner's aisle. Seen by night, hovering over graves or flitting across marshes, the luminous orbs could easily be taken for spirits and so provide rational insights into supposedly haunted places.

At the churches of Blythburgh and Bungay in the English country of Suffolk, ball lightning has even been invoked to try

to account for supposed diabolic intrusions. The events transpired during a thunderstorm on the morning of Sunday, August 4, 1577. At Bungay the devil in the form of a black dog reportedly rushed through the church killing and injuring several members of the

PSYCHIC TREMORS *Dowsers can locate water, mineral seams and even underground obstacles in the way of pipelines.*

congregation. At Blythburgh, some 7 miles (11 km) away, a similar event occurred: two men and a lad were killed and many others 'blasted'. To this day, a door in the church at Blythburgh shows black marks said to have been made by the manifestation. The phantom black hound is a common figure in East Anglian ghost lore, and it is possible that the frightened congregation might have hallucinated the canine details. The real culprit, many researchers have suggested, was ball lightning discharged during the thunderstorm.

But what is ball lightning? The term has no true scientific meaning, for lightning follows a forked path (sheet lightning is a reflection of forked lightning elsewhere). It is as mysterious in its way as phantom hounds, and many scientists doubt its existence. Their disbelief was tested in August 1982, however, when a ball of lightning struck Cambridge University's Cavendish Laboratories, where many Nobel prize-winners have worked. Eyewitness accounts from the staff were collected by the distinguished physicist Sir Brian Pippard and forwarded to *Nature*. 'It was most remarkable,' said Pippard. 'It went through a window as a secretary was closing it and passed by, without singeing her hair.'

Would scientists now recognise ball lightning? 'Well,' said the physicist, 'none of us actually saw it . . .'

# PUZZLES FROM THE PAST

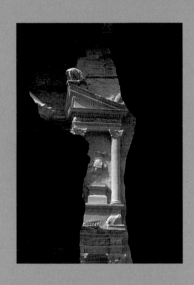

HIDDEN BEAUTY *A narrow gap reveals a glimpse of Petra's architectural glories.*

IS EGYPT'S GREAT PYRAMID ALIGNED TO A CONSTELLATION IN THE NIGHT SKY? WHY DID NATIVE AMERICANS LAY OUT THE GREAT SERPENT MOUND? WHO BUILT THE LOST AFRICAN CITY OF ZIMBABWE? WHAT DROVE A POLYNESIAN PEOPLE TO CARVE THE GIANT HEADS ON EASTER ISLAND? MYSTERY SHROUDS MANY SITES, AND THE QUESTIONS THEY RAISE CANNOT ALWAYS BE ANSWERED WITH CERTAINTY. BUT THAT DOES NOT STOP ENTHUSIASTS FROM TRYING TO PENETRATE THE SECRETS OF PLACES THAT RANGE FROM THE SITE OF THE WRECK OF THE TITANIC, LOCATED USING HI-TECH UNDERSEA EQUIPMENT MORE THAN 2 MILES (3 KM) BELOW THE SURFACE OF THE ATLANTIC, TO THE FABLED CITY OF TIMBUKTU IN WEST AFRICA.

MYSTIC GAZE *Easter Island's statues stare across the Pacific.*

# LOST REALMS, FABLED TREASURES

*Historical sites laced with fantasy and legend have long attracted archaeologists and adventurers alike. Lost or abandoned cities and buried treasure are made all the more alluring by the clouds of mystery that surround them.*

Ancient ruins bring out the romantic in most people. Standing in the shadows of a timeworn colonnade, peering through jungle foliage at the relics of an abandoned citadel, or exploring the crumbling battlements of a medieval castle, one feels the promptings of nostalgia for a heroic past that may never have existed. The fantastic rose-red city of Petra was not built by dream weavers but by hard-headed desert traders. The site of ancient Troy is surprisingly small when measured against the city of classical legend. The wizard Merlin probably did not cast spells of magic at the court of King Arthur – and if Camelot existed, it is likely to have been a tussocky hill topped by a timber fort mud-trampled by Dark Age warriors.

These relics of past civilisations, however, hold the keys to an understanding of human society today, and present many a fascinating enigma. Where did the builders of Mohenjo-Daro acquire their advanced skills of town planning over 4000 years ago? How extensive were Viking settlements in America? Who built the curious walled islands of Nan Madol in the Pacific? What caused the downfall of ancient Crete, civilisation of the labyrinth and the Minotaur?

The legends associated with mysterious places have a charm in themselves, and for fortune hunters none hold more interest than the tales of buried treasure linked with various sites scattered around the globe. Gold, revered as the 'sweat of the sun' by the ancient peoples of the Andes, was the lure that drew treasure-hungry *conquistadores* to the New World. The same voracious appetite for the yellow ore has more recently beckoned the

**WHEN THE DESERT BLOOMED** *Rich crops of corn, beans and squash were once stored in the D-shaped 'Great Houses' of Pueblo Bonito.*

hopeful to sites as different as Oak Island, Nova Scotia, and the small French village church at Rennes-le-Château, which, it is alleged, contains clues to the whereabouts of the treasures of the Temple at Jerusalem.

## PUEBLO BONITO, NEW MEXICO

*RUINS OF A HUGE, MULTISTOREY BUILDING IN THE DESERT WASTE.*

The D-shaped complex covers almost 3 acres (1.5 ha) of ground in the sagebrush desert of Chaco Canyon. Its intricate floor plan of circles and rectangles is so strange to the human eye that it might almost have been designed by a Martian. But the building material is local: tight-fitting sandstone blocks form the beautifully shaped walls, which dwindle gradually in thickness with each successive storey. Once, the curved complex contained 650 rooms rising five floors high. Who built it? When did they vanish – and why?

Pueblo Bonito is one of nine multi-storey constructions in Chaco Canyon. Known as 'Great Houses', the extraordinary buildings are connected by crisscrossing roads that sometimes end at stairways, cut into the surrounding cliffs to help people to get in and out of the canyon. Vegetation is sparse today, and it is hard to conceive of human communities thriving in this forbidding corner of New Mexico. Yet the Chaco once teemed with activity.

It is now known that the Great Houses were built by the Anasazi people, ancestors of today's Pueblos, who irrigated fields in the canyon to grow corn, beans and squash. Construction began around AD 900, using building stone quarried from the surrounding cliffs. Floors and roofs, however, called for timber, which was cut from forests as much as 50 miles (80 km) away. It is reckoned that 215 000 trees were used, and how they were transported is an enigma. But the greater mystery is the function of the huge circular chambers, known as *kivas*, found at all sites. Pueblo Bonito began as a semicircular cluster of rooms and *kivas*, and expanded over the centuries to reach completion in 1140. By that time it had acquired 37 *kivas*, of which the largest is an

underground chamber about 52 ft (16 m) in diameter.

The Great Houses themselves were once thought to have been giant apartment blocks, housing up to 5000 people. Recent research, however, indicates that only a small percentage of rooms was designed for habitation, with hearth and living room. 'Household suites' in each building probably accommodated no more than 100 people. Archaeologists believe that many of the rooms were designed for crop storage, and that the *kivas*' purpose was ceremonial as it appears that fires burned in them.

Pueblo Bonito and its neighbouring Houses are not seen today as self-contained townships isolated in the desert. Instead, they are thought to have been massive crop storage depots, where crowds gathered at seasonal intervals for ceremonial purposes. The Anasazi road system was much more extensive than once thought, stretching from New Mexico into parts of Colorado, Utah and Arizona. Since levels of rainfall varied considerably around the region, a good year's crop in one place might be matched by a bad year's crop in another. At the heart of the road network, the Great Houses stored surplus food for distribution to needy communities.

Times of poor rainfall throughout the region destroyed the system's delicate

**STONE AGE TOWN** *This tower (top) is among the remains of a settlement that flourished at Jericho 10000 years ago. Archaeologists have also dug up clay masks (above) of early inhabitants.*

balance: around the middle of the 12th century drought devastated crops everywhere. And that is probably why the Anasazi suddenly abandoned the Great Houses to migrate, famine stricken, from the Chaco and melt away into America.

## JERICHO, ISRAEL

*INTRIGUING RUINS OF WHAT HAS BEEN CALLED THE OLDEST TOWN ON EARTH.*

'Shout; for the Lord hath given you the city,' Joshua told his people in the Old Testament. According to the Bible, the Israelites only had to raise their voices in

LOST WORLD  *Bright Aegean sunlight falls on ruined Knossos (above), palace of the Cretan kings. A fresco from the 16th century BC (left) shows Cretan youths tempting fate in the sport of bull leaping.*

order to bring down the walls of Jericho. Historians believe that Joshua's sack of Jericho was an event that happened some time between 1400 and 1250 BC. Jericho has a further claim to the world's attention – it may well be the oldest town in the world.

The site lies about 1 mile (1.5 km) from the modern town of Jericho, in the valley of the River Jordan. A pocket of green in an arid land, the area owes its fertility to a benevolent stream gushing from a rock called Elisha's Fountain. The ancient settlement grew up beside the rock and is a huge mound today, formed by the accumulated ruins of successive cities built on the remains of earlier ones. Archaeologists have sifted through the many layers of Jericho's history, and have found some remains at a depth of 70 ft (21 m).

The lowest levels date back to 8000 BC, in the New Stone Age, when nomads first abandoned the wandering, hunting life in favour of farming. This was a momentous development that would wrench humanity out of the shadows of prehistory because

farmers need settled communities. With settlement came building skills, specialised crafts, the need for written records and the rule of law – civilisation had arrived.

The first builders of ancient Jericho erected rounded huts that resembled tents made of mud brick. These were succeeded by rectangular houses with smartly plastered rooms grouped around courtyards. Still at the threshold of settled life, the inhabitants had no pottery vessels yet, but clay models of animals suggest worship of a fertility cult. And a particularly enigmatic find has been a group of heads, modelled in plaster on real human skulls. Uncannily lifelike, they are the oldest examples of human portraiture in existence, showing the features of people who died 10 000 years ago.

Ancient Jericho was ringed by a huge town wall, implying that envious or marauding neighbours had their eyes on the inhabitants' possessions. Over the thousands of years that followed, the city gained strategic importance as the gateway from the desert to more prosperous Palestine. Its mighty walls were breached and rebuilt not

once but time and time again. In 1560 BC Jericho was destroyed (probably by the Egyptians) and was again rebuilt. But the town that rose on the rubble has been almost wholly obliterated as a result of erosion and human interference. It is an irony of this biblical city that, although infinitely older ramparts have been uncovered, no remains of the walls that were assaulted by Joshua survive.

## KNOSSOS, CRETE

*LEGENDS OF THE MINOTAUR CLING TO THESE ANCIENT COURTS.*

In Greek mythology, Crete was the island of King Minos, a tyrant who kept the monstrous Minotaur – a beast with a bull's head on a man's body. The creature inhabited a maze known as the Labyrinth, where it was fed on Athenian youths and maidens who were paid in tribute to Minos each year in revenge for the slaying of Minos' son by the Athenians.

Until the beginning of the 20th century the Crete of Minos was assumed to belong to the realm of pure fantasy. However, excavations at Knossos between 1899 and 1935 by the British archaeologist Sir Arthur Evans revealed the lost world that underlaid the myth.

Here was Europe's first civilisation – a society much older than Greece – whose people traded with the pharaohs' Egypt. Their great palace at Knossos was an extraordinary architectural feat, honeycombed with rooms, courtyards and corridors, and with bathrooms and flush lavatories among its comforts. Colourful frescoes show athletic youths and women in flounced skirts with coquettishly low-cut bodices, as well as bull sports in which performers executed thrilling and dangerous handsprings over the animal's horns.

The Labyrinth seems to have taken its name from the symbols of the double-headed axe (*labyros*, in Greek) that appear throughout the palace. Legends of the Minotaur were no doubt inspired by Crete's bull cult. But mysteries still linger about this vibrant civilisation. Its script, for example, has never been deciphered. Its form of government is not still understood; the curious absence of war-like images and bearded figures of authority has suggested to some historians that Crete may have been a matriarchy – a society ruled by women.

Above all, the downfall of Minoan Crete remains a subject of controversy. Around 1450 BC, this apparently peaceful and likeable society suffered some form of catastrophic destruction. Did civil war or rebellion break out? Was Crete overrun by warriors from Mycenae on the mainland? Or did a gigantic volcanic eruption wreak the damage?

It is known that the nearby island of Thera (Santorini) suffered a cataclysmic eruption in 1450 or 1500 BC. Millions of tons of rock were blasted from the heart of the island to spew thick clouds of volcanic ash over the surrounding islands. Tidal waves crashed over eastern Crete, causing some damage at Knossos and other palaces.

By the time that the local people recovered, and Knossos was rebuilt, Crete was under Mycenaean occupation.

Garbled reports of the eruption may have contributed to the myth of the lost city of Atlantis. It was Plato, the Greek philosopher, who created the legend when he wrote of a vast island power that had once flourished beyond the Strait of Gibraltar. Bulls and elephants roamed over the island, which had a circular walled city at the centre, and a majestic palace with hot and cold baths.

Crete does not lie beyond the Strait of Gibraltar, nor did elephants ever roam its shores. But the bulls and the baths hint at a connection, as does the finale to Plato's tale: 'There were violent earthquakes and floods, and in a single day and night of misfortune . . . the island of Atlantis disappeared into the sea.'

A memory of the Thera detonation? No one can say for certain. The people of ancient Crete wrote a fascinating chapter in the story of humanity, but it is a chapter with many blank pages.

## NAN MADOL, POHNPEI

*WHO BUILT THESE SEA-SPLASHED PACIFIC RUINS? WHEN? AND WHY?*

Sharks and rays haunt the blue canals lapping at the walls of the extraordinary man-made islets of Nan Madol. Likened by one explorer to a 'deserted Venice of the Pacific', Nan Madol consists of 90 artificial islands, bounded by walls up to 30 ft (9 m) high. The walls were built from many-sided basalt columns. Laid crisscross like the timbers of a log cabin, the columns have

CRYSTALLINE WALLS *Basalt logs form the ramparts of ancient man-made Pacific Islands.*

been cemented by coral masses to form resilient, darkly glimmering structures.

Lying among the Federated States of Micronesia, the island of Pohnpei is a lush, bejungled upthrust in the Pacific. Nan Madol, in the south-west, is in an isolated spot, and the first detailed account of it does not seem to have been written until 1853. In that year a shipwrecked Irishman, James O'Connell, explored the 'stupendous ruins' with a terrified islander who believed them to be haunted by spirits.

According to local tradition, wizards created Nan Madol by sorcery. Among outsiders, the ruins have been variously identified as the fortress of Spanish pirates, a relic of the lost prehistoric continent of Lemuria in the Indian Ocean, and the capital of a forgotten island empire. Scientific investigation has produced only sketchy results. Piecing together the scanty evidence, archaeologists have concluded that Nan Madol was built about 600 years ago, probably as some sort of ceremonial

AFRICAN CITADEL
*The granite walls and Tower (right) of Great Zimbabwe recall a lost Bantu civilisation.*

centre. It was clearly an important enterprise, for the basalt columns were brought from the island of Jocaz, 15 miles (24 km) away, towed on rafts and hauled with some difficulty to and from the shore. However, the building methods were very basic and the makers left no inscriptions – nothing suggests the hand of a people more advanced than the Micronesians themselves.

## GREAT ZIMBABWE, ZIMBABWE

### *WERE THESE RUINS OF AN AFRICAN SOCIETY KING SOLOMON'S MINES?*

Why would anyone want to build a granite tower 30 ft (9 m) high and solid throughout, without doors, windows or stairway? The ruins of Great Zimbabwe pose many

questions. Sprawling over 60 acres, the ancient citadel rises from green and fertile lands lying between the Zambezi and Limpopo rivers.

In 1871, the German geologist Karl Mauch came upon the huge, overgrown stone walls, and was so awed by their grandeur that he could not believe them to be the work of an African people. These, he reasoned, were replicas of the palaces of King Solomon and the Queen of Sheba, built by travellers from the north. Perhaps, it was even suggested, Zimbabwe was the site of King Solomon's Mines, the fabled source of fantastic riches alluded to in the Bible. Treasure hunters flocked to the area. By 1900, prospectors had registered 114 000 mining claims in the district.

Patient detective work by archaeologists has painted a very different picture of Great Zimbabwe, however. The first hilltop settlement on the site has been dated by carbon-14 analysis to the 2nd or 3rd century AD, and this was long before the towers were built, making nonsense of any connection with the Old Testament. In reality, the walls and buildings are hundreds, rather than thousands, of years old and appear to have been the work of the Mbire – a Bantu-speaking people whose skilled miners, craftsmen and traders formed part of a sizable African nation during the European Middle Ages.

Major construction work began at Great Zimbabwe around AD 1200, and there are two outstanding buildings, both walled by granite bricks laid without any form of bonding. Instead, they were precisely and skilfully shaped by the Bantu workmen so that they fitted neatly together.

The first is a hilltop structure nicknamed the Acropolis. It stands at the edge of a 90 ft (27 m) precipice – a maze of drystone-walled buildings merges into the natural contours of the rock to form an imposing fortress. The Acropolis looks down on a second notable building, the Great Enclosure, whose massive curved walls are 4 ft (1.2 m) thick, and soar to 35 ft (11 m) in places. Inside is a complex of passages, rooms and podiums whose precise purpose is hard to guess. Among them is the baffling Tower referred to above. If this was a lookout post, signalling spot or observatory for stargazers, why not provide a stairway?

Historians have interpreted Great Zimbabwe as the focus of a flourishing commercial network. To the west lay the goldfields of Matabeleland; to the east were trading ports on the Indian Ocean. The walled enclosures perhaps began as stock pens for cattle – an important unit of exchange – and grew as business flourished. The buildings' monumental size was probably designed to impress trading partners with the power of the inhabitants, who numbered over 3000 people at one time. However, their society was in decline by the beginning of the 16th century when food and timber reserves were exhausted. The people began to drift away, seeking better pastures elsewhere, and their citadel became a ghost town. Centuries later it was as puzzling to local people as it was to the first Europeans who stumbled across its creeper-clad ruins.

## SILBURY HILL, ENGLAND

*EUROPE'S LARGEST PREHISTORIC MOUND REMAINS A PUZZLE.*

Standing in a hollow, not far from an immense stone circle at the village of Avebury in Wiltshire, is one of the great enigmas of the British landscape. Silbury Hill is a colossal man-made mound that rises to 130 ft (40 m) from a base that covers 5 acres (2 ha) of ground.

The flat-topped cone, likened to an upturned pudding basin, was begun more than 4000 years ago and remains the biggest man-made hill in Europe. About 36 million basketsful of clay, turf and chalk are reckoned to have been needed, heaped up by teams of some 500 people working continuously for ten years. If Silbury Hill were placed in the centre of London, it would almost fill Trafalgar Square, reaching to three-quarters of the height of Nelson's Column. And yet, to this day, archaeologists have no idea why it was built.

According to one local tradition it is the grave of a legendary King Sil, buried within in golden armour, upright on horseback. And the first investigators, who sank a shaft in 1776, also assumed that it was some sort of burial mound, perhaps containing treasure. However, though they dug down from the summit to the heart of the hill, they found neither corpse nor relics. Several excavations have been undertaken at intervals since, but no grave or treasure has been found.

One thing has been made evident through excavation, however: the prehistoric makers of Silbury Hill built with exceptional care to ensure that their structure did not collapse. A central mound of clay and flint was covered by cut turf, and layers of chalk rubble were built up around

STRANGE STRUCTURE *No burial chamber exists to throw light on the purpose of Silbury Hill.*

it. Retaining walls of chalk blocks held the rubble in place at every level. The result is a sturdy and shapely structure that has withstood four millennia of natural erosion.

Many theories have been advanced to explain the hill's purpose, for example as a giant astronomical calculator, or a symbolic representation of the winter goddess.

Silbury Hill is clearly conspicuous from the megalithic complex at Avebury, and must surely have had some function associated with it. Did it serve as a podium on which priests or priestesses staged solemn rites? No one can say. Roughly contemporary with Wiltshire's world-famous monument Stonehenge, Silbury Hill is even more of an enigma.

## THE HYPOGEUM, MALTA

*A PREHISTORIC ECHO CHAMBER IN MALTA'S UNDERGROUND LABYRINTH.*

Workmen cutting into the rock of a building site in the Maltese town of Paola in 1902 suddenly burst into an immense underground complex carved from solid limestone. Here, archaeologists later explored a labyrinth of rooms that stretched three storeys into the ground. Reaching down to a depth of more than 100ft (30m), the complex consisted of cavities, natural and manmade, with pillars, niches and door lintels cut into the soft limestone by people using picks made of antler or horn. The extraordinary site was dubbed the Hypogeum, after the Greek for 'under the ground'.

There are temple buildings with similar architectural features such as pillars and lintels elsewhere in Malta. They were constructed between 3500 and 2500 BC by the island's Stone Age inhabitants, who worshipped the Earth Mother, represented in statuettes of a very fat woman. Sheep and cattle were sacrificed to her, and fragments of their bones were hidden in holes in the temple walls. The Hypogeum is remarkable, however, for being built entirely underground. The bones of 6000-7000 people were recovered from one of its chambers, indicating that it was as much a tomb as a temple. The Hypogeum has other enigmatic features. In a room nicknamed the Oracle

Chamber there is a cavity just large enough to contain one person. If a man sits inside and speaks in a normal voice the sound is carried by resonant acoustics all round the chamber (a woman's voice is too high in pitch to create the same effect). This, it has been suggested, was where oracles were consulted; answers given by hidden priests would have sounded eerily impressive.

But the idea is entirely speculative. No one knows quite what ceremonies took place in the Hypogeum: whether it was first

**SUBTERRANEAN WORSHIP** *Malta's Hypogeum (above) was a vast underground temple and tomb. Here the island's Stone Age inhabitants worshipped a plump Earth Mother goddess (left).*

conceived as tomb or temple. What is known is that at some time around 2500 BC, Malta's sacred sites were suddenly abandoned. Perhaps stricken by drought, famine or disease, the island's population vanished at the same time, leaving posterity with only tantalising glimpses of one of Stone Age Europe's most sophisticated societies.

## L'ANSE AUX MEADOWS, CANADA

*WAS THIS THE LOCATION OF VINLAND – FABLED SITE OF VIKING AMERICA?*

A needle and a spindle whorl might seem paltry finds for an archaeologist. Yet these two items, from a dig at L'Anse aux Meadows in Newfoundland, have been compared with the treasures of Tutankhamun in importance. For the bone needle and the soapstone spindle were of Norse origin, offering the first concrete evidence that the Vikings had travelled to North America.

Speculation about Viking America was first aroused by the Norse sagas. Handed down by word of mouth, these tales were committed to writing in the 14th century and told how Greenland Vikings sailed westward and discovered a strange new land. One, named Leif Ericsson, was said to have set out in AD 992 with a 35-man crew and made landfall at a fertile country where the winters were mild, the salmon bigger than the Norsemen had ever seen, and grapes grew wild. This place he named Vinland, after its vines. The Norsemen built huts there, mounted further expeditions and both traded and did battle with natives who went armed with bows and arrows.

Until recent times sceptics had dismissed the Vinland sagas as myth. But

NORSEMEN'S AMERICA *Turf huts like this would have been home to 11th-century Viking settlers in Newfoundland.*

excavations by the Norwegian archaeologist Helge Ingstad in Newfoundland challenged the sternest doubters. On the wide green plain of L'Anse aux Meadows, backed by

### CLAMS FROM VINLAND

Clam shells found on a Danish beach have provided further evidence that the Vikings reached America, it was reported in 1993. The clams, of the North American species *Mya arenaria*, were dated to 1245. Clams only float in their larval stage, and could not have been carried across the Atlantic by ocean currents. The likelihood is that they were brought by Norse navigators who used them for provisions.

woods and low hills, he uncovered an ancient settlement that closely resembled a typical small Norse farm complex, like those of western Greenland. Eight dwellings, dating from AD 1005-1025, were excavated, with a smithy where bog iron was smelted (a process unknown to Native Americans). The needle and spindle whorl clinched the argument. Not only did they indicate that Norsemen had reached the New World; they also

suggested that Norse women had come too, as spinning was women's work. The intention, it seems, was to settle the land.

L'Anse still presents mysteries, however, for it lies at a latitude too chilly for vines. If Vinland produced grapes, the country must have been farther south: in Maine or New Hampshire, perhaps. Some scholars believe that Leif Ericsson's settlement has yet to be discovered, and that L'Anse was founded by a later party led by the Norseman Thorfinn Karlsefni. Alternatively, the sagateller may have got things wrong: the 'grapes' may simply have been wild berries, which do grow in Newfoundland in profusion. Certainly, Norwegian Vikings fermented a kind of wine from the wild berries that grew near their own farms at home. Whatever the truth, L'Anse remains a place of abiding fascination: one small Norse fingerprint placed on the map of the Americas 400 years before Columbus set sail.

## PETRA, JORDAN
*A RUINED ROCK CITY THAT GLOWS ROSE RED IN THE DYING SUN.*

Visitors from the east approach through the sinister Siq – a dark gorge whose sheer walls soar to spectacular heights overhead. This valley of shadows twists between the mountains for more than 2 miles (3 km), narrowing at some points where the cliff walls almost meet to black out the sky. Beyond this menacing defile, however, an extraordinary vision bursts upon the eye: of gigantic rock-cut façades that flash and sparkle in the harsh midday light, flaming at sunset with sumptuous crimsons. This is Petra, 'a rose-red city, half as old as time', in the words of a Victorian poet, the Reverend John Burgon.

Who would build a city of such beauty in this desolate place? Petra was the capital of a people who were known as the Nabataeans, nomads in origin,

DESERT TRADE *Once a scene of bustling commerce, the market place at Petra, like the rest of the city, is now deserted except by tourists. In Roman times and before, Petra had a commanding position on the main north African trade routes. When the trade left, the city died.*

ROCKFACE WONDER *The splendid façade of Petra's Khazneh, dating from the 2nd century BC, leads into a temple hewn out of the living rock.*

death in 323 BC of the Macedonian conqueror Alexander the Great, one of his successors tried to win Petra for the empire he had inherited. The attack was not wholly successful, however, and as the general's Phrygian army returned from Petra burdened with prisoners and booty they had managed to capture, the Nabataeans burst from the wilderness and slaughtered much of the force.

With the spread of Roman power in the Middle East the Nabataeans continued for some time to hold on to their territory and their trade. In AD 106, however, they could no longer resist the might of the Roman army, and Petra was finally incorporated in the Roman Empire by the Emperor Trajan. The Nabataeans flourished for another century or so before a decline set in. Merchants were now switching their trade to easier and safer routes. In Petra the markets began to dwindle and the inns to close down. Around the city, desert sands trespassed on the neglected fields.

During the centuries that followed, Christian monks, Moslem invaders and Crusader knights all passed through the crumbling city, but its inhabitants eventually vanished and the buildings collapsed. Only tomb façades, a temple, monumental gateway, colonnaded street and theatre have survived. Hand-carved from pink sandstone they recall the splendour of a desert people who once found themselves at the crossroads of the world.

## BERINGIA, ARCTIC SEA

*A LOST LAND BRIDGE THAT WITNESSED EPIC MIGRATIONS IN PREHISTORY.*

Only a comparative trickle of water divides Asia from the Americas. The Bering Strait is just 55 miles (89 km) wide. The shallow channel takes its name from a Dane, Vitus Bering, who explored it in 1728 for the Russian tsar Peter the Great. In doing so,

who emerged from the deserts of northern Arabia around 400 BC. A hundred years later their fortress settlement at Petra was becoming an important trading post, controlling much of the caravan trade that passed along dusty desert routes leading from the southern coast of Arabia to the Mediterranean shore. Petra commanded

the region's main water supply, the Wadi Musa, while the mountains around provided excellent lookout posts for sentries. Here the merchants leading camel caravans laden with perfumes, incense and spices need fear neither thirst nor surprise attack.

The Nabataeans grew rich from the desert traffic, and powerful too. After the he proved a previously unknown fact: that Asia and North America are two entirely separate continents.

But they have not always been so. The evidence indicates that during the last Ice Age the sea level fell, revealing a land connection between the continents. To gaze across the grey waters today is to gaze across the site of a vast sunken walkway. Beringia, as the land is known, was the stage-setting of one humanity's greatest and most mysterious dramas, for it was over this bridge that bands of nameless Ice Age hunters first came from Asia to colonise the immense, empty landmass of the Americas. No humans had been there before.

When did this happen? There is plentiful evidence that people had reached the Americas 12 000 years ago, towards the end of the last Ice Age. But whether they were there earlier remains one of the most hotly discussed topics in archaeology. Some American archaeologists have argued that their land was inhabited more than 100 000 years ago, on the basis of bone tools found at sites in the Yukon. Their dating, however,

**THE FIRST AMERICANS** *Ice Age migrants from Asia cross the land bridge at the Bering Strait.*

is controversial. In 1986, a group of French archaeologists working in north-eastern Brazil came upon a rock shelter where prehistoric people had made a hearth. Radiocarbon tests on the charcoal suggested that people had been living there some 30 000 years ago, and that date is now accepted by many (but not all) for the first colonisation of South America.

Some experts suspect that the Americas' first settlers came in three separate streams, probably driven by a search for land as large areas of the northern hemisphere were covered in ice. The earliest, who worked their way down North and Central America and reached the southern end of South America around 9000 BC, may have belonged to the same ancient racial group as the Australoid races (today's Aborigines). They were followed by later migrations of Mongoloids: that is the racial group of the American Indians and Inuit, who have the same physical characteristics as the peoples of central Asia and northern China.

Fifteen thousand years ago the great thaw began, and by 10 000 years ago the climate was as warm as it is today. Floods caused by melting water drowned the Bering land bridge, locking the prehistoric settlers into their New World. There was no way back – boats do not seem to have been

invented at that time – and the first Americans were left to work out their destiny in isolation from the mother continents of the Old World.

## MACHU PICCHU, PERU

*A LOST CITY OF HEARTSTOPPING BEAUTY – WHY DID ITS INHABITANTS VANISH?*

Inca warriors of 15th-century Peru built an empire that incorporated some 10 million people. Sprawling from the southern borders of what is now Colombia, far south into central Chile, their realm measured some 2700 miles (4300 km) from end to end. A road network ran the length of the Inca empire, crossing some of the world's most hostile terrain in the heart of the great mountain range of the Andes. Yet for all its splendour, Inca civilisation lasted for little longer than a century. Already damaged by civil war, it was destroyed by the Spaniards in the 16th century.

Among all Inca sites, none is more remote or mysterious than Machu Picchu. Perched on a precipitous ridge among dramatic Andean crags, the forgotten citadel was brought to the world's attention by the US archaeologist Hiram Bingham in 1911. In the high jungle fastness he found white granite walls and dizzying agricultural

**INCA STRONGHOLD** *The builders of Machu Picchu terraced perilous Andean heights to shape their citadel. Animals may have been sacrificed on this stone (above).*

terraces, with stairways and water channels carved directly from the rock so that the whole complex appears to grow organically from its ridge.

The stonework of the buildings displays the astonishing precision that was characteristic of Inca masonry. Huge blocks are fitted together with mortarless joints so fine that a knife blade cannot be slipped between them. Beautifully crafted trapezoidal doors and windows graced some of the buildings. With a central plaza, royal palace and sun temple, Machu Picchu is in some ways a typical Inca city. But the extraordinary mountain top setting called for special ingenuity from the builders. And it poses the obvious question: why build a city here?

Stunned by Machu Picchu's beauty, Hiram Bingham imagined that it was a centre for sun worship, built high up in the mountains to be close to the shining heavens. It was, he believed, a lost city called Vilcabamba: the last refuge of the Inca ruler, to which the defeated king Manco Inca is said to have retreated in 1536. However, modern scholarship indicates that

Vilcabamba lay far away, at the edge of the Amazon rainforest. And though Machu Picchu certainly contained several places of worship, it was not large enough to constitute a religious capital. Instead, it is thought to have been a strategic site commanding the valley of the Urubamba River below. The Inca capital Cuzco lay 70 miles (113 km) upstream, and the mountain citadel would have provided a strategic view of advancing enemies.

The Spaniards knew nothing of Machu Picchu – mysteriously, the town was abandoned shortly before they arrived. There is no evidence of violent overthrow, though a mass flight from some invading tribe cannot be ruled out. It is also possible that the community fell victim to an epidemic. The cause of its desertion remains a subject for conjecture – perhaps the puzzle will never be resolved.

## HISSARLIK, TURKEY

*DO THE RELICS OF HOMER'S TROY LIE AMONG THESE MANY-LAYERED RUINS?*

According to legend, the abducted Helen of Troy possessed a face so lovely that it launched a thousand ships. The warrior king Agamemnon led a Greek force to recover the captive beauty, and after a ten-year siege the Greeks seized Troy by hiding men inside a wooden horse that the Trojans dragged into their city. The Greek warriors then destroyed Troy and sailed home across the wine-dark sea. Related by the poet Homer, the story of the Trojan War is among the best known of all Greek legends. But was it more than fantasy?

The Greeks themselves recorded the existence of Troy as historical fact, and the idea did not die in later times. Among the believers, the 19th-century German archaeologist Heinrich Schliemann had dreamed since childhood of discovering the lost city. From Homer's description of a hilltop citadel in the middle of a windswept plain, Schliemann came to believe the likeliest site to be Hissarlik, a 164 ft (50 m) high mount in Turkey, at the southern end of the Dardanelles strait. Ignoring the derision of scholars, he began excavations in

1870 on what turned out to be a bewildering mass of ruins, later identified as nine consecutive cities, built one on top of the other.

On June 14, 1873, the archaeologist was rewarded with a fantastic treasure haul of 8700 golden artefacts including cups, vases, bracelets and ear-rings. The dazzling prize was a diadem of 16 000 pieces of solid gold. Schliemann crowned his young wife with it, crying, 'You are wearing the treasure of Helen of Troy.'

In fact, Schliemann was mistaken. The diadem dated back to a period 1000 years before Helen's time. But much more is

GATEWAY TO TROY *The south gate at Hissarlik dates from the time of the war that probably inspired Homer's* Iliad. *Schliemann adorned his wife Sophia (left) with the jewels of Troy.*

known now than in Schliemann's day about the early history of the ancient Greeks. Scholars believe that the legendary Trojan Wars were based on an actual conflict between the Greeks and the Trojans in the 13th century BC, and that the German pioneer was right – Hissarlik is thought to be the site of Homer's Troy.

Among the nine strata of the mount, the legendary city has been identified as level six (Troy VI). This was a walled town dating back to the 13th century BC, with a substantial Pillar House near the south gate. Scholars believe that an earthquake badly damaged the city, and then around 1260 BC Troy was sacked and burnt. Much weaponry has been recovered from the site, including arrowheads, lanceheads and a knife of the type used by Bronze Age Greeks.

A wealth of evidence supports the notion that Hissarlik was Homer's city – except for one detail. The Troy of legend was a mighty citadel. Archaeology has uncovered quite a modest settlement: walled, certainly, but with an estimated population of no more than 1000 people. Did thousands more Trojans live in now-vanished wooden houses that lay outside the stone walls of the city? Did Homer use poetic licence to exaggerate Troy's grandeur? Or is it just conceivable that the real Troy was elsewhere, and still remains to be discovered?

## RENNES-LE-CHÂTEAU, FRANCE

*DOES THIS CHURCH OFFER CLUES TO THE LOST TREASURE OF JERUSALEM?*

A statue of the demon known as Asmodeus greets any visitors who enter the village church at Rennes-le-Château, and a mysterious moneybag appears in a fresco at the west end of the building. These are just two of many curious features that lend credence to the lore surrounding the place. For the moneybag hints at wealth and

Asmodeus was the legendary guardian of the treasure stolen from the great Temple at Jerusalem.

The village lies near Toulouse in the Languedoc region of southern France. During renovations to the church in 1891, the village priest, a man named Saunière, discovered coded parchments hidden in one of the hollow pillars supporting the altar stone. With help from churchmen in Paris, the manuscripts were deciphered and revealed references to a number of local landmarks as well as to Zion (Judaea) and to treasure. Mention was also made of a Frankish monarch Dagobert II, a ruler of the Merovingian dynasty who was murdered in the late 7th century.

His son later fled to Languedoc, and is said to have brought with him many of the dead king's valuables. Following up clues from the manuscript, Saunière did in fact bring various long-buried Merovingian relics to light. But he did more than that. Five years after discovering the manuscripts, the priest started spending money on a big scale, buying land and building villas. He explained to his bishop that the money had been given to him by some wealthy people whose identity he could not divulge.

Inevitably speculation was rife. Had the priest, a poor man, discovered a cache of Frankish gold hidden, perhaps, in one of Languedoc's many mountain caves and underground passages? Was it even the lost treasure of Jerusalem? Was this the wealth of ancient Judaea, plundered from the temple at Jerusalem when the Romans sacked the city in AD 70? Placed on display in Rome, the splendid ornaments were

SINISTER FIGURE *Father Saunière, parish priest of Rennes-le-Château until 1917, erected this statue of the demon Asmodeus, using mysteriously acquired wealth.*

seized by barbarian Visigoths when they overran the imperial capital in AD 410. The Visigoths subsequently swept across France and established themselves there, only to be supplanted in due course by the Franks.

Saunière died in 1917 without shedding further light on the affair. But he did spend fair amounts of his wealth on restoring the church; it was he who installed the guardian Asmodeus near the door and had the enigmatic fresco painted. Were they clues for researchers or practical jokes? A magnet for fortune-seekers ever since, Rennes-le-Château guards its secrets carefully.

## TOWER OF BABEL, IRAQ

*A MUD-BRICK STUMP EVOKES THE SPLENDOUR OF A BIBLICAL SKYSCRAPER.*

'And they said, Go to, let us build us a city and a tower, whose top may reach unto heaven. . . .' The words were spoken by Noah's descendants in the Old Testament story of the Tower of Babel. Using brick for the walls and slime for mortar, it is said, they

*CONDEMNED BUILDING
King Nebuchadnezzar II
started to restore this
staged pyramid at Babylon
in 604 BC, but the original
was built many centuries
earlier and may have
inspired the biblical Tower
of Babel. The brickwork
bull (above) was recovered
from the site of Babylon.*

and was acted out every year when the king slept with the high priestess. However, scholars doubt whether the tower-top provided the appropriate stage-setting for the ceremony. The riddle of the summit chamber is unlikely to be solved now, for the tower itself has vanished and only its stump survives to recall the skyscraping ambitions of its builder.

## CADBURY CASTLE, ENGLAND

*DID KING ARTHUR ONCE HOLD COURT
ON THIS TURF-TOPPED HILL-FORT?*

'Many-tower'd Camelot' was how the poet Tennyson described the ancient capital of King Arthur and Queen Guinevere. The very name of the court summons fairytale images of soaring medieval turrets and battlements, but if the great king really existed it must have been before the Middle Ages. The legends of the Knights of the Round Table were told by the 12th-century English chronicler Geoffrey of Monmouth, but they refer to a king who lived hundreds of years earlier. If Arthur was a historical character he probably lived around the late 5th or early 6th century AD. Historians have seen him as a war leader of the ancient Britons. After the Romans had left English shores, he perhaps survived as a champion of the Romano-British way of life, rallying resistance against the Anglo-Saxon invaders.

And where was his capital, Camelot? Despite the claims of various Welsh, Scottish and Northumbrian sites, most researchers believe that it was a stronghold in western England, strategically placed to defend the Britons' territories further west. Windsor, named by one 14th-century chronicler as the site, was ill suited to this function. The spectacular ruins of Tintagel Castle, on a rugged promontory of the Cornish coast, have also been associated with Camelot, but probably lay too far west. In the 15th century, Sir Thomas Malory more plausibly identified Camelot with Winchester in Hampshire. But for many, the likeliest site is a hummocky earthwork hill-fort known as Cadbury, in Somerset.

Half-hidden, as it is approached, by the trees on its flanking slopes, the turf-topped

proceeded to build so presumptuous an edifice that the enraged Lord confused their language. The builders could no longer understand one another, the tower was abandoned, and the people were scattered across the face of the Earth, babbling in their different tongues. This, it is said, was the origin of the world's languages.

Babel was in fact Babylon, a city of grandeur and infamy to the Bible writers, who denounced it as 'the mother of harlots and abominations of the Earth'. Babylon, lying on the Euphrates, was the heart of an empire that once rivalled Egypt. The Greek writer Herodotus described its gigantic ramparts, bronze gateways, palace, temple and colossal tower. Babylon, he wrote, 'surpasses in splendour any city of the known world'.

Floods, wars, revolts and invasions all ravaged Babylon at one time or another, and the city today is a vast field of ruins. These were first excavated in 1899 by a German team lead by the architect Robert Koldewey, and among the multitude of finds – relics of the magnificent main gate, bulls and lions in brightly painted glazed bricks – few have provoked more fascination than

the huge, square foundations of what is known as the Tower of Babel.

The building stood alongside the Temple of Marduk, chief god of the Babylonians, and took the form of an immense ziggurat, or staged pyramid, soaring some 295 ft (90 m) above the city. The tower known to the Old Testament writers was the work of Nebuchadnezzar II, who rebuilt an edifice, begun hundreds of years earlier, that had fallen into disrepair. Nebuchadnezzar was a mighty ruler who restored Babylon to her former glory, defeated the Egyptians, destroyed Jerusalem and brought the Jews into Babylonian captivity.

The king began restoring the Tower in 604 BC, creating a seven-storey building of sun-dried bricks, ascended by steps and ramps. It was crowned at the top with a room whose purpose remains mysterious. Was it a temple? Or an observatory for stargazing priests?

Herodotus believed that it was a bedchamber for sacred fertility rites, where a god came to spend the night with a woman of his choosing. It is known that a Sacred Marriage of the city's god and goddess was an integral feature of Babylonian religion,

fort covers some 18 acres (7 ha), commanding huge views over the surrounding countryside. Cadbury's summit is defended by four, and in places five, ramparts with ditches between them. Excavations have shown that the main defences were erected in the Iron Age, but major fortifications of timber and dry stonework were added around AD 500, in the historical Arthur's lifetime, making this the most impressive fortification of the era. Evidence of a large feasting hall has also come to light – was it once graced by a round table?

Cadbury was well sited to fend off West Saxon assaults from the Channel coast. The hill-fort was referred to as Camelot by the 17th-century writer John Selden, and the ghost of the name also survives in Cadbury's two nearby villages of Queen Camel and

**DREAM CASTLE** *Earthwork ramparts swirl around Cadbury Castle, said to be the original Camelot.*

West Camel. Nobody has yet proved that Cadbury and the 'many-tower'd Camelot' were one and the same place. But among all the sites that have claimed the title, there is no stronger contender.

## LAKE GUATAVITA, COLOMBIA

*THIS SACRED ANDEAN LAKE IS STEEPED IN THE LORE OF EL DORADO.*

By any standards, Lake Guatavita is mysterious. Lying among steep, scrub-cloaked hills in the Colombian Andes some 31 miles (50 km) north-east of Bogotá, the lake is an immaculate circle in shape. There is no lava or ash to suggest that its origin was as a volcanic crater, nor is there any evidence of iron or nickel to indicate that the round basin was formed by the impact of a meteor. The lake simply exists as a perfectly circular mirror for the sky. And it is a magnet for treasure-seekers, too.

For Lake Guatavita is widely regarded as the place that triggered the legend of El

Dorado. The name was given to a region fabulously rich in gold, rumours of whose existence hastened the Spanish conquest of South America. In the 16th century, warlike conquistadors mounted expeditions in search of the realm. But the likelihood is that El Dorado ('the Gilded One') was a man, not a country, and that Lake Guatavita was the place where his rites were observed.

The Gilded One was a ruler of the local Muisca people who coated himself with gold dust to make offerings at Lake Guatavita. The Muisca (or Chibcha) were skilled goldworkers who venerated the precious ore as the sacred metal of the sun god. An eyewitness account of 1636 describes how the heir to the throne was stripped naked and anointed with resin before being powdered with gold dust. Then he went out on a raft with his chiefs, all richly decked out with plumes, gold crowns and ornaments. Incense was burned, trumpets and flutes played and crowds sang on the bank as the raft moved out into the

lake. On reaching the centre, the Gilded One and his chiefs tipped shimmering piles of gold into the water in order to appease a monster that was said to haunt its depths. From the banks, his people tossed more treasures into the lake.

The voracious Spaniards extorted quantities of gold from the Muisca, and one of their number employed a labour force of 8000 Indians to cut a great notch in the rim of the lake, in an attempt to drain its waters

## SEARCH FOR EL DORADO

The English courtier and adventurer Sir Walter Raleigh mounted two expeditions to find El Dorado, in 1595 and 1616. His second search, along the Orinoco, was made following his imprisonment in the Tower of London for treason. The mission was a failure and he returned to certain execution.

off. The lake level did in fact drop enough for many emeralds and gold discs to be recovered from the shore. Investigation in the 20th century has yielded more valuable relics. And for any sceptic still doubting the rites of the gilded king, further evidence emerged in 1969. In that year, two farm workers looking for a lost dog in a cave near Bogotá discovered an exquisite model raft fashioned from solid gold. It showed eight oarsmen rowing with their backs towards the towering figure of a chief – surely El Dorado himself.

## TIMBUKTU, MALI

*A REMOTE CITY EMBODYING ALL THE*
*ROMANCE OF AFRICA.*

For Westerners, the very name summons images of an end-of-the-earth city – a place of ultimate mystery and allure. To the Victorians it was so remote as to seem almost a myth; the poet Tennyson likened it

RITES OF EL DORADO *Members of the Muisca people, presided over by a prince powdered with gold dust, tip gold into the waters of Lake Guatavita.*

to 'a dream as frail as those of ancient time'. Where is Timbuktu? And how did it acquire its mystique?

Originally founded in the 11th century as a Tuareg camp on the southern edge of the Sahara, the town developed in medieval times into a centre for caravan routes crossing the desert, eventually achieving prominence in the 14th century as a market for gold from the jungles of West Africa. The precious metal, which fed royal mints throughout much of Europe, was exchanged in Timbuktu for salt – weight for weight. It might seem a poor bargain to us, but salt then was a valued commodity, vital for preserving meat in the tropical, saltless lands south and west. Culture followed commerce; by the 16th century, Timbuktu was flourishing not only as a market but also as a great centre of Islamic learning.

In 1550 a Moor, Leo Africanus, wrote a description of the city that fired European imaginations: 'The rich King of Timbuktu hath in his possession many gold plates and sceptres, some whereof are 1300 ounces [37 kg] in weight, and he keeps a well-furnished and splendid court . . . Whosoever will speak to the king must prostrate himself at his feet and then taking up dust must sprinkle it upon his own head and shoulders.'

However, the trans-Saharan trade was controlled by coastal Arabs who guarded the heart of Africa against European penetration, so Timbuktu long remained a fabled but shadowy city. In 1824 the Geographical Society of Paris offered a prize of 10 000 francs to the first person to bring back to Europe an eyewitness account of it. Two years later a Scottish officer, Gordon Laing, managed to enter Timbuktu but was hacked to death by Moslem Tuaregs while making his way home.

The prize fell in 1828 to a penniless, uneducated French adventurer, René Caillé, who went in Arab disguise and succeeded in getting back after a 2000 mile (3200 km) journey across the Sahara. The Timbuktu Caillé found was a disappointment. 'The city presented, at first view, nothing but a

**MYSTERY CITY** *This mosque testifies to Timbuktu's days of fabled wealth as an important centre of trans-Saharan caravan routes.*

Timbuktu has long since declined in wealth and importance, a strange and intriguing aura still lingers about this city of stucco mosques, pale stone houses and crumbling mudbrick buildings mazed by narrow alleys. It is not easily reached; air transport or a four-wheel-drive vehicle provide the best means. The gold may have gone, but the mystery endures.

## MOHENJO-DARO, PAKISTAN

*RIDDLE OF A PLANNED CITY BUILT 4000 YEARS AGO.*

Standardised houses on ruler-straight streets, with municipal sewers for sanitation and sit-down lavatories in many homes . . . they all sound like features of a modern urban development. Yet this is Mohenjo-

Daro, one of the world's most ancient cities, which arose on the Indian subcontinent around 2400 BC. Excavated in the 1920s, the ruins astonished archaeologists. This was not because of any colossal statuary or temples – for Mohenjo-Daro had none. Nor did the experts come upon any colourful frescoes; homes were notable for their complete lack of decoration. What caused the amazement was evidence of incredibly advanced town planning by men with a totalitarian degree of control over their workforce. To this day, no one knows who they were.

Mohenjo-Daro is among the largest of nearly 100 similar towns built around the Indus Valley in present-day Pakistan, and occupied an area of roughly 1000 sq yd (800 m²). The towns were all created to a similar pattern, even sharing a uniform type of brick. Though the society flourished at the same time as ancient Egypt and Sumer, much less is known of its origins; the mystery of the Indus Valley civilisation is that it seems almost to have sprung ready-made into existence – and on a vast scale. With a 3 mile (5 km) perimeter, Mohenjo-Daro was a gigantic metropolis for its day. A dozen broad avenues divided up the

mass of ill-looking houses, built of earth.' Warring tribes had caused a decline, and the gold fields were largely exhausted.

Many would perish, either at the hands of the Tuareg or from disease, in trying to emulate the Frenchman. And although

residential blocks according to a strict grid, and the settlement also had a citadel built on a rectangular, man-made mound, where archaeologists have discovered the remains of a great granary and assembly hall.

Here, too, was a huge public bath, which was probably used for ritual bathing. The inhabitants were evidently very fastidious, for as well as homes boasting private baths and brick-built lavatories the city had an elaborate drainage system, with sewers that had manholes at intervals to permit maintenance workers to clear out waste.

Historians can only guess that some kind of elite ruled the Indus Valley civilisation, for no evidence of a god-king comparable to Egypt's pharaoh has come to light. The people were in trading contact with ancient Sumer, and it is conceivable that the diffusion of writing and other ideas from Mesopotamia triggered the rulers' sudden modernisation programme. However, the Indus people developed their own unique method of writing, and their script offers no clues to modern scholars, as it has never been deciphered.

The civilisation's decline was sudden and dramatic. Possibly the River Indus changed its course, causing disastrous floods, crop failures or desertification. Perhaps the inhabitants also provoked a crisis by felling too many trees from the forests around (timber supplied the fuel for baking bricks). Whatever the underlying causes for the decline, the death blow was clearly dealt, around 1700 BC, by human enemies. Skeletons recovered from the streets of

PLANNED TOWN *A sophisticated grid layout belies the ancient origins of Mohenjo-Daro in the Indus valley. The script (right) is still undeciphered.*

Mohenjo-Daro display evidence of sword cuts and axe blows to the head. The massacre victims probably fell prey to invading Aryans – ancestors of the modern Hindus – or to mountain tribesmen forced south by pressure from them.

Bodies were left to rot where they had fallen, shrouded only by the dust and silt that was to cloak them in the coming

centuries of neglect. When modern archae-ologists uncovered the ruins, they came upon a civilisation whose existence had not even been suspected.

## OAK ISLAND, CANADA

*WHO BUILT – AND BOOBY-TRAPPED –*
*THE INCREDIBLE MONEY PIT?*

The whole fascinating mystery might have been dreamed up for a boy's adventure magazine. In 1795, three local youths, ex-ploring tiny Oak Island in Mahone Bay, Nova Scotia, came upon a clover-covered depres-sion in the ground that suggested someone had buried something there. Fetching tools and helpers from across the bay, they began to dig, and uncovered a man-made shaft sealed at intervals with oak platforms. The youths got 30 ft (9 m) down before lack of resources caused them to abandon their quest, and it was nine years before the next assault was made on the shaft.

This time it was tackled by a properly equipped consortium. At a depth of 90 ft (27 m) the searchers unearthed a flat stone inscribed with a message that, once de-ciphered, read 'ten feet below two million pounds are buried'. Eight feet further down their picks struck an obstruction some took for a treasure chest. They went home that night rejoicing, but at dawn the next morning were horrified to discover that the Money Pit, as it was dubbed, had filled up with 65 ft (20 m) of water. No amount of pumping could lower the level.

In response to the calamity, a wholly new shaft was dug parallel to the first, reaching 110 ft (34 m) below ground. But no sooner did the searchers angle a tunnel towards the bottom of the Money Pit than they were met by a violent flood that sent them scrambling back to the surface. Whoever had dug the Money Pit had also booby-trapped it. In later years, researchers located flood tunnels dug from Smith's Cove on Mahone Bay that were filled by the Atlantic's high tide.

Further assaults on the treasure were made by companies using rotary drills, bulldozers, power winches and turbine pumps. New discoveries, of two drilled

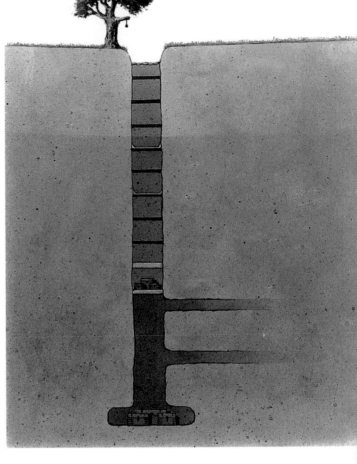

MONEY PIT *Amazing ingenuity was lavished on Oak Island's treasure shaft.*

rocks and an enigmatic stone triangle, suggested further treasure caches, and Oak Island became riddled with boreholes, shafts and craters. From the 1950s, thousands of tourists were coming annually to view the scarred island's wonders, and by the 1980s they were visiting two separate museums run by rival treasure companies. Not a single doub-loon has been recovered from Oak Island, yet fortunes have been lost on treasure-seeking. Theories on its origins have been wide ranging, from a UFO base to a repository for lost manuscripts of the plays of William Shakespeare – or for the Holy Grail.

Did a pirate hide his booty here? Carbon-14 dating on timbers from the Money Pit indicates that it was built sometime between 1525 and 1625, but researchers have doubted whether buccan-eers could have achieved such an engin-eering wonder. A disciplined military or naval force is more likely. Searching continues on the battered little island.

## QMRAN, ISRAEL

*DESERT CAVES THAT YIELDED NEW*
*LIGHT ON CHRISTIANITY.*

Treasure for archaeologists does not always come in the form of gold and jewels. One of the most important finds of modern times was made in 1947, when a Bedouin boy called Mohammed chanced upon a hoard of ancient scrolls that were wrapped in decaying linen cloth and had been de-posited in clay jars. Covered with bits of strange writing, the scrolls seemed to the young herdsman and his friends to possess little value, but when the manuscripts found their way into the hands of antique dealers they caused unheard-of controversy

and excitement. For despite early doubts about their authenticity, scholars found that they dated back to the time of Christ – and told of a religious community in the Holy Land whose traditions bore resemblance to those of the first Christians.

The Bedouins at first kept the source of the scrolls secret, but within two years it had been identified as a series of limestone caves in the barren cliffs near Qmran, north-west of the Dead Sea. In 1952 French and American researchers mounted an official investigation. The experts sweltered in cramped grottoes where temperatures were over 38°C (100°F), but the haul was impressive: from 11 caves, fragments of some 600 manuscripts were recovered, dating from 250 BC to AD 70.

This, it appeared, was the library of a Jewish sect known as the Essenes, whose monastery site lay on a nearby plateau. The sect's austere lifestyle was described by the Jewish historian Josephus, who once visited a community. The brethren wore plain linen loincloths, it seems, and ate frugally and in great quietness. The Essenes believed

**CAVE SECRETS** *The forbidding cliffs at Qmran served as hiding places for the Dead Sea Scrolls, manuscripts that provide evidence about a community contemporaneous with the early Christians.*

themselves to be a community of the elect, and anticipated an apocalypse that they alone would survive. Much of their time was spent studying scriptural law; the Dead Sea Scrolls include texts of many Old Testament books, commentaries, prayers and psalms as well as material relating to their community and the forthcoming Day of Judgment. It is thought that the manuscripts were hidden in the caves for safe keeping during the Jewish revolt of AD 66-70, when the Romans laid Qmran waste.

Was there a direct connection between the first Christians and Qmran's elect? There were marked differences between the two groups; for example Christ's followers went out into the world, preaching among Jews and Gentiles, while Qmran's brethren were an inward-looking, exclusive sect. Yet there are some curious echoes of Essenism in early Christian practices. Both groups renounced earthly riches. The Qmran faithful shared a sacramental meal that has been likened to the Christian celebration of the Last Supper. The Essenes practised a ritual cleansing comparable to Christian baptism; indeed, the River Jordan, where John the Baptist baptised the faithful, is not far from Qmran, and John has been suggested as a possible link between the two groups. John spoke of a coming Messiah, and scrolls from the caves also allude to Messianic figures who would usher in the apocalypse. In 1991 new studies

of the scrolls revealed some references to a 'Dying Messiah' with mention of 'piercings' and 'wounds'. Christ Himself may not have been an Essene (as commentators once speculated), but the caves at Qmran have provided fascinating insights into the setting in which Christianity arose.

## HAUSLABJOCH GLACIER, AUSTRIA

*IN AN ALPINE ICE RIVER, A 5000-YEAR-OLD BODY CAME TO LIGHT.*

In 1991 the world was astonished by reports of a prehistoric 'Iceman' trapped in a remote glacier in the Otztaler Alps, on the border between Austria and Italy. The glaciers that grind their way down through the folds, ridges and pinnacles of this great range have occasionally yielded up the bodies of mountaineers who had succumbed to lonely deaths in modern times. But this body was different: reports described the well-preserved corpse of a man holding a copper-headed axe, whose tattered leather footgear was stuffed with hay. A stone knife was found, too, along with a belt pouch and a quiver of fur with flint-tipped arrows. On his back he had worn a fur pannier with a U-shaped hazel-rod frame. Tests revealed that the body was of a man aged perhaps 35-40, who died some 5300 years ago.

The equipment he carried offered fascinating clues to the nature of everyday life in the late Stone Age. A birch-bark container held grass and maple leaves wrapped around charred embers. Fire-making was a time-consuming business among hunter-gatherers, who would carry with them some embers from the hearth of their last camp (as nomads still do to this day). Though the man appeared virtually naked, traces of his clothing had survived, including remnants of loincloth,

## CARBON-14: THE PROBLEM SOLVER

Many an ancient mystery has been solved – and many a myth exploded – by radiocarbon dating. This provides archaeologists with their chief means of determining the age of organic remains such as wood, plants and bone. The technique was developed in 1955 by an American physicist, William F. Libby, and hinges on the fact that all living things absorb small quantities of the isotope carbon-14 from the air around. When a living thing dies, the level of carbon-14 starts to fall at a set rate. So, by measuring the level of carbon-14 lost, an object's age can be estimated.

Conventional radiocarbon dating has its limitations and is not very reliable with dates reaching back more than 30 000 years, However, a recent invention called the Accelerated Mass Spectrometer has pushed the limits back further. It works by separating and detecting atomic particles of different mass, and can date objects from 70 000 years ago. Another advantage is that the sample required is over 1000 times smaller than in the

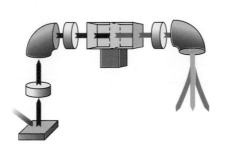

DATING THE PAST *Carbon atoms are sped through an Accelerated Mass Spectrometer, using high-voltage electricty. Then they pass through a magnetic field, allowing carbon-14 to be separated out.*

conventional technique. A single seed or a smudge of charcoal from a prehistoric hearth is sufficient for a date. New techniques have shed invaluable light on the Ice Age communities, the age of the Neanderthals and the prehistoric settlement of the Americas. But radiocarbon dates can only tell when a living thing was alive, and not when it was turned to human use. For example, bone tools, alleged by some American archaeologists to be 100 000 years old, have been recovered from the Yukon. However, even if the controversial date is accepted for the bones, it does not mean that the tools were from the same period. Bone is preserved almost indefinitely by freezing – prehistoric hunters could have come upon them at almost any time and turned them to their use.

leggings and cap, with fragments of matted grass indicating he had worn a kind of straw coat as protection against the elements. His feet were wrapped in leather packed with grass for warmth; the footgear recalls that of present-day Lapps. In addition, the man's body was marked by tattoos, probably done with a bone needle and charcoal. They take the form of small sets of parallel lines on his back, wrist and ankles, as well as cross marks inside the right knee and beside the left Achilles tendon. Medical examination indicates some degeneration in the bones of back, knee and ankle joints; it may be that the Iceman suffered from aches and that the tattoos were done for therapeutic purposes – branding and puncturing have often been used for treatment in folk medicine.

What was he doing so high in the frozen Alps? Threshing remains in his ember carrier show that he had some sort

ICEMAN *This Neolithic hunter, mummified by the enfolding ice, was recovered from an Austrian glacier in 1991.*

of contact with a settled farming community, but a copper axe was a prized item in Neolithic times, and it has been suggested that he may have been a specialist prospector for metals looking for ore deposits. Others have explained his apparently lonely calling by proposing that he was a priest enduring a period of solitude in the mountains. A more plausible explanation is that he was an itinerant hunter or herdsman who frequented the high pastures above the treeline. Some disaster may have occurred in his village – a family feud, or an attack by warlike neighbours – prompting him to take refuge in the inhospitable heights. If so, was he alone, or was he with companions who left him when he died?

## AMARNA, EGYPT

*CAPITAL OF EGYPT'S RENEGADE PHARAOH, LOST FOR OVER 3000 YEARS.*

It was one of the strangest events in world history. Shortly after coming to the throne, the pharaoh Amenophis IV swept aside the

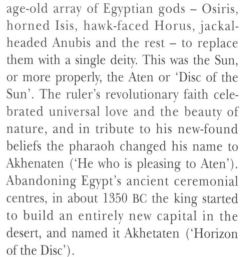

**SUN WORSHIPPER** *All images of Akhenaten and his queen Nefertiti (left) were destroyed or buried to expunge the memory of the heretical pharaoh.*

age-old array of Egyptian gods – Osiris, horned Isis, hawk-faced Horus, jackal-headed Anubis and the rest – to replace them with a single deity. This was the Sun, or more properly, the Aten or 'Disc of the Sun'. The ruler's revolutionary faith celebrated universal love and the beauty of nature, and in tribute to his new-found beliefs the pharaoh changed his name to Akhenaten ('He who is pleasing to Aten'). Abandoning Egypt's ancient ceremonial centres, in about 1350 BC the king started to build an entirely new capital in the desert, and named it Akhetaten ('Horizon of the Disc').

Until recent times historians knew virtually nothing of these events, for Egypt's high priests and other traditionalists had been so outraged by them that when the heretic died they sought to erase every trace of Akhenaten's memory. While the old gods were restored to their niches, statues of Akhenaten were smashed and his name was hammered from inscriptions. If any reference was made to his reign it was alluded to as the 'era of the rebel'. His new capital was destroyed, rubble was dispersed and the temple foundations were buried under a layer of cement. Covered by desert sands, the ruins slept undisturbed until their discovery by European Egyptologists more than 3000 years later.

The site lies near modern Tell el-Amarna, about 200 miles (322 km) south of Cairo, on a sandy plain flanked by a natural amphitheatre of cliffs. Something in the setting clearly made a deep impression on the pharaoh, for it had few natural advantages, lying on barren land at some distance from the Nile's banks. Akhenaten nonetheless felt its sanctity, for in a carved inscription in the cliffs he vowed never to leave this hallowed ground.

It was in the 19th century that archaeologists began to uncover the ruins with their groundplan of temples, palaces, villas and workshops. Some spectacular finds came to light: while excavating a sculptor's studio, German archaeologists discovered the now-famous painted bust of Akhenaten's queen, Nefertiti, which ranks among the greatest treasures of Egyptian art. Freed of traditional constraints, artists of the Amarna period generally expressed a new naturalism in their works, and stone carvings have yielded some vivid pictures of the royal family's daily life. The king and queen are often seen dandling their children on their knees in unmistakably affectionate domestic scenes. Unmistakable, too, is the pharaoh's curious physique: broad-hipped and paunchy, with drooping shoulders and elongated face. Doctors have suggested that Akhenaten suffered from a condition known as Frohlich's syndrome, resulting from a malfunction of the pituitary gland.

Was he a saint or a madman? Or was he, as some Egyptologists believe, a reactionary using a traditional sun cult to reinstate autocratic kingship and break the power of the priests? The stones of Amarna answer only with their ancient silence. What can be said, however, is that Akhenaten was a man of extraordinary spirit – a spirit so strong that, for a time, the whole pantheon of Egyptian gods counted as nothing against his decrees.

## COCOS ISLAND, COSTA RICA

*DOES A FORTUNE IN GOLD STILL LIE CONCEALED ON THIS TREASURE ISLAND?*

'Oxen and wain-ropes would not bring me back again to that accursed island; and the worst dreams that ever I have are when I hear the surf booming about its coasts, or start upright in bed, with the sharp voice of Captain Flint still ringing in my ears: "Pieces of eight! Pieces of eight!"'

So wrote Robert Louis Stevenson, in the final lines of *Treasure Island*. The classic tale is thought to have been inspired by the real-life mystery of a small and remote Pacific isle, some 300 miles (480 km) southwest of Costa Rica.

The Cocos Island enigma begins in 1821 when South American rebels rose in revolt against their Spanish overlords, laying siege to Lima, capital of Peru. Fearful for their wealth, and for the Cathedral's riches, the city's nobility had their treasures stowed aboard a brig called the *Mary Dyer*. The vessel was English, but her captain,

Thompson, had a reputation as an honest trader. Loaded with gold, jewelled caskets, cedarwood coffers, sacred bones and precious ornaments, the treasure ship set sail from the port of Callao with an escort of six soldiers. However, within a few days the gold-hungry crew had murdered the guards, fed their corpses to the sharks and struck out for Cocos Island. There, in a cave, they hid the bulk of the loot – including a spectacular effigy known as Our Lady of Lima, a life-sized statue of the Virgin Mary wrought from solid gold.

The mutinous crew were eventually arrested in Panama, where only Thompson and his Mate, Forbes, escaped execution, on the promise that they lead the Spaniards back to the treasure. Returning to Cocos, however, the two miscreants escaped their guards and hid in the jungle until the Spaniards gave up the search. The fugitives survived on the island for a year before being rescued by a passing ship. So far as is known, neither Thompson nor Forbes ever returned to Cocos Island, but the Captain did pass on a map, with instructions on how to find the cave. Many attempts to recover the Treasure of Lima followed, with false maps being circulated to mislead rivals.

A Newfoundland sailor, John Keating, is reputed to have found the cave and taken $110 000 from it in gold while moving portions of the treasure to a new location

on the island. Others have been less successful. A German, George Gissler, devoted 20 years of his life to fruitless fortune-hunting on Cocos. A Victorian admiral, Henry Palliser, landed 300 sailors on the island and made them dynamite, tunnel and dig for the treasure – all at the expense of the British taxpayer. In 1926 the world land-speed record-holder Sir Malcolm Campbell added his name to the list of fortune-hunters. Among dozens since, one of the most recent was the British actress Moira Lister. In 1989 she went in search of a legendary cache of silver said to have been hidden on Cocos by a Portuguese pirate named Benito. However, her hi-tech metal-detecting equipment found nothing.

The Cocos mystery is clouded by the fact that the island is volcanic and prone to earthquakes, which have destroyed landmarks and caused cave-blocking rockfalls. Add to this the passing of documents from hand to hand, dying words and deliberate deceptions, and the puzzle becomes ever more baffling. The surf booms on around the island coasts – after more than 170 years, Our Lady of Lima still awaits her discoverer.

# ENIGMA AT STONEHENGE

Among the huge megaliths loom-ing dramatically against the sky-line at Stonehenge are some 80 blue-grey stones that form two incomplete rings in the middle of the monument. Known as 'bluestones', they are volcanic in origin and have no business being on the chalk downland – they are known to come from the Preseli mountains in south-west Wales. The distance is about 240 miles (386 km), and the bluestones weigh up to 7 tons each. Textbooks have long taught that the prehistoric builders must have brought them most of the way by water, floating them on rafts or barges around the coast of South Wales, then shipping them across the mouth of the Severn and up a network of rivers to leave themselves only a short overland haul to the site of Stonehenge itself.

A plausible theory – but is it true? Among the multitude of megalithic mon-uments scattered across western Europe there is no evidence elsewhere for large stones being transported for more than 3 miles (5 km) or so. Indeed, some scholars doubt that human effort was involved at Stonehenge; in 1991 the geologist Dr Richard Thorpe proposed that the blue-stones were formed from 'erratics' – rock debris left on Salisbury Plain by the retreat of giant glaciers during the Pleistocene era.

The issue is still a subject of debate, illustrating precisely how little is known about the largest and most complete megalithic monument in Europe. Standing on its bare plain, the great stone circle has provoked astonishment at least since the Dark Ages when the Saxons gave it its name (Stonehenge means 'hanging stones'). Some medieval writers referred to it as the Giants' Dance, while in the 12th century the chronicler Henry of Huntingdon named it among the wonders of Britain; here, he wrote, 'stones of an amazing size are set up in the manner of doorways . . . nor can anyone guess by what means so many stones were raised so high, or why they were built there!'

One early legend explain-ed them as the work of the wizard Merlin, while later theories proposed variously that they were relics of a Druid temple, a prehistoric sports stadium, royal palace, battle ring, burial place, covered market, ley centre, UFO land-ing base or the sanctuary of the people of Atlantis. In the 17th century, the architect Inigo Jones, who studied Stonehenge at the request of King James I, concluded that it was a Roman temple.

Who built Stonehenge, and why? Recent research indicates that the monument was dev-eloped in three separate phases over a period of about 1700 years. Work started in 2750 BC – before the Great Pyramid was begun in Egypt – when a Neolithic people laid out a

CROSSPIECE *Each giant lintel was linked to its supports by a ball-and-socket joint cut into the stone and visible on top of the upright stone rising to the left.*

circular bank and ditch marked out with 56 equally spaced holes in the ground (known today as Aubrey holes after the antiquarian John Aubrey, who first noticed them). The Aubrey holes appear to have contained cremation burials, and may have symbolised entrances to the underworld. The 'heel stone' at the entrance to the site was erected at this stage.

The second phase of the construction began around 2100 BC and was the work of the 'Beaker Folk', so called because they buried pottery beakers with their dead. These were the people who erected the two bluestone rings, one inside the other, in the centre on the earth bank, and they also built a wide avenue leading north-east to the River Avon.

The final part of the work was carried out by early Bronze Age people. Between 2000 and 1100 BC they repositioned the bluestones within a colossal arrangement of sandstone uprights. Averaging 30 tons in weight and 16 ft (5 m) high, the giant sandstone blocks were connected by lintels (crosspieces) shaped in a slight curve so that when fitted together they made a circle running around the top, with carefully crafted ball-and-socket joints linking the lintels to the upright stones for stability.

**AERIAL VIEW** *Stonehenge's outer circle of sandstone megaliths has a diameter of about 100 ft (30 m).*

Scholars have pictured the builders hauling the immense stones on sledges, using oak logs as rollers and levers, and also stacking logs up in towering decks to raise the blocks into the correct position. The biggest stones were used to construct the sandstone trilithons – the groups of three stones, two upright with a lintel linking them across the top, that make up the inner horseshoe. These weigh 50 tons and would have required 800 men to haul them.

The uplands around are littered with standing stones, barrow tombs and other monuments. However, Stonehenge is the supreme achievement, and most archaeologists today agree that its purpose was religious, and probably also astronomical.

It seems to have been connected in some way with the observation of heavenly bodies, for people noticed long ago that on midsummer day the Sun can be seen from the centre of the stone circles rising almost exactly over the 'heel stone'.

With the help of a computer, the US astronomer Gerald Hawkins has proposed a number of other important alignments: sightlines for the rising and setting of both the Sun and the Moon throughout the annual calendar, as well as more complex astronomical calculations that include the movement of the constellations and the prediction of eclipses.

The findings remain controversial, however, and nothing whatever is known of the ceremonies that may once have been enacted here. Awesome in its partial ruin, Stonehenge still yields only glimpses into the secrets of its past.

**MEGA-MYSTERY** *Sunrise over Stonehenge's inner circle is an intensely atmospheric moment.*

# STRANGE RELICS

*With levers, ropes, sledges and ramps men of ancient times raised colossal megaliths, pyramids and statues that astonish the eye and baffle the mind to this day. Other relics, smaller in scale, provoke equally tormenting questions.*

Sites such as Tollund Fen owe their aura of mystery to the human relics recovered from them and the detective puzzles that they pose. Who were the victims? What do their remains tell about their lives?

Other sites seem mysterious only because their purpose has been forgotten. Such is, perhaps, the case at Mystery Hill in the United States, where some remarkable stone constructions revered by New Age mystics have been identified by archaeologists as fairly recent farm buildings with no magical function whatsoever. Other sites again evoke age-old riddles of existence.

Such are the ceremonial monuments raised by peoples of the past to connect themselves with the universe. The Great Pyramid at Giza, for example, was more than just a memorial to a vainglorious pharaoh – its astronomical orientations reflect how the Egyptians felt their destiny to be related to the cosmos and recall their faith in a life beyond death. Celestial alignments have also been discerned at pyramids in Mexico,

at Stonehenge and at a multitude of other megalithic sites in Europe.

The astronomical knowledge combined with the awesome building achievements of our ancestors have so astonished some commentators that they have explained them in terms of extraterrestrial intervention. Alien astronauts, it has been said, imported esoteric knowledge from outer space and gave a jump-start to civilisation on Earth. The theory has been used to explain the appearance of huge pyramids on both sides of the Atlantic, despite the fact that there was no known contact between the Old and New Worlds.

Such extreme claims have been dismissed by professional archaeologists, who have pointed out, for example, that the pyramids of Egypt and Mexico were very different in their form and their purpose. But it remains evident that ancient peoples all around the world were fascinated by the movements of the Sun, Moon and stars, often saw in them messages from the gods, and sometimes orientated their most awe-inspiring and labour-intensive monuments towards positions of the heavenly bodies.

## EASTER ISLAND, CHILE

*WHO CARVED THE IMMENSE STONE HEADS ON THIS REMOTE PACIFIC ISLAND?*

Gigantic stone statues brood over Easter Island, a tiny, barren place pitted with the craters of extinct volcanoes, lying lost in the South Pacific. The island appears as a solitary speck in the vast map of the ocean – it is nearly 1243 miles (2000 km) from its

ETERNAL GAZE *Some of Easter Island's 600 statues stare out to the far horizon.*

nearest island neighbour, and double that distance from the coast of South America. Yet this, one of the loneliest spots on Earth, provides the stage setting for some of the most awesome megalithic statuary ever shaped by humankind.

Fierce controversy once surrounded the origins of the mysterious statues. The Norwegian writer and explorer Thor Heyerdahl proposed that they were erected by settlers from South America, and in a well-publicised expedition sailed his raft, *Kon-Tiki*, on a 101-day drift voyage as far as Tahiti to prove that the journey was possible. However, the historical evidence strongly indicates that the first inhabitants were Polynesians, Stone Age navigators who crossed immense tracts of uncharted ocean to colonise the Pacific islands from the west. They reached Easter Island, the most easterly point of their voyage, some time before AD 400. And there, in the following centuries, they acquired considerable skill as sculptors, building ceremonial terraces known as *ahu* of finely cut volcanic rock. These were funeral places, where bodies were exposed after death, and the bones

later interred beneath. The settlers also made small statues at this time, but it was not until the period 1150-1500 that they produced their famous giant sculptures.

Hundreds of the huge statues were made, stylised male figures with long heads, long ears and jutting chins, carved from grey volcanic tuff. Some were also given curious topknots of red tuff. The statues were carved to adorn the ceremonial terraces and probably dragged on sledges from their quarry sites to be levered into place using large wooden posts (the island was once better forested than today). The biggest statue ever made at Easter Island was 65 ft (20 m) long and weighed a massive 270 tons. This, though, proved too heavy to move and remains unfinished in its quarry, along with other incomplete examples.

What was the statues' significance? Captain Cook, an 18th-century visitor, was told by the islanders that each statue had a name – often including the title *ariki*, or chief. Since ancestor-worship is found on other islands in the South Pacific, it is a fair guess that the giant effigies represented dead tribal leaders. Though built for eternity, many ancestral images were toppled in a calamitous period after 1500, when feuding and warfare broke out on Easter Island.

It seems that at the height of the culture, monument-building intensified and became competitive. Meanwhile, as the population grew, forests were cut down to increase agriculture. The loss of trees caused soil erosion and crop failure, and hunger was widespread. Amid raids, violence and destruction, Easter Island's civilisation collapsed, leaving a colony of enigmatic stone giants as testament to its former grandeur.

## MYSTERY HILL, NEW HAMPSHIRE, UNITED STATES

*WERE HUMANS SACRIFICED AT THE SITE DUBBED 'AMERICA'S STONEHENGE'?*

Intriguing stone structures are sited in North Salem, New Hampshire. Grey rocks are piled up here in a cluster of 22 small dry-walled formations, some roofed with

ANCIENT OR MODERN?
*Stonehenge-like structures*
*such as this 60 ton boulder at*
*North Salem may be no more*
*than the remains of 18th or*
*19th-century farm buildings.*

boulders, others having corbelled vaults. Their discovery sparked controversy among investigators, some of whom likened them to monuments of the Celts or even earlier megalith-builders of ancient Europe. Certainly, they bore no resemblance to anything known to have been built by the native American. What were they doing here in America? And what in particular was the purpose of a prominent slab, resting on stone supports, bared to the sky with a gutter cut into its upper surface, apparently to drain off liquid? One investigator in the 1970s interpreted it as 'a sinister altar in proper proportions for human sacrifice'.

Taken at face value, Mystery Hill (also known as 'America's Stonehenge') seems to provide dramatic evidence of a European presence in the New World before both the Vikings and Christopher Columbus. A scattering of similar sites has also been located in Massachusetts and Vermont, some with chamber entrances orientated towards the south and east, in ways that appear to recall ancient Celtic practices. Curious signs on the stones have been interpreted as messages in Ogam – an Old Irish alphabet dating from the 4th century AD. Should the history books be rewritten?

Not according to conventional archaeology. In the course of one excavation at Mystery Hill, scientific investigation yielded some 7000 items – but none of them was Celtic in origin. They were either prehistoric Native American artefacts, dating back to a time before the structures were built, or bits of pottery, brick, nails and plaster made by European settlers in the last century.

In the view of the sceptics, the stone chambers at Mystery Hill and elsewhere are nothing more than 18th or 19th-century farm complexes. The purpose of the baffling chambers seems to have been quite banal: they were shelters for the cold storage of fruits and vegetables. One researcher even found 18th and 19th-century publications offering advice on how to build them.

If the structures had a Celtic look, it was probably because the builders were Scots or Irish emigrants, using crofters' building methods that did indeed go back to the time of the ancient Celts – but were still in use in Europe in the 20th century. The 'Ogam inscriptions' were, as likely as not, crude strokes for the record-keeping of stocks. And the 'sacrificial altar' strikingly resembled a lye stone of a type that was not uncommon in England; on its surface, soap was made by leaching wood ash.

Mystery Hill is still a place of pilgrimage for New Age believers, who continue to interpret it as a place of long-forgotten magic and ritual. Orthodox archaeologists are satisfied with a mundane 19th-century explanation. All agree that the buildings are historical curiosities, but beyond that there is little consensus.

## THE GIZA PYRAMIDS, EGYPT

*WERE EGYPT'S SPECTACULAR*
*MONUMENTS ALIGNED TO THE STARS?*

It is the world's most celebrated graveyard. Five miles to the west of the River Nile, just beyond the outskirts of Cairo, stand the Giza pyramids built more than 4000 years

FAMILY PLANNING  *Father, son*
*and grandson were buried in*
*the three great pyramids at*
*Giza, each orientated to ease*
*the passage to heaven.*

ago as burial places for the pharaohs. The first and largest, the Great Pyramid, constructed for the pharaoh Khufu (who died in 2567 BC), incorporates some 2.3 million limestone blocks weighing an average of 2½ tons each. Some weigh considerably more; monstrous 50 ton granite slabs roof Khufu's burial chamber deep inside. The base of the pyramid covers an area of some 13 acres (5 ha), while the summit is 481 ft (147 m) above the desert sands.

The whole giant hunk of solid geometry was once sheathed in a smooth and shining limestone casing that must have created an impression of dazzling splendour. Near by looms the pyramid of King Khafre, son of Khufu, which is scarcely less imposing; the third pyramid is the tomb of King Menkaure, son of Khafre. With the Great Sphinx for guardian, these stone mountains rank among the greatest human achievements of any time or place.

Construction of the pyramids evidently involved a massive deployment of manpower. The Great Pyramid is reckoned to have soaked up the energies of some 4000 workmen toiling over a period of 20 to 30 years. Complex mathematical and surveying skills were required of the architects. The base of the Great Pyramid is level to

## GREAT WALL OF FRANCE

Napoleon's soldiers, who won a famous victory in Egypt at the Battle of the Pyramids in 1798, were astonished by the grandeur of the Giza pyramids. The army surveyors calculated that there was enough stone in them to build a wall around France 10 ft (3 m) high and 3 ft (1 m) thick.

within 1 in (2.5 cm), and the 750 ft (229 m) sides differ by less than 7 in (17.8 cm) in length. Particular care was taken over orientation; the pyramid is sited so that its sides face north, south, east and west, accurately within one-tenth of a degree.

Egyptian astronomers probably aligned the Great Pyramid with a prominent star, likely to have been Alpha Draconis, which was, at that time, close to the north celestial pole. But why align the monument with the

heavens at all? The answer must be found in Egyptian ideas concerning life after death. The Egyptians believed in the afterlife, and each tomb was conceived as a house for the occupant's spirit, or ka. For the ka to survive, the earthly body had to be embalmed and laid to rest with material provisions such as food, furniture and other trappings of daily life. Fantastic grave offerings were buried with the pharaohs, thought to be god kings, whose true home was in the heavens. 'He is no longer upon Earth, he is in the sky! He rushes at the sky like a heron; he has kissed the sky like a falcon,' runs a pyramid hymn.

Some authorities believe that the pyramids were conceived specifically to allow the pharaoh's spirit to soar heavenward at will, return for sustenance to his tomb and soar again. In the Great Pyramid, they have pointed in particular to two small shafts leading north and south, upwards to the outer air. These are said to have been entrances and exits for the royal ka.

Are the celestial connections more elaborate? Researchers have long wondered why the three Giza pyramids, so accurately designed individually, should have been laid out of line with one another: Menkaure's pyramid seems to lead off at a tangent. A new theory, published in 1994, suggests that the three Giza pyramids were laid out to mirror the three stars of Orion's

SNAKING EARTHWORK *The bizarre Serpent Mound winds its way across the Ohio landscape.*

belt, which are similarly out of alignment. Whether the theory is true or not, it is clear that the pyramids were more than mere memorials. They were colossal stonework machines designed to engineer immortality for their royal occupants.

## THE GREAT SERPENT MOUND, OHIO, UNITED STATES

*THE RIDDLE OF A GIANT SNAKE FASHIONED OVER 2000 YEARS AGO.*

The weird earthwork reptile winds its way along a wooded hilltop in Adams County, above the stream of Bush Creek. Ohio's great Serpent Mound is more than 1300 ft (400 m) long, from coiled tail to a gaping mouth that seems to be holding an oval ring, or perhaps swallowing an egg. Modern visitors are able to view the serpent from a tower near the tail, but the enigma presented by this sinuous effigy is deepened by the fact that – like the Nazca patterns in Peru – it is best seen from the air. This has led aficionados of the paranormal to suggest that its makers must have possessed powers of levitation, or of mind projection, that permitted remote viewing.

The precise purpose of the creature can only be guessed at today, but something is known of its origins. Archaeologists have determined, for example, that the Serpent was probably shaped in the 1st century BC. The builders first set out the pattern in stones, then overlaid it with clay from the valley below, heaping it up to waist height to create the relief design. The Mound has yielded no evidence of skeletons or grave goods. This, it appears, was a sacred symbol rather than a place of burial.

Who built it? Likely candidates are the Adena people, a Native American culture that was already flourishing along the Ohio river in 700 BC. Besides hunting and gathering wild foods, the Adena also grew crops from seed and threw up earthwork circles, squares, pentagons and other shapes at various sites in the Ohio area. Thought to be sacred enclosures, they measure as much as 328 ft (100 m) in diameter. The people also set up burial mounds, sometimes incorporating log tombs containing more than one body. Many of the dead found in the larger sites were stained with red ochre, and were laid to rest with grave goods such as carved stone tablets, copper bracelets and tubular stone pipes for smoking tobacco. The smoking ritual seems to have spread from South America, and the plant was more potent than the type cultivated by the white settlers in later centuries. Its effect was narcotic and intoxicating. The shamans, or tribal priests, may have used it to induce trance states among the people.

Energetic as they were as mound-builders, the Adena never achieved any other creation to compare in scale and elaboration with the Serpent Mound. And this has led some experts to believe that it may have been the work of the more advanced Hopewell people who started to appear in Ohio around 100 BC, more or less when the Adena culture was at its

height. The Hopewell built bigger, more complex earthworks, and buried their dead with exquisite ornaments such as stone-carved tobacco pipes bearing images of panther, hawk, raven and bear. Cutout pictures were wrought from mica and beaten copper, representing bird talons, human hands and swastikas. The serpent was another recurrent motif. In legends widespread among Native American tribes the horned snake symbolised the power of water to fertilise and regenerate. And perhaps this was what the Great Serpent Mound embodied as it wound its way along the hilltop above Bush Creek.

## FILITOSA, CORSICA

*WARLIKE FACES SCOWL FROM STANDING STONES AT A MEGALITHIC SITE.*

Lying among the rocks and scrub of the Corsican mountains are intriguing mega-lithic monuments that recall the island's prehistoric past. Here are dolmens, communal tombs roofed with massive stone slabs, and menhirs, or upright pillars. Dating back at least 5000 years they are products of the same European civilisation that raised stones as far north as Scandinavia and Orkney. But in Corsica, monument-making took a particular turn.

**FROWNING ROCK** *The hint of a beetle-browed face peers out from this standing stone at Filitosa.*

At Filitosa, near Propriano, the menhirs come to life. Faces emerge from the standing stones – of stern warriors, with carved indications of weapons and cloaks. They stand like sentinels, menacing but impressive too, for these are among the first statues known in European art – crude precursors of Donatello and Michelangelo.

The monuments at Filitosa lie in tangled heathland, on an outcrop overlooking a valley wooded here and there with old olives and holm oaks. In 1989, while clearing away the maquis, or scrub, not far from the site, investigators discovered the ancient granite quarry where the settlement's occupants obtained their blocks, splitting them off along fault lines in the rock. Who were the builders? The evidence suggests that the megalith-makers were peaceful Stone Age farmers and herdsmen, overrun around 1400 BC by warriors with metal weapons whose occupation lasted until after 800 BC. And the statues appear to be portraits of the invaders: one figure carries a longsword and a sheathed dagger, and another has a breastplate, sword belt and horned helmet.

Although the identity of the new arrivals cannot be known for sure, they probably came from the eastern Mediterranean, where similar arms and armour were known. Scholars have identified them as Torreans, a people who are named after the tower-like fortresses that they built on the hilltops of several other Mediterranean islands. At Filitosa the Torreans built defensive walls from massive blocks of stone, and they also erected a temple where fires burned on the earth floor and sacrifices of some kind were offered on an altar with a drainage channel cut into it.

The slopes around are covered with slab-sided buildings whose origins – megalithic or Torrean – are hard to interpret. Meanwhile, the ghost eyes of the statue-menhirs confer additional mystery on this, one of the most impressive of all Europe's ancient sites.

## CARNAC, FRANCE

*THE RIDDLE OF BRITTANY'S VAST*
*AVENUES OF ANCIENT STANDING STONES.*

North and east of the Breton resort of Carnac is the area that contains Europe's largest concentration of megaliths. About 3000 standing stones can be seen, ranged in bizarre avenues across the heathland. According to local tradition these were

Roman legionaries chasing after the early Christian St Corne'ly. Finding his escape barred by the sea, the saint turned and blessed his persecutors, who promptly turned to stone – and stand there in petrified ranks to this day.

One formation marches towards the hamlet of Le Menec: 1099 stones arranged in 11 avenues that stretch as far as the eye can see. The stones are not laid out in perfectly straight lines, but follow a slight curve. They also increase in size from the eastern end of the formation (where they barely reach waist height) to the western end, where they tower overhead at 12 ft (4 m). Other similar rows of stones are laid out at Kermario and Kerlescan nearby, and the local monument builders did not restrict themselves to avenues.

Individual upright stones, known as menhirs, may have had significance in fertility rites. Until very recent times, it was still the custom for young married couples to visit a menhir called Le Vaisseau at Carnac by moonlight; there, under the eyes of their parents, they ran naked around the stone to assure themselves of offspring. Similar rites were performed by villagers at other menhirs in Brittany, suggesting some deep-rooted association of the stones with fertility. The avenues, however, are not so easily explained. What was the purpose of the stone alignments?

It has been suggested that they were great places of assembly for their New Stone Age builders, or ceremonial pathways for funeral processions. During the 1970s Alexander Thom, a former professor of engineering, surveyed the Carnac megaliths and concluded that the whole complex had been designed as an astronomical observatory, to study lunar movements in particular. They formed what he referred to

STONE SOLDIERS *Local legend tells that Carnac's megaliths are ranks of petrified Roman legionaries.*

HORSEPOWER *The chalk-cut figure on White Horse Hill gallops across the downland.*

as a 'megalithic graph paper' on which Neolithic astronomers plotted their sightings of the rising and setting moon at different times of the year. Other experts remain unconvinced. All at Carnac suggests a great creative vision and a huge, orderly work force to turn the vision into reality. The meaning of the vision remains elusive – perhaps it will never be understood.

## WHITE HORSE HILL, ENGLAND

*WHO CUT THE ANCIENT EMBLEM*
*INTO ENGLAND'S UPLAND HEART?*

The bold, barbaric image is branded into an English downland crest just below the Iron Age hillfort of Uffington Castle. This is not a naturalistic picture but a stylised effigy that seems to embody some spirit of animal energy. The mouth is oddly beaky, and two legs are detached. Is it even a horse? The chalk-cut creature looks down on a curious flat-topped hummock known as Dragon Hill, where St George is alleged to have slain the dragon – according to one belief the galloping steed represents the dragon itself.

Surging to 856 ft (261 m) from its ridge on the Berkshire Downs, the summit of White Horse Hill commands panoramic views out over the ancient heartland of

England, inviting the imagination to soar and wander. The castle was built on the prehistoric Ridgeway track, and a walk along it leads to Wayland's Smithy, an eerie Neolithic burial chamber brooding among tall beeches. King Alfred was born at Wantage to the west, and an old tradition holds that he had the White Horse cut to commemorate a great victory over the Danes in AD 871.

However, most archaeologists now believe that the image was carved from the hillside long before King Alfred was born. It was probably the work of the Iron Age Celts who built Uffington Castle, and they may have been members of the Dobunni tribe, for one of their coins was discovered at the site. Stylised horses, not unlike the Uffington figure, are depicted on Celtic artefacts, and a horse goddess called Epona was revered in Celtic tradition.

The image may have been carved around 100 BC, and it is tempting to imagine Druidic rites being enacted to celebrate the event, with fires lit and sacrifices offered. But how was the design laid out? One of the White Horse's enigmas is the fact that the figure is tilted skyward; the best views of it are from the air. Viewed from the foot of the hill, the picture is foreshortened and indistinct. Climb the turf-topped slopes and it becomes indecipherable – a confusion of long white scars in the grass. From the ground the best views are obtained from some miles away. Did the artist stand here and direct the cutting by some type of relay?

White Horse Hill guards its mystery. Back in the 14th century it was already famous as one of the Wonders of Britain, second only to Stonehenge, and the chalk-cut figure is now so woven into national lore that it almost seems an ancestral totem. The priest and writer G.K. Chesterton wrote:

> *Before the gods that made the gods*
> *Had seen the sunrise pass,*
> *The White Horse of the White Horse Vale*
> *Was cut out of the grass.*

## NEWGRANGE, IRELAND

*CARVED SYMBOLS ADORN EUROPE'S FINEST PREHISTORIC BURIAL CHAMBER.*

The midwinter solstice, on December 21, is the darkest day of the year – the day when the hours of sunlight are shortest. For Europe's prehistoric tribes it must have been a disquieting time, when the shadows of night lingered long over fields and homes, prompting fears that the sun might abandon them for ever. But it was also a turning point, marking the beginning of

INNER SANCTUARY *The domed exterior of the Newgrange tomb conceals a vaulted burial chamber approached by a long, stone-walled passage (above).*

the new year. Soon the dead earth would start to revive – the green shoots rise again.

The extraordinary burial chamber at Newgrange, County Meath, was built to take advantage of this seasonal drama. Constructed at some time in the 4th millennium BC, it was so orientated that at dawn on the midwinter solstice the rising Sun would send a shaft of direct sunlight into the tomb via a specially constructed 'roof-box' above the entrance. Pencil-fine at first, the beam widened to bathe the tomb with golden light, illuminating the superbly carved stones deep within the inner sanctuary. Then the shaft of light dwindled again. After 15 to 20 minutes, its beam was obscured.

Here was a superb metaphor of hope – in the new life to come for cattle and crops, and perhaps for the dead, too, whose cremated bones once filled the chamber. Were these the remains of great chieftains? Or of respected elders? Newgrange guards its secrets, but what can be said is that this was a remarkable feat of engineering for a people who had only stone and wood technology. The most impressive of some 50 000 megalithic burial chambers scattered around Europe, Newgrange takes the form of a great, egg-shaped mound, carefully layered with river gravel and clay sods, and surrounded by a kerb of 97 large stones. A 60 ft (18 m) long passage leads to the cross-shaped burial chamber at the centre. While many prehistoric tombs were simply roofed by a capstone laid across uprights, the inner sanctuary at Newgrange has a vaulted roof 20 ft (6 m) high. This was achieved by corbelling: the roofing slabs were placed in stepped layers, getting closer together towards the top.

Many of the stones at Newgrange are wonderfully carved with spirals, zigzags and circles that may well contain symbolism related to magical or astronomical phenomena. Their meaning can only be guessed at today. But it is evident that the Newgrange area, on a hill above the River Boyne, was one of immense ritual significance, for it is strewn with large numbers of prehistoric graves and standing stones. In one Irish myth, the hill was the underground citadel of 'three times fifty sons of kings'; in another, it was the abode of the Celtic high god, Dagda Mor. This is a landscape imprinted with ancient mystery – a place to conjure up dreams.

## THE NAZCA PATTERNS, PERU

*BAFFLING DESERT MARKINGS VISIBLE ONLY FROM THE AIR.*

The gigantic image of a spider, 148 ft (44 m) long, sprawls across the desert landscape near Nazca in southern Peru. Vast effigies of monkeys, lizards, llamas, whales, snakes, hummingbirds and condors are laid out here too, amid fantastic geometric patterns of crisscross lines, zigzags, trapezoids (four-sided shapes) and spirals. Altogether, the patterned area covers some 193 sq miles (500 km²) between the Andes mountains and the Pacific Ocean.

It is not hard to understand how the drawings were made. The desert plains comprise an immense natural blackboard on which the patterns were etched by removing the surface covering of reddish-

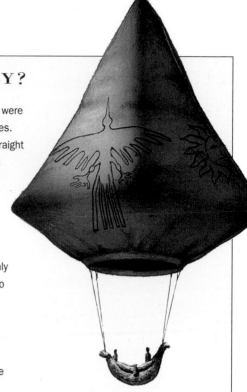

### COULD ANCIENT MEN FLY?

A number of ancient symbols, from Ohio's Serpent Mound to England's chalk-cut White Horse, have provoked puzzlement through the fact that they are best viewed from the air. Images may have been pointed skywards in order to please the gods, but how did the makers obtain vantage points from which to direct their designs?

In the case of the Nazca patterns in Peru, it has been seriously proposed that the makers could fly. In the 1970s Bill Spohrer, an American member of the International Explorers' Society, noted that some Nazcan fabric had a tighter weave than that used in modern parachute material or hot air balloons. Additionally, objects that could be interpreted as kites or balloons with trailing streamers were depicted on Nazcan pottery wares. And at the end of many long, straight lines drawn on the Nazca plains there are roundish patches of blackened rock. Were fires lit here to launch hot-air craft?

In 1975 fellow members of the Explorers' Society launched a simple airship, made using only materials of the type available to the Nazcas. Two men, Jim Woodman and Julian Knott, sat aboard a reed gondola hanging below. Though the men were jettisoned soon after take-off the balloon, Condor 1, did fly successfully for some 20 minutes. In theory, prehistoric flight was possible – but there is no evidence that it happened.

**UP AND AWAY** *Condor 1 was built to determine whether flight was feasible for the Nazcas.*

brown stones to reveal the paler soil below. The long, perfectly straight lines could have been laid out without too much difficulty by setting up sighting poles and stretching cords between them. But the patterns are so huge that they can only really be interpreted from the air, and this has invited adventurous speculation. The Swiss writer Erich von Daniken, in particular, argued in his bestselling book *Chariots of the Gods* that the markings are an airfield used by aliens for landing vehicles from outer space.

Sceptics will look for a more rational explanation, and though much remains baffling about the Nazca patterns it is at least possible to place them in a historical context. There can be little doubt that the lines were laid out by the Nazca Indians, whose culture flourished in southern Peru from about 370 BC to about AD 450. Quantities of their pottery have survived at various grave sites, bearing images that are strikingly similar to those sketched on the high desert plains. Broken pottery was also found on the Pampa Corrida, a 30 mile (48 km) long plateau that has the greatest concentration

**NAZCA HUMMINGBIRD** *An aerial view reveals the subject of this complex pattern etched on desert plains.*

of ground drawings. Since the area is too forbidding for long-term settlement, the fragments may well have been left by the workers who laid out the patterns, or by pilgrims come for ceremonial purposes.

The Nazca mystery has never been resolved. It is a fair guess that the pictures were dedicated to the sky gods, or to the spirits of ancestors, for if designed for human eyes they would surely have been made easier to appreciate at ground level. According to one theory the crisscross lines were sacred ritual pathways, though there is no compelling evidence for the notion. Other researchers have suggested that the lines point to prominent stars, or to the Sun. Computer studies do not indicate more definite alignments than would have occurred by chance.

Altogether, the ground drawings remain profoundly puzzling, and the Nazcas themselves bequeathed no clues to their purpose. They were a farming people who had no writing, and left few buildings of any size. In due course they were assimilated by the Huari culture expanding from a mountain capital further north, and the Nazca draughtsmen abandoned their great desert sketchpad to the elements.

## HELL CREEK, MONTANA, UNITED STATES

*ERODED GULLIES THAT ILLUMINATE THE MYSTERIOUS DEATH OF THE DINOSAURS.*

Primeval memories of vanished life forms are exposed in Hell Creek's battered ravines. The site lies in the badlands of Montana, rough and remote country where cowboys and sheep-herders started reporting strange bones almost a century ago. Here are thick, grey sediments laid

DINOSAUR FIND *This skeleton of a Tyrannosaurus rex was discovered in the Rockies in 1990.*

down by rivers that flowed eastwards for millions of years during prehistoric times. In these fossil-rich beds, now turned to sandstones and siltstones, are the remnants of innumerable creatures, from fishes, lizards and frogs to giant dinosaurs. The first skeleton of a *Tyrannosaurus rex* was found at Hell Creek in 1902, and the site has attracted fossil-hunters ever since.

What has fascinated them has been the study of beds dating back some 65 million years, the time when the dinosaurs vanished from the Earth – along with many other animal species of their time. This period, at the end of the Cretaceous and dawn of the Tertiary, provides one of the great puzzles of the planet's past. On one side of the fossil line there are dinosaur remains aplenty; on the other, almost none. What caused the mass extinction? During the 1980s, some geologists thought they had found the answer. They discovered that all around the world, rocks laid down 65 million years ago contained strong concentrations of iridium, an element found in abundance in meteorites. Their theory was that a giant meteorite, or some other extraterrestrial body, had struck the Earth, causing a global catastrophe akin to a nuclear winter, with dust clouds veiling the sun,

freezing temperatures and dying vegetation. If the immediate impact did not cause the disaster, it has been argued, it may have split the Earth's crust and triggered widespread volcanic eruptions with comparable results (iridium is also found at the Earth's core and can be released by volcanoes).

Catastrophe theories make exciting reading, and it is now generally agreed that an impact by an extraterrestrial body did occur. But did it cause the death of the dinosaurs? The ancient streambeds at Hell Creek suggest not. Studying their strata, experts have discovered the iridium layer as expected. But they have also found evidence that the dinosaurs were dying out before it was laid down.

A researcher, J. Keith Rigby, employed an unusual technique to chart the decline: counting the number of dinosaur teeth per ton of rock. He discovered that well before the end of the Cretaceous Period there were about 200 teeth per ton. But the figures then decreased markedly, and in the rock dating from just before the impact, teeth numbered only 30 to 35 per ton. Dinosaurs, evidently, were dwindling in numbers before the explosion occurred. What was more, some of them survived well beyond the catastrophe. Rock from after the

COSMIC RING *Boulders form a huge wheel high above the Great Plains.*

Cretaceous Period still yielded 18 dinosaur teeth per ton, and the evidence showed that some dinosaurs were still living a million years after the supposed impact.

The Hell Creek researchers believe that the dinosaurs were at their peak earlier than many people think, about 100 million years ago. They began to decline, both in species and in number, as dropping temperatures and other environmental changes – possibly even the appearance of new mountain ranges – altered their habitat, particularly in relation to the availability of food. The impact cannot have done anything to help their situation, but it was not in itself a key factor in their disappearance.

## BIGHORN MEDICINE WHEEL, WYOMING, UNITED STATES

*RIDDLE OF A MAGIC CIRCLE*
*LAID OUT ON A US MOUNTAIN TOP.*

Nomadic tribes of the Great Plains lived on the move, travelling light to follow the buffalo herds. They left little but the faint indentations of tepee rings as evidence of their passing, but across the landscape from Wyoming to Alberta lies a scattering of more substantial relics, enigmatic stone circles of ritual significance to the tribal people. More than 80 'medicine wheels' have been identified in North America, the largest at an altitude of 10 000 ft (3000 m) in the Bighorn Mountains of Wyoming. It is a dramatic site, commanding sweeping views to the distant plain. Here the tribes' medicine men must have felt very close to the sky and sensed the awesome power of the Great Spirit. Protected as a National Monument, the Bighorn Medicine Wheel is also venerated to this day by the local Arapaho people.

The design takes the form of a circle of boulders with a rock pile, or cairn, at the hub. Twenty-eight spokes lead to the outer rim 80 ft (25 m) in diameter, where six more cairns are laid out. What was its purpose? Archaeologists believe that the wheel was a symbol for the sun. One important alignment points to the summer solstice: the sun's rising point on the horizon, on the longest day of the year. This was a key calendar event in many ancient societies where sowing and harvest times depended on the rhythmic patterns of seasonal change.

Researchers have noted the site's resemblance in layout to the Plains Indians' Sun Dance Lodges: open structures made of wooden poles, often with entrances facing the rising sun. Inside, a ceremonial dance was performed at the summer solstice, and no doubt in the Medicine Wheel, too, sun-related rites were enacted.

The wheel had further cosmological significance, incorporating alignments that marked the rising points of three bright stars, Aldebaran, Rigel and Sirius. This, it seems, was an observatory of some complexity, suggesting that the Plains Indians knew more about the sky than is generally thought. But precisely how the Medicine Wheel was used, what meanings were read into celestial events, and what

*STRANGE SERENITY The Iron Age man recovered from Tollund Fen appeared oddly tranquil, in view of evidence that he had been strangled.*

ceremonies were held here is unknown. To this day the monument cannot even be dated with any certainty. Elders of the local tribes believe the site to be haunted by spirits which should not be disturbed. High on its windswept peak, the Medicine Wheel guards many secrets.

## TOLLUND FEN, DENMARK

*MACABRE SITE OF AN IRON-AGE*
*KILLING. WAS THE VICTIM SACRIFICED?*

For centuries now, peat cutters have been recovering bodies from the fenlands of northwest Europe – gruesome remains of people misshapen by the pressure of the decomposed vegetation above them. In some cases the bones were decalcified, leaving only the twisted skin and organs. But in others, the state of preservation was extraordinarily good. The acidity of the bog water had combined with cold temperatures and a lack of air to deter micro-organisms.

Decay was arrested; ancient faces and fabrics were so efficiently embalmed that the bodies were sometimes mistaken for recent murder victims.

Several hundred corpses have come to light this way, in Germany, Denmark, Holland, Britain and Ireland. Many are Iron Age bodies, and a surprising number bear the stamp of violent death. Victims had been clubbed, hanged or strangled; had their throats slit or been decapitated. The corpse of an Iron Age man unearthed in 1984 at Lindow Moss, Cheshire, bore signs of massive 'overkill'; he seemed to have been bludgeoned and garrotted – and had his throat cut for good measure.

Denmark has yielded a remarkable number of finds, particularly from north and central Jutland. The most famous of all turned up in 1950 in a bog called Tollund Fen. Lying on its right side was the body of a man, naked but for sheepskin cap and belt, whose 2000-year-old features were astonishingly well preserved. 'The face,' wrote the Danish authority Peter V. Glob 'wore a gentle expression – the lips softly pursed, as if in silent prayer.' This was in spite of the noose of plaited skin rope around his neck which showed that he had been strangled. Other victims, male and female, were found in the same area. Here, it seems, was an Iron Age killing ground.

The victims may have been executed criminals but finds also show ritual elements. Many bodies had been stripped partially, like that of Tollund Man, or wholly. Some were found staked down into the bog. Professor Glob and others have suggested that the victims were people sacrificed to a fertility goddess in winter rites held to hasten the coming of spring. Examination of Tollund Man's stomach contents revealed that shortly before death he had eaten a gruel of barley, linseed and sorrel; the absence of summer or autumn foods indicates death in winter or early spring. Lindow Man's last meal, a similar gruel, contained pollen of mistletoe – a plant with mystical properties for the Druids.

The Roman historian Tacitus (AD 55-120) described human sacrifices to the gods among the northern tribes of Europe. But he also wrote: 'Traitors and deserters are hanged on trees; cowards, shirkers and sodomites are pressed down under a wicker hurdle into the slimy mud of a bog.' Was Tollund Man a victim of fertility sacrifice or criminal execution? The evidence of the eerie fen is inconclusive; the face serene but silent.

## LASCAUX, FRANCE

*WHAT WAS THE PURPOSE OF THE CAVE'S AMAZING PREHISTORIC PAINTINGS?*

In 1940 four boys exploring a cave at Lascaux in the Dordogne wriggled through a narrow chute and dropped into an astonishing painted gallery. Walls and

ANIMAL MAGIC  *Lascaux's cave ceilings are riotous with images of Stone Age animals.*

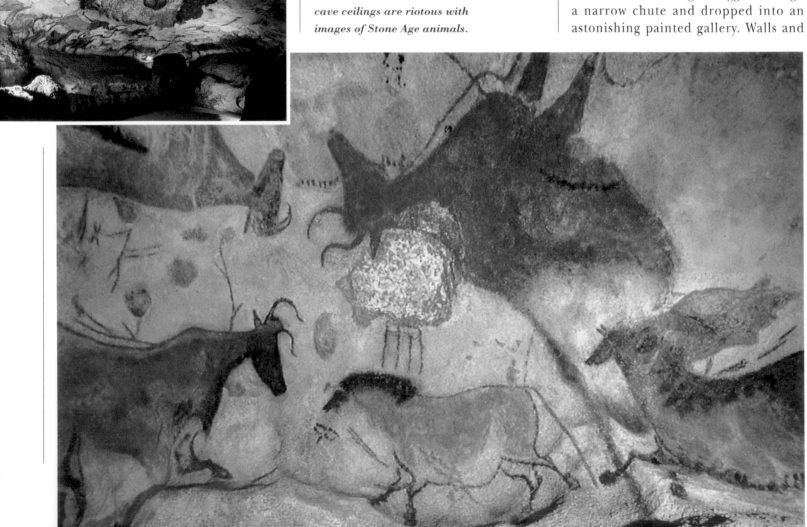

ceilings swirled with magnificent images of bulls, horses, bison and swimming deer, and what has impressed visitors ever since is not only the number and vibrant colour of the scenes but also their expressive sense of movement. Painted at least 17 000 years ago, the cave at Lascaux quickly won fame as the finest example of prehistoric art to be found anywhere in the world. Changes in the moisture level caused by thousands of visitors caused the paintings to deteriorate, and the cave was closed in 1963. Today, only five visitors a day are permitted, and those only by prior arrangement. Instruments constantly monitor temperature and humidity; the entrance is through a series of airlocks.

Though protected with exceptional care, Lascaux is not unique. Dotted around south-west France and north-west Spain are more than 100 caves adorned with images that recall the life and spirit of Palaeolithic man. This is a limestone landscape riddled with grottoes and overhangs that, for thousands of years, offered ready-made shelters for our ancestors. The climate was colder than today, and they used weapons of flint, antler and bone to kill reindeer, mammoth and woolly rhinoceros. In many paintings the detail of the animals is strikingly accurate, reflecting the hunters' long and patient observation; human figures are, by contrast, caricatures – little more than stick men.

Much is known of how Lascaux paintings were made. The artists worked by the light of hollow stone lamps with moss wicks floating in animal fat. For paint brushes they used feathers or twigs of animal hair, while colours were mixed from natural pigments such as iron oxide and red and yellow ochre. Charcoal provided black. Pestles and mortars were used to grind the minerals, which were blended on stone palettes. It seems that the paint was mixed with fat to make it waterproof, and there is evidence at Lascaux that scaffolding was used to reach ceilings.

What was the purpose? It is thought that the paintings had some kind of magical significance in hunting ritual. To depict a chase would guarantee that a chase would

take place; to show a kill would ensure a kill. The animals depicted are chiefly the grazing creatures on which Stone Age men depended for food, and many images represent animals either wounded or falling into traps. At Lascaux, one scene shows a herd of horses being stampeded over a cliff – a common means of slaughtering this favourite prey. Conceivably, Lascaux and other caves were used for initiation ceremonies in which the young members of the tribe were introduced to the mysteries of the hunt. Whatever precise function the images served, they were not casually painted for decoration only. This was a place of Stone Age sorcery – a cathedral dedicated to the kill.

## PULEMELEI MOUND, WESTERN SAMOA

*HUGE, OVERGROWN PYRAMID ON A SOUTH PACIFIC ISLAND.*

Scattered around the islands of Samoa, a volcanic chain in the South Pacific Ocean, are several curious man-made platforms with stone protrusions radiating from their

*PACIFIC MYSTERY   An unknown ancient people evidently lavished great care on the construction of Pulemelei Mound in Samoa – in spite of which no record survives of what it was used for.*

bases. They are known as 'star mounds' among archaeologists, who are at a loss to know why they were built. The Samoans are Polynesians whose seafaring ancestors are thought to have colonised the islands from Asia around 1500 BC. Samoan myths tell how their land is the 'cradle of Polynesia', fashioned at the Creation by the great god Tagaloa. But despite a rich culture based on customs stretching back for many centuries, Samoan traditions offer no explanation for the mounds. There are no burials at the sites, and though investigators have guessed that they were made to stage religious ceremonies, there is no evidence to support the hypothesis. A more common explanation is that the mounds were raised as platforms for the sport of pigeon-snaring.

On Savai'i island stands the most intriguing monument of all. Not far from the

SIFTING THE EVIDENCE
*Soviet researchers found
evidence of radiation
in the Tunguska soil.*

scenic Olemoe Falls, half-hidden from travellers by thick jungle vegetation, Pulemelei Mound is the biggest ancient structure in the whole of the Pacific. At its base the two-tier pyramid measures 200 ft by 164 ft (61 m by 50 m), with side ramps leading up to a 39 ft (12 m) summit where postholes and cairns have been identified. The monument is orientated roughly north-south, east-west. A stone walkway leads north to a smaller platform, where additional mounds and platforms are laid out in other directions. No mention is made of the mounds in Samoan lore, and scholars are reluctant to speculate on its purpose.

## TUNGUSKA, RUSSIA

*SITE OF A COSMIC CATASTROPHE THAT
LIT UP THE NIGHT SKY ACROSS EUROPE.*

Just after 7.15 am, local time, on June 30, 1908, an explosion of astonishing force rocked Siberia's central plateau. Its scorching heat laid waste an area the size of St Petersburg, and caused the skies above to glow with an eerie brightness that could be seen as far away as the United Kingdom, more than 4000 miles (6440 km) distant. There, people were reportedly able to play night-time cricket and read newspapers by the weird nocturnal glow.

Closer to the epicentre – the explosion's centre – in the remote valley of the Tunguska River, forests were devastated, herds of reindeer incinerated and violent gusts of wind felt for hundreds of miles around. Local newspapers reported that peasants had seen a fireball brighter than the sun, trailing a vast black smoke cloud, and heard a mighty bang, as if of cannon fire.

An Irkutsk journal described villagers 200 miles (320 km) from the blast running in panic into the streets. 'The old women wept and everyone thought the end of the world was approaching.' Nearer to the town of Tunguska, a farmer standing on his porch felt the shirt almost burn off his back in the sudden flash of light. 'Afterwards it became dark and at the same time I felt an explosion that threw me several feet from the porch. I lost consciousness for a few moments and when I came to I heard a noise that shook the whole house and nearly moved it off its foundations.'

What had happened? The region of Siberia's space disaster is one of the most inaccessible on Earth, and it was not until 1927 that an expedition, headed by the Soviet mineralogist Leonid Kulik, managed to investigate the site of the explosion. The team found that the forest trees had been flattened and uprooted to a distance of some 40 miles (65 km) from the epicentre, while evidence of the earth tremors extended some 70 miles (110 km).

Kulik had expected to find a meteorite. However, there was no huge crater of the type that is normally associated with a meteorite impact. Though the ground was dented here and there, at the very epicentre were a frozen swamp and a group of trees that had survived curiously intact. Whatever had caused the explosion, it had never reached the ground.

In 1930 an English meteorologist, F.J.W. Whipple, suggested that a small comet might have entered the Earth's atmosphere and shattered in mid-air. However, no comet had been seen in the sky before the fireball suddenly arrived. More recently, two British physicists put forward the theory that an atom-sized black hole had entered the atmosphere at a collision speed over Tunguska, passed straight through the Earth and emerged on the opposite side. However, the notion is flawed because such an event would have triggered shock waves

# SONAR — ECHOING ENIGMAS

Research into seabed mysteries has been revolutionised in recent years by the use of increasingly sophisticated sonar equipment. The invention of echo-sounding devices goes back to the 1920s, when scientists devised a means of transmitting sound waves towards the ocean floor. By measuring the time taken for the echo to be bounced back to the device it was possible to estimate the depth. This is the principle underlying sonar (from the initials of an American system, 'Sound Navigation and Ranging'). Modern sonar works by sending out an ultrasonic pulse – one beyond the range of human hearing – that is generated electronically and takes into account problems which occur when a signal is distorted by ocean currents or masked by layers of water with differing salt contents or temperatures. Unlike a simple echo-sounder, which merely sends sound beams down vertically, the most advanced systems send out pulses

that can fan out over an area of 38 miles (61 km) diameter. The echoes create an acoustic image resembling a photograph of the sea floor.

Since the 1960s, sonar has solved many riddles of the deep. It has, for example, located the wrecks of the *Titanic* and *Lusitania* as well as an assortment of sunken Armada galleons and treasure ships. In 1981, £45 million in gold bullion was recovered from the wreck of the Second World War vessel HMS *Edinburgh*, located in freezing seas off the coast of the Soviet Union, north of Murmansk. In 1985 the wreck of the *Atocha*, found by the American treasure-hunter Mel Fisher, yielded a haul of silver bars and coins estimated at $200 million in value. And in 1993, 3 million coins and 2000 tons of silver ingots were reported to have been recovered from the *John Barry*, an American military freighter sunk in 1944 by a German U-boat 125 miles (200 km) off Saudi Arabia. The silver bars were a war loan from the United

States to the British in India, and the coins were a gift for the Saudi government. The total value was estimated at £200 million.

Sonar has also mapped much of the ocean floor with its fantastic landscape of ridges, canyons, trenches and craters. For

aficionados of myth and legend, however, there has been some disappointment: a marked lack of evidence for the lost Atlantic continent of Atlantis, or its Pacific counterpart, Lemuria.

WRECK FINDING *Sonar is used to locate a sunken ship before a submersible is lowered.*

underground, while the only seismic effects were on the surface. Moreover, there is no record of an explosion in the North Atlantic (where the mini black hole would have emerged). The most startling hypothesis is that the Tunguska blast resulted

TRAGIC LINER *The wrecked Titanic was finally located by a search team in 1985. A robot camera took these striking shots of encrusted guardrails and surviving pieces of china.*

from a nuclear explosion in an alien space ship – a suggestion owing more to imagination than to research.

Most scientists accept the comet explanation as the likeliest. Though nothing resembling a meteorite was found at the site, investigators have discovered traces of cosmic dust that could be the vaporised remains of a comet's head. As to why its approach was not observed, it probably came from the direction of the rising Sun and so was hard to detect. Could a similar explosion happen tomorrow – perhaps over a

big city? The answer has to be yes, and the prospect is alarming. However, we can take comfort from scientists' calculations that the chance of a comet colliding with the Earth is about one in 40 million years.

## THE TITANIC WRECK, ATLANTIC SEABED

*RUSTED SEA FLOOR RUINS RECALL THE MAJESTY OF A ONCE-GREAT LINER.*

'Here I was on the bottom of the ocean, peering at recognisable, man-made artefacts designed and built for another world. I was looking through windows out of which people had once looked, decks along which they had walked, rooms where they had slept, joked, made love. It was like landing on the surface of Mars only to find the remains of an ancient civilisation similar to our own.'

The words are those of Dr Robert Ballard, head of the joint French-American expedition which located the wreck of the 'unsinkable' *Titanic*. The story of how the giant liner went down has entered the folklore of the modern world. Pride of the White Star fleet, the *Titanic* was the largest ship ever built and also the most luxurious. A swimming pool, tennis court and gymnasium were among her comforts, and there were two verandah palm courts where orchestras played amid the foliage of exotic pot plants.

As far as safety was concerned, the thick steel hull divided into 16 watertight compartments was thought to make the liner 'unsinkable'. Yet sink she did, on her maiden voyage, in the early hours of April 15, 1912. The ship struck an iceberg about 450 miles (720 km) south of Newfoundland and went down with the loss of 1513 lives.

The idea of finding the wreck in the vastness of the North Atlantic long seemed the stuff of fantasy fiction. Yet that was the feat eventually achieved by Ballard's team on September 1, 1985, when, employing the latest in hi-tech underwater search aids, they identified the massive, rusted hull 2½ miles (4 km) down on the ocean floor. A deep-sea sonar device first located the wreck, and the scientists later obtained close-up photographs by guiding a robot from a three-man submarine named *Alvin*. The submarine touched down on the bow and the bridge,

while the robot camera, named Jason Junior, proceeded to explore the Grand Staircase and the staterooms. From the impenetrable shadows of the Atlantic depths came photographs of the giant liner's silverware and still-hanging chandeliers to astonish TV viewers worldwide.

The *Titanic* lies there still, her back broken amidships, her hull split in two. Here indeed is a place of mystery – an undersea ghost town, haunted by the shades of the men, women and children whose fate was sealed when they entered her steel-rimmed precincts in 1912.

## ALTAMIRA, SPAIN

*CAVE PAINTED BY STONE AGE MEN WITH A MAGNIFICENT ARRAY OF ANIMALS.*

'Look Daddy – painted oxen!' cried the daughter of the antiquarian Marcelino Sanz de Sautuola. The year was 1879 and they were exploring a cave at Altamira, 17 miles (27 km) south-west of Santander in northern Spain. The cave had been discovered ten years earlier by a local man following

his dog, but it was the antiquarian's bored daughter, waving the lantern about, who first saw the now-famous painted ceiling. Here was a superb parade of bison, etched in vibrant shades of red with wonderfully confident, impressionistic strokes. Sometimes the artist even took advantage of swellings in the rock surface to add a sense of volume to the creations.

More pictures were found in other caverns in the Altamira complex, and so bright and lively was the whole assembly that many scholars dismissed them as fakes. However, their authenticity was settled in 1901 by the great French archaeologist Henri Breuil, and it was reinforced by the discovery of scores more painted caves in northern Spain. Among them Altamira remains the most spectacular, having no rival for splendour apart from the French masterpieces at Lascaux.

INTERIOR DECORATION *A fine stag is among the figures that adorn the prehistoric caves at Altamira in Spain.*

The caves date back to about 1200 BC and incorporate 150 animal paintings, including bulls and boars. Bison, however, predominate: painted in red ochre with manes, tails and hooves done in black manganese. As at Lascaux, it has been widely assumed that the paintings served a purpose in hunting magic, but some sexual symbolism in the works has suggested to other researchers that the cave was a sanctuary for fertility rites.

Probably the full purpose will never be known – and nor will the glorious freshness of the paintings ever be quite recovered. For since the caves' discovery there has been some deterioration in the murals due to surplus moisture – caused by the breath of many thousands of visitors – in the atmosphere. Closed in 1977, Altamira was reopened in 1982 but admits only limited numbers of people each day by prior arrangement.

## TALATI DE DALT, MENORCA

*STONE CIRCLES AND UNDERGROUND*
*CHAMBERS ON A SPANISH ISLAND.*

The Balearic Islands off the east coast of Spain are renowned today for their sweeping tourist beaches. However, in Roman times they were known as a home of mercenary warriors famous as 'stone-slingers', or *balearii* (hence the name). Earlier still the islands were inhabited by monument-builders who left them strewn with megalithic remains, and among these none is more atmospheric than the complex at Talati de Dalt on Menorca.

Here, on a hill cloaked with large and venerable olive trees, are relics of a settlement assumed to have been built by the seafaring Torreans, or Tower People. The mysterious raiders (also thought to have built the monuments at Filitosa) invaded Menorca around 1500 BC, and at Talati de Dalt they built a remarkable settlement consisting of five towers and assorted stone circles, underground chambers and round houses with pillared and roofed courts.

The cone-shaped ruins of the main tower stand on the top of the hill, and it is

---

### STANDING STONES

Prehistoric Europe's largest surviving menhir, or standing stone, is the 385 ton Grand Menhir Brisé at Locmariaquer in Brittany. Originally more than 65 ft (20 m) high, the great stone is now broken into four pieces. Perhaps it fell victim to an earthquake or lightning; perhaps it crashed to the ground as the builders tried to heave it into place. The tallest stone still standing, at Kerloas in Brittany, rises to 39 ft (12 m).

---

easy enough to imagine it as a watchtower and fortified retreat for the inhabitants. Other remains are harder to interpret; a solitary menhir, pierced by a hole, looms enigmatically from a spot near the southern margin of the site. Elsewhere, a curious pattern of low stones is laid out like the prows of a boat.

Most perplexing of all is a great T-shaped megalith known as a *taula* (meaning 'table' in Catalan). Comprising a huge standing stone topped by a smaller, horizontal stone, the *taula* was a characteristic creation of the Torreans, and the centrepiece of their ritual sanctuaries. There is no evidence, however, that it served any

*MENORCA MYSTERY The taula, or T-shaped megalith, at Talati de Dalt has a diagonal stone propped against the horizontal. Its function is unknown.*

astronomical purpose, as Stonehenge may have done; and the capstone is much too high to be a convenient altar for sacrifices.

Since bronze bulls have been found at certain sites, some scholars have speculated about a bull cult among the Torreans; the T-shape could be a stylised representation of a bull's head and horns. However, the example at Talati has an extra, diagonal stone laid against one end of the capstone, thus altering the straightforward T shape for no discernible reason (the extra stone is unnecessary for support). Altogether, the sanctuary at Talati – a solemn, almost overpowering presence among the ancient trees – presents a considerable challenge to the imagination of scholars.

## TASSILI N'AJJER, ALGERIA

*DID HIPPOPOTAMUSES ONCE WALLOW*
*AND SHEEP GRAZE IN THE SAHARA?*

The scorched heart of the world's largest desert is a place of annihilating heat. Temperatures in the sprawling sandstone massif of Algeria's Tassili mountains can soar to 70°C (158°F). From among the eroded cliffs and ravines rise wind-scoured, sand-blasted rockstacks that loom like battered cathedral spires against the sky. It is not easy to believe that this desolate landscape was once lush and green. Yet that is what the study of world climate suggests – and key evidence comes from the mountains' rich heritage of prehistoric art.

Thousands of ancient paintings and carvings grace the cliffs and caves. Revealed to the outside world by the Frenchman Henri Lhote during the 1950s, the scenes show dark-skinned huntsmen chasing wild sheep, elephants, buffaloes and hippopotamuses. Some huge, round-headed beings are shown too, and have generally been interpreted as gods or creatures from mythology. (In 1961 a distinguished Soviet physicist, Professor Agrest, caused controversy by suggesting that these might be representations of visitors from outer space – aliens who triggered the rise of civilisation in Egypt and the Near East.)

The hunting scenes date back to 6-4000 BC, many centuries before the Egyptians produced their wall paintings of the same subjects. Later images indicate a transition to the pastoral life, showing huge herds of long-horned cattle being tended, while women and children work by village huts. Ritual celebrations with music and dance are also represented. Later still, enigmatic images of armoured, chariot-riding soldiers crop up in the paintings. They could be Egyptians, their auxiliaries or their enemies. Did they trade with or conquer the cattle herdsmen? Nothing is known for sure.

What is certain is that from about 4000 BC the Sahara was drying out, during an arid phase in the climate, exacerbated by the prevailing winds, and that by Roman times it was as arid as it is today. Whatever fate befell the draughtsmen, the desert claimed their massif – no more paintings were made on the Tassili rocks.

SAHARA PASTURES *Prehistoric paintings at Tassili N'Ajjer demonstrate that the Sahara once teemed with life. The rock engraving (above) shows an ornate cow's head.*

# SACRED SITES

## 2

ANCIENT GOD *Fantastic sculptures grace the jungle city of Angkor Wat in Cambodia.*

ON FEBRUARY 6, 1989, SOME 15 MILLION PEOPLE ASSEMBLED AT ALLAHABAD ON THE GANGES IN INDIA TO TAKE PART IN A HINDU RELIGIOUS FESTIVAL. THIS IS RECKONED TO HAVE BEEN THE GREATEST NUMBER OF HUMAN BEINGS EVER ASSEMBLED FOR A COMMON PURPOSE, AND ITS STATISTICS SHOW THAT RELIGION TODAY REMAINS ONE OF THE MOST DYNAMIC FORCES IN HUMAN AFFAIRS. IN PAST AGES IT HAS PROMPTED CRUEL WARFARE AND PERSECUTION, BUT IT HAS ALSO INSPIRED SUBLIME ACHIEVEMENTS IN ART AND ARCHITECTURE. THE MYSTERIOUS RUINS OF ANCIENT TEMPLES AND THE

GRAND DESIGN *The Maya worshipped at Palenque.*

WORLDWIDE VENERATION OF OTHER HOLY PLACES ALL TESTIFY TO AN AGELESS SENSE OF A WORLD LYING BEYOND VISIBLE EXISTENCE.

# ANCIENT OF DAYS

*Ruined temples, tombs and treasure-decked skeletons cause the imagination to roam around the ultimate mysteries of God and humanity. Here are grand and colourful enigmas, with evidence also of the dark side of religious faith.*

When the stolid French naturalist and explorer Henri Mouhot first discovered the temple citadel of Angkor Wat in 1860, it was a jungle-choked ruin whose overgrown courtyards were bounded by shadowy galleries where bats hung in flocks from the tottering roofs. And yet the stupendous architecture, riotous with sculpted reliefs, could not fail to elicit excitement even from someone with his phlegmatic temperament. The sight, he wrote, made the traveller forget all the fatigues of his journey. 'Suddenly, and as if by enchantment, he seems to be transported from barbarism to civilisation, from profound darkness to light.' The local Indo-Chinese could offer no coherent explanation. 'It was built by giants,' Mouhot was told; 'it built itself'; or 'it is the work of Pra-Eun, the king of the angels.'

Borobudur, Palenque, Abu Simbel, Ellora, ruined temples and tombs of lost civilisations, provoke a special kind of wonder, tinged by the spiritual mysteries of the faiths that inspired them. It is as if the visitor is in the presence not just of the ancient people who shaped the buildings but of their gods too. Standing silent and aloof amidst derelict temples, the

SEATED IN SPLENDOUR *Four giant statues of Ramses II guard Abu Simbel's entrance.*

statues of neglected deities invite the mind to contemplate the timeless puzzles of glory and decay.

While the great religious ruins may open the mind to eternity, the exploration of sacred sites has also yielded disquieting relics: sacrificial altars where blood was let, for example, and macabre burial remains. One of the notable pioneers of archaeology was the Italian Giovanni Belzoni, a former circus strongman who won international renown for hacking and blasting his way into the tombs of ancient Egypt. In 1820 he wrote of his work that he sometimes could not move without brushing his face against that of an ancient corpse. 'I could not avoid being covered with bones, legs, arms and heads rolling from above. Thus I proceeded from one cave to another, all full of mummies piled up in various ways, some standing, some lying and some on their heads.' Always informative, sometimes exciting, tomb-searching has never been a job for the fainthearted.

## ABU SIMBEL, EGYPT

*GIANT PHARAOHS CARVED FROM CLIFFS BY ONE OF EGYPT'S SHOWIEST RULERS.*

Ramses II earned his title of 'the Great' by thinking big. Whether waging war or siring children (Ramses boasted more than 100), the pharaoh did things on a gigantic scale, and in his building works he was equally extravagant. Two huge temples hollowed out of a sandstone cliff at Abu Simbel, a site by the Nile near the border with present-day Sudan, survive in testimony to their creator's monumental ego. The façade of the Great Temple is dominated by four colossal statues of Ramses. The second temple, which is not much smaller, also has immense statues – on this occasion, four of the king and two of his queen, Nofretari. With the two leading members of the royal household immortalised in this way, people could scarcely forget who ruled Egypt.

The great pharaoh was sovereign for 66 years during the 13th century BC, and he built the temples in what used to be called Nubia, lying some distance from his centre of government to the south of Egypt.

It was almost an act of provocation, for the gold-rich Nubians were fierce warriors and had often rebelled against Egyptian overlord-ship. The pharaoh's workmen tunnelled deep into the cliff to create the temple chambers, and sculpted the rock face with magnificent façades. Each of the four statues of Ramses outside the great temple is 66 ft (20 m) high – and seated. Should the monster pharaohs choose to rise, you feel, they would blot out the sun.

These mighty works were not just political propaganda. The Great Temple was dedicated to three great deities: Amun, king of the gods; falcon-headed Horus; and Ptah, god of craftsmen. The power of the pharaoh and the grandeur of the gods were closely linked in the Egyptian mind, and inside the Great Temple the pharaoh is depicted as Osiris, lord of the afterlife. Ritual offerings to the gods were made by lamp-light inside the cave temple, which was so orientated that at certain times of year the rays of the rising sun would flood through the entrance and touch the inner sanctuary with golden light.

During the 1960s, Abu Simbel came under threat from the new flood level of Lake Nasser created by the Aswan High Dam. To save the temples from inundation, an international rescue effort was launched, and the entire temples, with their statuary, were cut in sections from the rock face and reassembled 200 ft (60 m) higher up. It was a fantastically complex undertaking – and it worked. Even the orientation remained the same, so that the rising sun still enters the Great Temple as its ancient architects intended. Here was a project worthy in its breathtaking ambition of the masterbuilder, Ramses II himself.

## THE CARTHAGE TOPHET, TUNISIA

*MACABRE PRECINCT WHERE THE ASHES OF SACRIFICED CHILDREN WERE BURIED.*

Diodorus, a Greek historian born in Sicily, described nightmarish rites practised in Carthage in the 1st century BC. Quoting from an eyewitness account, he wrote that Carthaginian parents brought their children out at night for sacrifice. Masked dancers cavorted and loud music was played as the infant, generally between two and three years old, was presented before a great bronze statue of the god Baal Hammon. At a certain stage in the proceedings, the child was taken off by a priest to have his or her throat cut. The little body was then placed on the statue's outstretched arms, whence it rolled into the flames of a sacrificial fire.

Not much remains of ancient Carthage, the North African city that once rivalled Rome for grandeur. After its defeat in 146 BC the great metropolis was levelled by the Romans, who built a city of their own on its ruins – which was destroyed in turn by the Arabs. The writings of Greek and Roman contemporaries, however, have survived to provide a picture of Carthaginian society.

Carthage was founded by Phoenician traders and retained the Phoenician religion. Baal, the 'Lord', was the Phoenicians' fertility god, worshipped in one guise or another throughout the Near East, and nourished like many other deities by offerings and sacrifices. Human sacrifice was not unknown in the Bible lands (allusion to it is made in the Old Testament story of Abraham and Isaac), but quite why the primitive rite flourished in otherwise sophisticated Carthage remains a mystery.

However, clear evidence that it did comes from Carthaginian walled sanctuaries, known as tophets, which were marked by carved gravestones and urns containing the ashes of the dead children. One tophet at Carthage has yielded the remains of thousands of sacrificed infants, all coming from the wealthier classes. Evidently,

the honour of dedicating a child to Baal in this way was granted only to high-born Carthaginians. Diodorus reported that bereaved parents were required to watch without shedding tears as the priests carried out the appalling sacrifice.

During the last centuries of warfare against Rome, it seems, Baal thirsted with particular eagerness for freshly spilt blood. Diodorus wrote that Carthaginian aristocrats at one time took to substituting the children of slaves for their own in the cruel ceremonies, and that Baal's wrath was expressed through defeats in war. The need to propitiate the god therefore became more urgent – and archaeology confirms an upward trend in child sacrifices. From finds in the sacred precinct, it has been estimated that, towards the end of the Carthaginian era, ritual killings numbered 500 a year. Weed-grown today, some broken and some fallen, the carved stones of the Carthage tophet record a bloodbath.

## TULA, MEXICO

*RITES OF THE PLUMED SERPENT – AND HUMAN SACRIFICE – TOOK PLACE HERE.*

Giant carved columns in black basalt brood in silence over the central pyramid at Tula. These stone warriors once supported the roof of the priests' temple at the summit, and look across the ruins of a city that was once home to some 30 000 people. Tula is

TOLTEC REMAINS *Stone warriors surmount the Tula pyramid, and a carved jaguar feasts on human hearts.*

believed to be Tollan, the ancient capital of the Toltecs whose civilisation flourished from the 10th to the 13th century AD. And its relics bear eloquent witness to the grim rites of the rain god Tlaloc, who feasted on freshly sacrificed human hearts.

The Toltecs were a shadowy people who had vanished long before the conquistadors overran Mexico. Spanish chroniclers were told by local Indians that the Aztecs had been strongly influenced in their art, architecture and religion by this earlier society. 'They cut jade and they cast gold, and made other works of the craftsman and feather worker,' a Franciscan friar was informed. 'And these Toltecs enjoyed great wealth; they were rich; they were never poor. Nothing did they lack in their homes.' Legends about the Toltec capital, Tollan, recur in Mexican folklore, but it was not until 1940 that the site was identified at the dusty village of Tula de Allende, lying some 50 miles (80 km) north of Mexico City.

Here, in a sun-scorched valley, archaeologists uncovered pyramid temples and images of the plumed serpent symbolising

## CASTING A DIVINE SHADOW

The El Castillo pyramid in the ancient Mexican city of Chichen Itza is so constructed that, at the spring and autumn equinoxes, sunlight sends a shadow image of the plumed serpent god Quetzalcóatl winding down each set of steps .

the god-king Quetzalcóatl – revered by the earlier peoples of Teotihuacán and worshipped by the Aztecs. *Quetzal* is the name for a brightly plumed bird of the rainforest; *cóatl* means serpent; and the feathered snake was the emblem of Tula's founder, who came to be venerated as a god-king. Here, too, were grislier relics: temple reliefs depicting eagles and jaguars feasting upon human hearts.

More sinister still were the stone images of the rain god Tlaloc in a reclining position, holding a bowl to catch the freshly sacrificed hearts of the victims that the priests brought to him. Such sacrificial

altars are not unique to Tula; at Maya sites they are known as *chacmools* after Chac, the Maya equivalent of Tlaloc, although the Maya were less inclined towards human sacrifice than the more bloodthirsty Toltecs. The Toltecs were a tough, warlike people, and their soldiers, who carried obsidian-edged swords, overran the older Maya centres, taking their gods and their ceremonies with them. The Toltec gods thirsted for human sacrifice, and their warriors provided victims aplenty; at Tula, archaeologists discovered a skull rack where victims' heads were displayed.

### LESHAN, CHINA
*A GREAT BUDDHA*
*OVERLOOKS THREE RIVERS.*

Mere statistics cannot convey the immensity of this sacred effigy – the world's largest Buddha. Carved from the red rock of the riverside cliffs, Leshan's seated Grand Buddha is 230 ft (70 m) high, dwarfing New York's Statue of Liberty (a mere 150 ft – 46 m – high): his ears alone are 23 ft (7 m) long, and a picnic could be held on his big toenail.

The historic town of Leshan lies in Sichuan, a province at the heart of China. Over 1000 rock tombs were cut in the neighbourhood under the Eastern Han Dynasty (AD 25-220). Its proudest boast, however, is the Buddha. Overlooking the confluence of the Dadu, Quingyi and Minjiang rivers, the statue was the brainchild of a Buddhist monk called Haitong, who began it in AD 713 in order to protect boatmen from the rivers' swirling waters. It was not only the Buddha's tranquil gaze that offered protection, for surplus rock from the sculpture was used to fill in depressions in the river bed that caused dangerous eddies.

Known locally as Dafo, the figure took some 90 years to complete, and incorporates a water-drainage system designed to prevent erosion. This has not been wholly

COLOSSUS *For more than 1000 years the Grand Buddha of Leshan has meditated on eternity.*

successful; green foliage has trespassed into moist pockets, so that ferns flourish around the Buddha's topknots and flowers bloom on his colossal hands. These signs of neglect have not interfered with Dafo's survival as a focus for pilgrims and tourists, however. Hundreds of narrow stairs lead from the riverbank up to a Grand Buddha temple that rises from a promontory near Dafo's head, while a passenger boat operating from Leshan pier offers visitors a view of the statue from its deck.

### TEOTIHUACAN, MEXICO
*CENTRAL AMERICAN CITY OF THE*
*GODS, ADORNED BY A PYRAMID.*

At the height of its power around AD 500, the ancient metropolis of Teotihuacán was bigger than imperial Rome. Rising from a high plateau and laid out on a grid plan, the site sprawled over 7 sq miles (18 km$^2$)

and contained a population of over 150000 inhabitants. Once thought to be the work of the Aztecs, the city was in fact built by a much earlier people of whom little is known. The Aztecs knew its ruins, however, and held them to be sacred: Teotihuacán is an Aztec term meaning 'the great city where men became gods'.

Courts and palaces line the ceremonial heart of the city, but this was, above all, a great religious centre. Its skyline was dominated by a colossal Pyramid of the Sun, rising to 210 ft (64 m). As large around the base as the Great Pyramid in Egypt, the spectacular monument was raised on the site of an earlier shrine. Nearby stood the smaller Pyramid of the Moon, at the north end of the 2 mile (3 km) long Street of the Dead. The avenue's name was invented by the Aztecs, who mistook its many small ceremonial platforms for tombs. The Street of the Dead was in fact the city's principal avenue, a sacred way lined by more than 100 religious buildings. One of these, situated in an enclosure known as the Citadel, is the Temple of Quetzalcóatl, adorned with elaborate stone carvings of the feathered serpent and the goggle-eyed rain god Tlaloc. Both were deities of great importance to the Central American peoples, and would reappear later in the Toltec and Aztec pantheons.

SACRED WAY *The pyramid of the Sun rises on the left of Teotihuacán's main avenue. A carving of Quetzalcóatl (right) ornaments the temple of the feathered serpent.*

Teotihuacán flourished from about 100 BC to AD 750 as the first great metropolis of the Americas. Its mysterious rulers and priests were so confident of their power that they built no formal defences around the city – a misplaced confidence, as it turned out, that must have contributed to Teotihuacán's eventual collapse. It is evident that a decline set in towards the end of the Teotihuacán era, when a drop in annual rainfall affected farming in the area. Relatively unprotected, with a falling population, the city fell prey in AD 750 to nameless invaders, who looted its buildings and set them ablaze.

## THE ROMAN CATACOMBS, ITALY

*VAST SUBTERRANEAN CEMETERIES CONTAIN EARLY CHRISTIAN GRAVES.*

While wealthy Roman citizens might furnish themselves with a tomb, the mass of the Roman people cremated their dead. The early Christians, however, regarded the funeral pyres with alarm; they believed firmly in the resurrection of the body, and to burn a corpse would put the soul in jeopardy. They also believed that the poor were as worthy of attention as the rich, and one early Church father, Ambrose, declared that in order to secure a proper Christian burial it was even permitted to melt down and sell sacred vessels.

Burial within the walls of Rome was forbidden by law, and so the early Christian believers tunnelled out a vast system of underground passages and tombs outside the city walls. These are the catacombs, a secret realm of the dead that eventually extended for 150 miles (240 km) around the original perimeter of the city.

Built chiefly between the 2nd and 4th centuries, Rome's catacombs contain the bodies of some 75 000 people. Many tunnels were made in abandoned quarries where Roman masons had obtained a soft volcanic rock known as *tufa*. Some were burrowed from wells, others from virgin ground, and others still from existing tombs. Believers especially prized sites close to the tombs of Christian martyrs. The simplest resting places were hollows dug into the passage walls in which the body, wrapped in linen, was laid. More elaborate family chambers, which housed successive generations, were also cut. In some catacombs, pictures of the *fossores*, or tomb-diggers, have survived; they wear short tunics and carry picks and lamps with chains and spikes that could be hammered into a wall to leave the hands free.

Though there is no evidence to suppose (as is often claimed) that the early Christians hid in the catacombs in times of persecution, they entered them regularly to visit the tombs of martyrs and of their own families. St Jerome (AD 342-420) describes boyhood visits, made on Sundays, to corpse-lined crypts where 'everything is so dark that it seems almost as if the psalmist's words were fulfilled: "Let them go down alive into hell." Here and there the light, not entering through windows but filtering down from above through shafts, relieves the horror of the darkness. But again, as one

MULTI-STOREY TOMBS *Rome's catacombs contain burial chambers that were dug out layer upon layer.*

cautiously moves forward, the black night closes round . . .'

In medieval times, pilgrims to Christian Rome paid scant attention to the great labyrinth of tombs, some as many as six storeys deep, which lay underneath the holy city. During the 17th century, however, increasing numbers began to explore what were now 'monstrous, unwholesome and stinking places', in the words of one visiting bishop. Relic-hunters plundered the catacombs, destroying as they went, and it was only in the 19th century that careful investigation was carried out in them in the interests of science and religion. They proved to be treasure-troves for researchers as tomb paintings found there are almost the only forms of Christian art surviving from the early years of persecution. New catacombs have been discovered at intervals throughout the 20th century. An underground city of ghosts, this shadowy metropolis beneath Rome sheds invaluable light on the character of a dawning faith.

## YAZD, IRAN

*THE DEAD WERE EXPOSED TO EAGLES IN ZOROASTRIAN TOWERS OF SILENCE.*

The town of Yazd lies at the desert edge some 325 miles (520 km) south-east of Iran's capital, Tehran. Silk fabrics and Persian carpets are among its leading products, but apart from its textiles the town is also known as an ancient centre of the Zoroastrian religion, founded by the Iranian prophet Zarathustra in the 6th century BC. Zarathustra was a priest of the Aryan faith, which venerated fire as the element of the great god Ahura Mazda. About eight centuries after the prophet's time his religion became state orthodoxy, and fire altars were set up all over the country, in both temples and open spaces, where flames were kept permanently burning.

Fire has remained the key feature of the religion as practised by Parsees, who are the modern descendants of the Zoroastrians. To this day they tend perpetual fires in their temples, and their priests wear veils to prevent their breath from contaminating the purity of the sacred flames.

Two other elements were sacred to the Zoroastrians, in addition to fire. These were earth and water, and the pollution of any of the three was held to be an act of desecration. These notions created difficulties when it came to disposing of the dead. A corpse could not be buried without defiling the earth, or burnt without contaminating the fire. The solution was to build *dakhmes*, or Towers of Silence, huge circular structures of stone or brick with high walls but no roofs.

The most impressive – and certainly the most photographed – rise from hilltops outside Yazd. In the Towers of Silence the naked bodies of the dead were deposited on one of three concentric circular platforms: the men were placed on the outer platform, the women on the inner one, and the children on the central one. Exposed to the open sky, the bodies were quickly stripped of flesh by vultures and eagles. The bones, baked and bleached by the sun, were disposed of months later in a central pit in the *dakhme*.

Modern Parsees continue to maintain these ancient funeral traditions. The towers

FUNERAL PLATFORMS *The sky, not the earth, claims the dead at Yazd in Iran.*

themselves are closed to everyone except the corpse-bearers, but on one day every year a special festival is held in honour of Farvardin, the god who presides over departed souls. On this day the people gather on the hills around the towers and pray for the dead.

## ANGKOR, CAMBODIA

*THE WORLD'S LARGEST RELIGIOUS COMPLEX IN THE HEART OF THE JUNGLE.*

It has been likened to a journey through the universe. The jungle city of Angkor once sprawled over nearly 38 sq miles (100 km²), incorporating moats and canals that glimmered like the cosmic oceans of myth, terraces and galleries representing the earthly continents, and giant temples symbolising Mount Meru, the Hindu home of the gods. All these were built by successive rulers in order to glorify their capital city and emphasise their own divinity.

The existence of the immense ruined city seemed little more than a rumour until 1860, when the French naturalist Henri Mouhot, with backing from the British Royal Geographical Society, travelled deep into the heart of the Cambodian jungle to uncover its splendours. Then, invading creepers and the colossal roots of banyan trees held the ruins in their grip, and during the 20th century the crumbling metropolis has again been threatened during decades of warfare. Yet Angkor still stands, provoking questions about who shaped its glorious architecture.

The ruined city was once the capital of the Khmers, a people whose empire flourished between the 9th and 14th centuries AD in modern Cambodia, extending into parts of southern Vietnam, Laos and Thailand. Khmer prosperity was founded on rice. This they were able to cultivate on a huge scale thanks to a vast irrigation network fed by the Mekong River system and its monsoon waters. Wealth derived from

swollen rice harvests turned Angkor's rulers into god-kings who lived in great splendour.

Angkor's temples celebrated the god-kings and their Hindu beliefs. The most stupendous of all is Angkor Wat, built by Surayvarman II (AD 1113-50), which covers almost 1 sq mile (2.6 km²), an area larger than the Vatican, and is the world's largest temple complex. It rises in tiers from terraces adorned with galleries and pavilions, to

**JUNGLE MARVEL** *The temple of Angkor Wat still amazes, despite centuries of neglect and the depredations of the forest that engulfs the ancient Khmer capital.*

form a pyramid crowned by a cluster of five towers, the tallest soaring to 213 ft (65 m). Dedicated to the god Vishnu, Angkor Wat was also its builder's burial place and faces west towards the land of the dead.

Nearby stand complexes of comparable grandeur, protected by moats once stocked with crocodiles and with gateways big enough to allow the royal elephants easy passage. Hosts of sacred dancers, known as *apsaras,* are commemorated in countless carved reliefs, along with battle pictures and scenes from the Hindu epics. Among the most striking images are gigantic stone faces of the Buddha set up by Jayavarman VII (1181-*c.*1215), the last great king, who was a devout Buddhist.

The Khmers' shift from Hinduism to Buddhism may help to explain their decline. The Buddhist sect that came to hold sway promoted a doctrine of renunciation, non-materialism and self-denial that was at odds with the empire-building traditions of the tyrant god-kings. In 1431 Angkor was sacked by neighbouring Thai armies, and the people put up only limited resistance. With the collapse of authority the great waterworks fell into disrepair, and the capital, which had once boasted a population of well over half a million, was abandoned to the ever-spreading jungle.

## PALENQUE, MEXICO

*ANCIENT CARVING OF A MAYA KING —*
*OR A VISITOR FROM OUTER SPACE?*

In his international bestseller *Chariots of the Gods* (1967), the writer Erich von Daniken proposed that alien beings from a distant galaxy created intelligent man and were worshipped as gods by early peoples because of their advanced technology. Among the archaeological finds von Daniken quoted to support his theory was a figure carved on a sarcophagus lid at Palenque. This was said to represent an ancient astronaut. 'There sits a human being, with the upper part of his body bent forward like a racing motor-cyclist; today any child would identify his vehicle as a rocket.'

In reality, tomb inscriptions deciphered in the 1970s identify the figure very clearly as King Pacal, a king of the Maya who died in the year AD 683, and his 'rocket' is a no more than a maize plant, symbolising rebirth. The Maya relics at Palenque are so impressive, however, that it is easy to see

ANCIENT ASTRONAUT? *Some have interpreted this image (above) as an alien and a rocketship. In fact, it represents a Maya king with a maize plant. It comes from a sarcophagus in the crypt of Palenque's Temple of the Inscriptions (right).*

how they might cause some observers' imaginations to run riot.

The Maya are a mysterious people who built cities in the jungles of Central America and possessed extensive knowledge of science, mathematics and astronomy. Yet at the height of their culture, around AD 800, their civilisation ended. The ruling elite vanished; temples were left unfinished and towns were abandoned.

Set against the emerald splendour of the rain forest, Palenque is perhaps the most beautiful of the Maya's forgotten cities. It lies in the foothills of the Usumacinta mountains, a ceremonial centre rich in palaces, stairways, plazas, aqueducts and pyramids. The outstanding Temple of the Inscriptions, which contains King Pacal's sarcophagus, stands at the summit of a nine-stepped pyramid.

# THE SACRED BALL COURTS OF THE MAYA

The ancient peoples of central America were passionate enthusiasts for a ball game known to the Maya as *pok-a-tok* and to the Aztecs as *tlachtli*. This was a sacred sport played with a solid rubber ball on a long, narrow court shaped like a capital 'I'. The court was flanked with sloping or vertical walls, into which two stone rings were set at right angles just above the players' heads. The aim of the game was to get the ball through one of the rings – a difficult feat considering that players were not allowed to throw or kick the ball. Instead, they had to bounce it off the hips, knees or elbows – as protection they wore heavily padded clothing. Two teams competed, passing the ball between players, and high stakes were wagered on the result, including jade, gold, slaves and houses. Skilled players were hugely admired, and the rewards for success were high: the winners were entitled to the jewellery and clothing of the spectators. Failure, however, incurred displeasure – the losers were sometimes sacrificed.

Elaborate ceremonies accompanied the contests, which clearly had some ritualistic significance. The courts were often sited by the temples, which may have served as viewing stands for the upper classes. In the ruined Maya city of Chichén Itzá, for example, the ball court adjoins the impressive Temple of Jaguars.

**SPORTING VENUE** *In the sacred ball court at Chichén Itzá, losing players were sometimes beheaded.*

In 1949 a team of archaeologists led by the Mexican Alberto Ruz Lhuiller discovered an interior chamber under the temple's flagstone floor. Stone steps blocked with rubble led down through a tunnel into the core of the pyramid, where Ruz found the skeletons of six young victims of human sacrifice. Breaking through a triangular doorway, the archaeologists entered a darkened vault. Lights picked out wall carvings of nine gods of the Underworld standing guard over the sarcophagus of King Pacal.

Inside lay the body of a man whose teeth were painted red and who was covered with green jade jewellery, including a magnificent mask of jade mosaic, with shell and obsidian inlay for the eyes. Following tradition, the dead man had also been buried with a jade bead in his mouth so that his spirit could buy food in the afterlife. The most curious detail was a small duct that began at the side of the sarcophagus and ran along the corridor and up the stairway to the floor of the temple. This hollow tube is believed to have been designed to relay incantations from the priests in the temple to the spirit of the dead man below.

No one knows precisely what rites were enacted in the temple, but one thing is certain: finds as eerie and extraordinary as those as Palenque do not require tales of spacemen to make them more interesting.

## VILLA OF MYSTERIES, POMPEII, ITALY

*SECRET RITES OF DIONYSUS REVEALED IN PAINTINGS OF ANTIQUITY.*

'A thick and ominous smoke was spreading over the Earth . . . we were enveloped by night. It was not a moonless night, or one dimmed by cloud, but the pitch darkness of a sealed room without lights. Only the shrill cries of the women, the wailing of children and the shouting of men could be heard . . .' So wrote the Roman politician Pliny the Younger in an eyewitness account of the catastrophe at Pompeii. For two days in the summer of AD 79, Mount Vesuvius hurled out a vast tonnage of ash and lava that buried the entire city. Centuries later, archaeologists would find preserved in the compacted ash the bodies of people who

**MYSTERY FRESCO** *A Pompeian initiate into the cult of Dionysus is beaten by an angel.*

were overcome by poisonous volcanic smoke as they sought to flee or take shelter from the disaster. Streets, forum, baths and theatres have been excavated, revealing graffiti that provide minute insights into everyday life.

Among the private houses, none is more fascinating than a villa situated slightly to the south of the town, famed for its life-size frescoes depicting the secret rites of the god Dionysus. The Villa of Mysteries, as it is known, presents a complete cycle of paintings that show a woman's initiation into the cult. In one scene she stands veiled while a naked child reads a lesson under the watchful eye of a solemn matron. In another, a bearded Pan plays his lyre while three women sit around a table. In yet another, the kneeling initiate is being scourged by a female figure resembling a winged angel.

What is the meaning of these strange, compelling images? Scholars remain baffled, though something is known of the cult's history. Dionysus, who features in the villa's scenes, was the Greek god of wine. Known to the Romans as Bacchus, he was originally a nature god of fruitfulness and vegetation whose rites were celebrated every spring in Greece. The phallus, symbol of male fertility, was conspicuous in his rituals, and there was always an orgiastic element in his worship, revellers seeking to become possessed by his spirit through wild dancing and drinking.

The cult came to republican Rome via southern Italy, and at first the mysteries were for women only. Subsequently, admission was extended to men. The 'Bacchanalians' held clandestine meetings by night, in caves and cellars where they danced by torchlight. Wine was consumed in great quantities, and the grossest depravities were attributed to the participants. Besides sexual misconduct, all kinds of crimes and political intrigues were alleged by the authorities to take place, and in 186 BC more than 7000 men and women were executed or imprisoned in an attempt to suppress the cult.

In spite of this repression, however, the secret worship of Bacchus never entirely died out. And from the scenes in the Villa of Mysteries it is clear that the cult had a deep seriousness. Whatever their precise meaning, these allegorical images speak of an authentic solemnity and reverence. The true Bacchanalian, it appears, was much more than a drunken reveller.

## AACHEN CATHEDRAL, GERMANY

*DO THE MEGALITH-BUILDERS' SECRETS SURVIVE IN CHARLEMAGNE'S THRONE?*

Not many years ago, the German photographer Hermann Weisweiler discovered by accident some remarkable features in the cathedral at Aachen, west of Bonn. Waiting for favourable sunlight to photograph the interior of the Octagon Chapel he was startled to notice a ray of sunlight suddenly burst in through a window.

Intrigued, he made a closer study of the way that sunshine illuminated the interior of this historic chapel, construction of which started in AD 786 on the orders of the great Frankish emperor Charlemagne. It was to be the sacred heart of his capital city. The photographer found that on June 21 – in other words, Midsummer's Day – sunlight

SEAT OF POWER *The throne of Charlemagne in Aachen Cathedral was carved from ancient Roman stone.*

entering through the eastern octagon window would light up the crowned head of the emperor as he sat upon his throne. At the equinoxes, sunbeams falling at other angles also bathed the throne in light, suggesting that the architects had employed sophisticated astronomical knowledge to stage-manage mystical lighting effects for their emperor.

Charlemagne, who wanted the world to see him as an imperial sovereign in the great Roman tradition, attracted scholars from all over Europe to his court at Aachen, and he is known to have taken a personal interest in astronomy. It is not impossible, then, to believe that careful thought was applied to the precise placing of the throne – on which imperial coronations would be held throughout the Middle Ages. Situated at the west end of the chapel, the raised chair was approached by six steps; they were made from marble fashioned from ancient pillars, as if to reinforce links with the great tradition.

More extraordinary – and much more controversial – was Hermann Weisweiler's finding that there are similarities between the palace chapel's ground plan and that of megalithic Stonehenge in England. If the plan of Stonehenge's lintel ring and inner horseshoe is superimposed at the same scale on the Octagon Chapel, their features make a rough fit.

It is an additional curiosity that Aachen and Stonehenge both lie close to latitude 51°N. Does the Octagon Chapel enshrine ancient secrets that were known to the megalith-builders – preserved, perhaps, by monks and craftsmen in Europe, or by men of learning brought to Aachen from the British Isles? Or are these things no more than coincidences?

## ELLORA, INDIA

*FANTASTIC CAVE TEMPLES ADORNED*
*WITH SCULPTURES CARVED FROM ROCK.*

The gigantic Kailasa temple at Ellora in west India is the world's largest monolithic structure; carved out of a single outcrop of rock, this stupendous edifice has dimensions twice those of the Parthenon in Athens – 275 ft (84 m) long by 155 ft (47 m) wide and 110 ft (34 m) high.

Dedicated to the god Shiva, it was constructed by kings of the Rastrakuta dynasty ruling in the Deccan region of western India between about AD 755 and 975. The site incorporates a central temple set in a courtyard and supported on a frieze of elephants. The temple has a gabled front and a tower in three tiers beneath a cupola. Among its glories is a shrine to the holy Shiva lingam, a stylised stone phallic symbol surrounded by flowers and lit by candle-light, and a frieze showing the demon king Ravana trying to lift the Hindus' holy mountain, Kailasa. Shiva, unperturbed, puts his foot down to thwart the efforts of the evil one.

Starting at the top of a cliff, battalions of stonecutters worked in shifts to shape this wonder, and in the process they removed 3 million cu ft (84 000 m³) of rock. Yet, incredibly, the Kailasa temple is just one of 34 sculpted caves at Ellora. Built between AD 600 and 1000, they celebrate the Buddhist, Hindu and Jain faiths of their

CAVE TEMPLE *Sculpted out of a cliff, the immense Kailasa Temple took 150 years to create. The interior of Cave 29 (far left) is another of Ellora's rock-cut wonders.*

makers in one colossal rock-cut library of mythology. Here calm Buddhas sit under trees and parasols, and ferocious Hindu goddesses do battle, while lovers, lion thrones, peacocks, eagles and monkeys all feature. Many of the caves are dark, and some of the sculptures are so inaccessible that visitors wanting to take photographs require the services of a guide with a mirror. Yet the glory of the builders' creative spirit shines through at every turn.

How did the great work begin? Over 2000 years ago, Buddhist monks took sanctuary in smaller caves that they excavated out of the rocks at Ajanta, not far away. These they decorated with wall paintings and sculptures depicting the life of the Buddha and tales from the Buddhist fables. Some of the caves were left mysteriously unfinished, and the site itself seems to have been suddenly abandoned. The monks evidently moved to Ellora, where they began working in the same tranquil tradition.

The Buddhist impetus had tailed off around AD 800, but their practice of cave-making and adornment was taken up by the Hindus and by followers of the ascetic Jain religion, who worked side by side at Ellora, without apparent feuding, for centuries. The Jain temples are less dramatic in their imagery than the Hindu ones, but are notable for their exquisite attention to detail.

Ellora represents a rare example of different faiths enjoying a wholly peaceful coexistence, and, taken collectively, its remarkable rock-cut temples survive as the supreme testament to the varied magnificence of India's sacred art.

## ELEUSIS, GREECE

*DEATH WAS THE PRICE FOR REVEALING THE RELIGIOUS RITES ENACTED HERE.*

About 14 miles (23 km) from Athens, the busy little industrial town of Eleusis contains the site of the most famous religious ceremonies in ancient Greece. Despite their fame, these rites were shrouded in secrecy; very little was ever divulged about what transpired in the Eleusinian mysteries. The Athenian politician Alcibiades was condemned to death (though later reprieved) for parodying part of the ceremony, and

CULT CENTRE *Ancient Eleusis witnessed the secret ceremonies of the goddess Demeter. The goddess Demeter and her daughter Persephone (above left) send a gift of corn for mankind.*

Aeschylus, the tragic dramatist born at Eleusis, was almost lynched on suspicion of disclosing details on the stage.

The rites originated in an agrarian fertility cult, and the main deities worshipped were the corn goddess Demeter and her daughter Persephone. Persephone was kidnapped by Hades, god of the dead, and taken down to the underworld, but Zeus was moved by Demeter's sorrow and allowed her daughter to return to Earth for part of the year. For the Greeks the myth symbolised the regeneration of living things in the spring. Ceremonies at Eleusis recalled the descent into the underworld and culminated in a rite enacted in a darkened hall, where the worshippers were shown visions in flashes of light. The nature of the revelations is unknown, but the Roman orator Cicero derived great spiritual comfort from the experience.

Situated on a rocky ridge close to the shore of the Bay of Eleusis, the site was excavated by the Greek Archaeological Society after 1882. Visitors wander today among the remains of the ancient paved road of the Sacred Way, the monumental gateways, and the Telestrion or Hall of Initiation, which dominated everything else. About 170 ft (50 m) square, the great hall was surrounded on all sides by steps partly cut into the solid rock. These served as tiers of seats for some 3000 initiates watching the sacred pageant staged below. To explore these precincts is to tread ground that, for 2000 years, was forbidden to the uninitiated – on penalty of death.

## WIELICZKA, POLAND

*EXTRAORDINARY CHAPELS AND STATUES OF SAINTS CARVED OUT OF ROCK SALT.*

This is a prime candidate for the world's strangest place of worship. Some 8 miles (13 km) south-east of Cracow lies a salt mine reaching more than 325 ft (100 m) below the ground. The workings date back to the 10th century, and were often visited by the kings and princes of medieval Europe. A 17th-century Frenchman wrote that 'the salt mines of Wieliczka are as remarkable as the pyramids of Egypt', adding that they were a lot more useful, too. Flights of steps connect seven different levels of workings, and among the subterranean maze of white corridors, chambers and galleries is the immense Crystal Cave whose walls, garlanded with salt crystals, soar to a roof 262 ft (80 m) high. There are glimmering underground ponds

SALINE SOLUTION *For worship at work, Wieliczka's miners cut chapels from the rock salt.*

here, too. The most remarkable sites are the chapels at the back of the mine, richly ornamented with altars and statues.

The St Anthony Chapel was carved from a block of rock salt in 1675. The Holy Cross Chapel takes its name from a large crucifix of salt and was cut in the same century, while the St Cunigonde Chapel is a 19th-century creation, commemorating a medieval saint, Cunigonde, wife of the Holy Roman Emperor Henry II, who became a nun in her widowhood. These were not wrought from the salt as whims but expressed the sincere religious faith of the miners, and their hopes for divine protection amid the dangers of their everyday life.

## BOROBUDUR, JAVA

*SHADOWY KINGS MAPPED BUDDHIST BELIEF IN A MOUNTAIN TEMPLE.*

'The inhabitants make wine from coconut palm blossoms and when they drink it, they become drunk.' So wrote a Chinese ambassador, describing the people of ancient

Java. In the 8th century AD this Indonesian island was a patchwork of wealthy kingdoms set against a backdrop of volcanic mountains and lush vegetation flourishing under the tropical sun. But if the inhabitants' fondness for coconut wine conveys a sense of indolent luxury, that is illusory. The fighting galleys of Javanese warlords struck terror throughout the South China Sea; the raiders were reputedly 'black, skinny, terrible and wicked like death'. And one principality has won renown for displaying energy of a different kind. Its people were builders on the colossal scale, and their temple of Borobudur, rising from a green plain in southern central Java, is a gigantic testament to the Buddha's tranquil faith.

Some 2 million cu ft (56 000 m³) of stone, 27 000 sq ft (2500 m²) of bas-reliefs and 440 statues were incorporated in the building, which rises from a square base through ten successive levels of concentric terraces that represent the successive stages in the pilgrim's progress from ignorance to enlightenment and, as a whole, make up a symbolic diagram of the universe. On the vertical surfaces is carved a continuous relief depicting events from the Buddha's life and key aspects of his teachings. The summit is graced by three circular terraces supporting 72 *stupas*, bell-shaped shrines containing images of the Buddha, who is only partially visible through their latticed stonework. A single, crowning central *stupa* represents nirvana – the supreme goal of Buddhism – in which the soul is freed from all earthly bonds.

Who was responsible for building this amazing cosmography in stone? Borobudur was conceived by a mysterious dynasty of kings known as the Shailendra, or 'sovereigns of the mountain'. It is known that they ruled central Java in the 8th and 9th centuries, and began work on the temple around AD 800.

BLESSED RELIEF *Followers of the Buddha are depicted on this carved relief from Borobudur (above). The great temple represented the stage-by-stage ascent to nirvana.*

Though they seem to have imported Buddhism from mainland south-east Asia, historians believe that the Shailendra kings were themselves Indonesian in origin. Evidence suggests that the Javanese villagers worked willingly on their great undertaking, and that the kings were perhaps regarded as *bodhisattvas*, saints who would be united with Buddha in nirvana after death. But not much more is known; the Shailendra kingdom fell around AD 900 with as little noise as it had made coming into existence. The rulers left no boastful monuments of conquest, but hundreds of thousands of pilgrims still come to Borobudur every year to read their eternal message in stone.

## LAKE TITICACA, BOLIVIA/PERU

*DAZZLING BLUE WATERS WHERE THE INCAS' SACRED HISTORY BEGAN.*

Travellers reaching the shores of Lake Titicaca will probably find themselves gasping for breath, for the air is thin about this vast expanse of water that, on its high Bolivian plateau, mirrors a shining blue sky.

Lake Titicaca is not only the largest lake in South America; at 12 506 ft (3812 m) above sea level, it is also the highest navigable body of water in the world. The people of the surrounding uplands have developed extraordinary physical characteristics to cope with this breathless altitude. Lung development is almost a third greater than is normal for people elsewhere in the world, and the heartbeat is slower.

Stony and sparse in vegetation, the high terrain might seem a strange place in which to find the ruins of a civilisation. Yet at Tiahuanaco, 12 miles (19 km) south of the lake, are the remnants of a city dating back before the time of the Incas. Built between AD 500 and 1000, its great Gate of the Sun, Acapana pyramid and Temple of Kalasaya are relics of one of South America's oldest civilisations, whose hieroglyphics have still to be deciphered. Little is known of the people who founded the city, but they seem to have been overrun by the Incas who, while destroying their culture, borrowed some of its ideas. One of these was a reverence for Lake Titicaca.

According to Inca legend, the lake was the home of Viracocha, the invisible Creator God, who had the power of self-multiplication, some of his offspring becoming local gods themselves. When he emerged from the lake's icy depths, he made the sun, moon and stars and set them on their regular courses. The sun god, Inti, sent Manco Capac and Mama Ocllo, the founders for the Inca dynasty, down to earth and from them all the Inca kings were descended, so the lake was venerated as the womb both of gods and of kings.

Ruins of both Inca and pre-Inca civilisations survive on the sacred Isla del Sol, or Island of the Sun, situated in the Bolivian section near the southern end of Lake Titicaca. It was here that, according to legend, the Inca founders arrived on Earth, and gold and silver offerings have been found buried there. The chief destination

for pilgrims in past times was a gold-plated rock projection on the tip of the island, dedicated to the sun god. In this place where the legends of succeeding civilisations have become entwined, much is still not known.

## THE EXTERNSTEINE, GERMANY

*A RUINED CHAPEL, CAVES AND CARVINGS AMONG WEATHERED ROCK PINNACLES.*

The shrine is carved high up in one of the many natural rock pillars that form the Externsteine, near Detmold in Germany. Reached by a precarious footbridge, it has a circular window orientated towards the midsummer sunrise. The shrine is roofless now, but it would once have been a place of darkness, broken by the sunbeam as it illuminated a niche on the facing wall. To this day, no one can say for certain who

HOLY WATER *Lake Titicaca was sacred to the Incas and their predecessors in the Andean highlands. This carved monolith (below) comes from ancient Tiahuanaco.*

ROCK CHAPEL *A curved walkway leads up to the shrine at the Externsteine.*

carved this sacred light-box, but all the evidence suggests prehistoric origins among a people who, like the builders of Stonehenge, regarded the midsummer solstice – the day on which the sun reaches its highest point in the sky in the northern hemisphere, and therefore the longest day of the year – as a vital astronomical event. The belief was to linger, for the Nazis tried to revive solstice celebrations here as part of their drive to restore Nordic pagan rites under the Third Reich.

Certainly, the sanctuary lies in wooded country bristling with standing stones. The forest, known as the Teutoburger Wald, was a major centre of pagan worship, and nowhere can have made a stronger impression on the pre-Christian priests than the Externsteine where five huge, eroded pillars rise a good 100 ft (30 m) above the trees. There is abundant evidence that pagan worship did take place here – indeed, there are records of the ancient rites being suppressed at the Externsteine by the Frankish emperor Charlemagne, a 9th-century champion of Christendom.

Subsequently, the site was taken over by Christian monks who also left their imprint here, using an assortment of rock-cut chambers as hermitages for their own meditations. Around AD 1120 they carved a relief at the Externsteine of the Deposition from the Cross, in which Christian imagery triumphs over the pagan Irminsul, or world pillar. Altogether, this is a place steeped in mystical associations; its intermingling strands of nature worship and Christian faith are hard to disentangle.

## GLASTONBURY, ENGLAND

*LEGENDS OF KING ARTHUR CLING TO THIS MYSTICAL PLACE.*

If a special aura has long been attached to Glastonbury, it must have something to do with its Tor, a hill that rears up with dramatic suddenness from the flat landscape of the Somerset Levels. A realm of fairies in ancient myth, the hill is crowned by a solitary tower, which is all that survives of a 13th-century church dedicated to St Michael. Seen at dusk, it provides a supremely romantic silhouette wholly fitting to this, one of the most mystical sites in the British Isles.

In 1191 the monks of Glastonbury Abbey, situated below the Tor, announced that they had discovered the graves and corpses of King Arthur and his queen Guinevere, which they reburied in their church. The site of Arthur's supposed burial place is now marked off on the greensward among the abbey ruins. Archaeologists in the 1960s confirmed that a burial had taken place here, though the grave's owner could not be identified.

Historians date the abbey back to around AD 700, but legend places its origins much further back in time. The abbey, it is said, was founded by Joseph of Arimathea, the man who prepared the body of Christ for burial. According to tradition, he came to Glastonbury and here leaned on his staff in prayer. The staff took root and became the famous Glastonbury Thorn, a plant that blooms around Christmas-time. Pilgrims and visitors still arrive in midwinter to see descendants of the Thorn come into flower in the

abbey grounds and by St John's church. Joseph is also said to have brought to England the Holy Grail, the chalice used at the Last Supper, in which he received the Saviour's blood at the Cross. The Grail is supposed to be hidden in Chalice Well, which lies between the Tor and the abbey.

The waters are rust-coloured due to their iron content, but tradition asserts that the redness comes from the blood seeping from the sacred vessel. (Chalice Well was once known as Blood Spring.)

As if the intermingling strands of Christian and Arthurian legend did not weave enough magic around this sacred place, it is also imprinted with occult lore.

**HALLOWED GROUND** *Legend asserts that Glastonbury's ruined abbey was founded by Joseph of Arimathea. The tower-topped Tor (left) is visible from miles around.*

In a theory that has been current from the 1920s onwards, Glastonbury forms part of a huge zodiac outlined in natural and man-made features of the landscape. This Glastonbury Zodiac, or Temple of the Stars, has attracted the interest of hippies and UFO-spotters. Ancient in its sanctity, Glastonbury has also become a place of pilgrimage for all those who interpret the end of the 20th century as the dawning of an Aquarian New Age.

## KAKADU, AUSTRALIA

*CROCODILE DUNDEE COUNTRY IS THE HEARTLAND OF ABORIGINAL DREAMTIME.*

The Aborigines have erected no great temples; to the native people of Australia, the whole land is a living cathedral created by ancestral beings in the mythical era known as Dreamtime. The goal of life is to live in harmony with the sacred earth, and, although certain sites have particular importance in ritual, the whole landscape is imprinted with spiritual significance.

Among the ritual centres, none is more venerated than the Kakadu wilderness, bounded on the south and east by the Arnhem Land escarpment, in the Northern Territory. Here is a varied landscape, with fantastic rocky outcrops, forests of euca-lyptus, grasslands, mangrove swamps and dunes edging the coast. From December to March torrential monsoon rains flood the lowlands in the season known locally as 'the Wet', while from May to October, 'the Dry', the land is parched.

Kakadu is the homeland of an Aboriginal people called the Gagudju. In their trad-itions, the landscape was created by Warramurrungundji, a female being who emerged from the seas. Ginga, a giant crocodile, made the rock country and can be seen here petrified in the form of a rocky outcrop resembling a crocodile's back.

Dangerous spirit forces still survive everywhere as well. Dark streaks in the cliff face of sacred Mount Brockman, for exam-ple, are said to be bloodstains, marking the place where serpent creators once fought. The reptile beings are said still to haunt the pools of Serpent Dreaming, which must not

**ANCIENT PAINTINGS**
*Aboriginal rock paintings at Kakadu go back 18 000 years. A river turtle (right) is depicted in the Aborigines' so-called 'X-ray' art style.*

be disturbed in case they arise and sunder the mountain.

Ancient rock paintings have been found at many places around Kakadu, and thou-sands adorn the cavernous overhangs of Nourlangie Rock, a distinctive lowland outcrop. Here, aborigines of prehistoric times depicted everything from kangaroos to curiosities such as the Tasmanian devil, a carnivorous marsupial long since extinct on mainland Australia. The rock artists also developed a distinctive 'X-ray' style of representation that involved painting the internal organs or skeletons of magpie geese, goannas (monitor lizards), mullet and the huge fish known as barramundi – all important to their diet. The oldest images date back to the Ice Age; the most recent are 20th century. Kakadu's rock paintings span 18 000 years, making the wilderness among the oldest art galleries in the world.

# THE HOLY GANGES

From its source high up in the Himalayas to its outlet in the Bay of Bengal, the mighty Ganges flows for some 1560 miles (2500 km), and its waters sustain more than 300 million people – more than the population of the United States. Yet the spiritual nourishment that the river supplies is even greater in importance, for 'Mother Ganges' is the Hindus' holy of holies, in whose sacred waters pilgrims from all over India and beyond come to purify themselves. Here they bathe, they cast garlands of orange marigolds and rose petals into the stream, and they push out little boats made of dried leaves and lit with a wick soaked in *ghee* (clarified butter) to sanctify their offerings to the river goddess. Shrines are strung out along the Ganges, and the main centres of pilgrimage teem with activity as the visitors flocking to perform their dawn ablutions mingle with fishermen, labourers, caterers, flower-sellers, beggars, street entertainers and the solitary *saddhus* (holy men), who sit in a trance of prayer amid the continuous rhythmic slapping of men and women pounding and ringing out their colourful laundry on the *ghats*, or stairs, leading down to the water.

The origins of the great river are explained in a legend that tells how, in ancient times, a king named Sagar sought to conquer Indra, the king of heaven. In the course of their quarrel, Sagar sent his

PILGRIM THRONG *Millions of people annually crowd the Ganges' banks for the great Hindu festivals.*

60 000 sons out on a rampage, but the god Vishnu, the Preserver, reduced them all to a mound of ashes. For thousands of years their souls remained in limbo until an ascetic descendant of Sagar persuaded the gods to free their souls by having Mother Ganges descend from heaven and wash the ashes away. To this day, Hindus believe that the sacred river will cleanse the souls of those who have their ashes scattered in her purifying waters. It is also believed that salvation can be ensured with a few drops of Ganges water on a man's tongue at the moment of death. So pilgrims come to the river not only for ritual bathing but also to die by or even in it, and to be cremated. Many visitors are advanced in years, and some are people known as *sannyasin*, or 'renouncers', who have given up their worldly goods to wander the roads as beggars, in orange robes, with a staff and drinking vessel.

Among the holiest places on the Ganges is Varanasi, considered the chief *tirtha*, or crossing place, between heaven and earth. An ancient city, still also known by its old name of Benares, this is the place where most devout Hindus would choose to end their days. To die in the city was to be guaranteed salvation, and in the past people came here expressly to kill themselves. Reginald Heber, Lord Bishop of Calcutta, wrote in the 1820s of how pilgrims would tie themselves between two large, empty kedgeree pots and use them as floats to paddle into the stream, 'then fill the pots with the water which surrounds them and thus sink into eternity'.

Today, fires still burn almost incessantly on the cremation *ghats*, and smoke loads the air, lightly scented with the odours of camphor, mango leaves and *ghee* used to lend fragrance to the pyres. Beside the main cremation *ghat* stands the Manikarnika Ghat, the holiest place in the whole Hindu world, where it is believed that the world was created – and will be destroyed. Here Lord Shiva promised to liberate souls from the cycle of reincarnation; Varanasi is protected by Shiva, the supreme Hindu deity, and amid its labyrinth of narrow lanes are hundreds of shrines devoted to him.

The city of Allahabad (Prayag) is also a place of key significance, situated at the confluence of the rivers Ganges and Yamuna, at a sacred intersection called the Sangham, where they are said to be joined by a third river, the mythical Saraswati (personified by a goddess of learning and eloquence). Every year in the months of January or February, the Magh festival here attracts up to a million pilgrims, who come to bathe at the Sangham in order to cleanse their souls. In 1954 the stampede to enter the water was so great that 350 people were crushed to death.

It is an irony of the symbolically purifying Ganges that it is, in reality, among the most polluted rivers in the world, contaminated by human and industrial waste from the many cities along its banks. Partially burnt corpses can sometimes be seen in it because poorer families cannot afford enough wood to finish a cremation.

Nonetheless, despite government warnings against drinking the water, ancient traditions endure, and the pilgrims still stream to the *ghats* at dawn to plunge into the Ganges – often blue-lipped and shuddering under the shock of the cold water, yet eager to expiate their sins and attain salvation.

WATERS MEET *Allahabad, at the sacred confluence of the rivers Ganges and Yamuna.*

# HOLY MOUNTAINS, PILGRIM CENTRES

*Braving shipwreck, brigandage, foul weather and thieving landlords, believers have for centuries journeyed to the world's great pilgrim centres. Holy places or sanctified tourist attractions, they are still sites of potent appeal.*

Christianity is generally reckoned to be the religion with the largest following: some 1833 million followers, about one third of the world's population, were credited to it in 1992. The Church's great pilgrim centres – Jerusalem, Lourdes, Rome – annually attract teeming multitudes of visitors. These are not the only places of spiritual magnetism and power. The River Ganges, hallowed among Indians, is among the world's oldest pilgrimage destinations; every pious Hindu yearns to be washed clean in its purifying waters. Mecca annually draws the Muslim faithful in their millions. Buddhism was originally a religion without ceremonial, yet at Bodhgaya, revered through association with the Enlightened One, pilgrims flock to see a bo tree said to have been grafted from the original under which the Buddha attained illumination.

Pilgrimages may be undertaken for one of many reasons. Some travellers wish to perform an act of simple piety, others one of penance, to expiate sins; others still make pilgrimages in expectation of divine favour or of miracles. In medieval times Christian pilgrimage was often undertaken to secure relics or indulgences (pardons for sins). The sale of easy forgiveness and of saints' limbs – often animal bones – provoked scandals that rocked the Church, and vendors of cheap

DOME OF THE ROCK *Jerusalem's great mosque glimmers above the Wailing Wall.*

rosaries and plaster madonnas continue to congregate in hordes at Christianity's sacred centres to this day. Yet still the pilgrims stream to the holy places, drawn to locations touched by divine grace and hence charged with mysterious significance.

In many faiths, believers are attracted to significant religious buildings for obvious reasons, but the holy mountain is another widespread focus for pilgrimage. Have high peaks always been revered because they seem close to heaven? Or do they recall some primal mound rising above the great Flood of world mythology? Whatever the reason, mounts Ararat, Olympus, Fuji, Tai Shan, Kailas and others are rich in myth and legend – and offer pilgrims satisfying ordeals of ascent.

### JERUSALEM, ISRAEL

*HOLY CITY OF SUPREME SIGNIFICANCE TO JEWS, CHRISTIANS AND MUSLIMS.*

Three great world religions, all professing faith in one god, hold Jerusalem in special reverence, and its symbolic importance was such that medieval mapmakers placed it at the very centre of the world. For Christian pilgrims the most venerated place is the Church of the Holy Sepulchre, which stands at the end of the Via Dolorosa (Way of Sorrows), the traditional site of Christ's crucifixion and resurrection. Here, too, are the Garden of Gethsemane and the Mount of Olives, both steeped in the tragedy and mystery of Christ's martyrdom.

Muslims honour Jerusalem for its associations with Muhammad. The glory of the city's buildings is the gold Dome of the Rock, a mosque built on a huge rock from which the Prophet is said to have soared to paradise on a Night Journey described in the Koran. This is also reputedly the site where Abraham prepared to sacrifice his son Isaac in obedience to God. The rock is furthermore claimed by Christian and Jewish fundamentalists as the place where Armageddon – the final battle before the Messiah's Second Coming – is to be fought.

For Jews, the symbolic importance of Jerusalem can hardly be overstated. The city was the royal capital of King David, who in 1000 BC won it from the Philistines and went on to unite all the tribes of Israel. Solomon built the first Temple here to house the Ark of the Covenant, and the Bible devotes over eight pages to details of the great building's construction.

Solomon's Temple was razed by the Babylonians in 586 BC, and a Second Temple, erected by Herod the Great, was destroyed by the Romans in AD 70. However, the western wall of this later building, known as the Wailing Wall, survives intact and is the most sacred place of Judaism. For more than 1000 years of their often harrowing history Jews have gathered here to pray and mourn over the Temple's destruction and the dispersal of their people. Sacred scrolls are contained in lockers along the Wall, while ordinary pilgrims write personal prayers and slip them into the cracks.

### MOUNT KAILAS, TIBET

*A MAGICAL, DOMED PEAK VENERATED BY HINDUS AND BUDDHISTS ALIKE.*

For Hindus, Mount Kailas is the throne of ferocious, four-armed Shiva, the Destroyer. One of the most important gods in Hindu religion, Shiva also represents the principle

**THRONE OF THE DESTROYER**
*In Hindu belief, Tibet's Mount Kailas is the seat of Shiva.*

of generation, symbolised by the lingam, or phallus. It was to his home on Mount Kailas that Shiva brought the goddess Parvati, and their embrace, it is said, made the whole earth tremble.

Buddhists venerate Mount Kailas as well. It was here that the 11th-century Tibetan Buddhist saint Milarepa was supposed to have defeated the magician Naro Bon-chung in a celebrated duel of supernatural powers that ended with a race to the summit. (Milarepa won by flying to the top on a sunbeam.) And the mountain's spiritual associations do not end there, for followers of the Jain faith – founded around the same time as Buddhism, in the 6th century BC – also venerate it, since it is the place where their first saint found spiritual liberation.

Rising to 22 000 ft (6700 m), the peak is not, by Himalayan standards, especially high, so what caused it to be venerated by so many groups? One answer must lie in its physical appearance. The summit of Mount Kailas soars high above its surrounding

GRANITE SPIRES *Dramatic rock pinnacles soar against the skyline in Dakota's Black Hills.*

massif, and it is snow-crowned throughout the year. Furthermore, the mountain is a major watershed: four great rivers – the Indus, Brahmaputra, Karnali and Sutlej – all rise in the surrounding region. Watering long valleys to the north, south, east and west, Mount Kailas has always seemed a life-giver. The 'Jewel of Snow' (its Tibetan name) is a mountain graced by both nature and a distinct personality.

Pilgrims and hermits have been coming here for at least 2000 years to gain spiritual nourishment on the mountain's slopes. One was the celebrated 8th-century guru Padmasambhava, the 'Lotus Born One', who took refuge in a cave in a valley on the western flank. To this day it is customary for pilgrims to complete a 32 mile (51 km) walk around the mountain, following a well-established route that only the very hardiest manage in a day.

There are monasteries along the way, as well as hermit caves, and supposed footprints and handprints left in the rock by saints. Several curious rock formations include dome-shaped outcrops resembling the *stupas* of Buddhist religion. Yaks carry luggage for some who make the circuit,

while the more rigorous pilgrims perform ritual cleansing ceremonies in the cold turquoise water of a cliff-edged sacred lake.

Few visitors ever get any closer to Mount Kailas itself, for to proceed further into the massif the pilgrim must complete 13 circuits of the mountain on foot. Dangerous moraines combine with sacred tradition to protect the mystery of Shiva's abode.

## BLACK HILLS OF DAKOTA, UNITED STATES

*A PINE-CLAD RANGE HELD SACRED BY THE INDIAN TRIBES.*

Rising forbiddingly out of the prairie, South Dakota's Black Hills owe their name to the dark forests of conifer with which they are clothed. In truth, these are mountains rather than hills, with towering granite spires that rise above the pines to a summit of 7242 ft (2207 m) at Harney Peak. When Sioux tribes, migrating westwards in the later part of the 18th century, came upon the range they were awestruck by its *wakan* (spiritual power).

From 1765, when the Indians' own calendar or 'winter count' records their

discovery, the mountains became sacred to them as a gift from Wakan Tanka, the Great Spirit. The *Pa Sapa* ('black hills' in Sioux language) became the beating heart of their culture, and the tribes cut their tepee poles from the sacred mountains' pine forests.

It was by the Sylvan Lake in the heart of the hills that the young warrior Sitting Bull had a vision that changed his life. He heard a lovely song echoing across the water, and on top of a lakeside rock he made out what seemed to be the figure of a man; as he approached, however, the figure turned round to look at him, and Sitting Bull saw that it was an eagle. When the Indian drew closer, the eagle flew away. Convinced that this was no ordinary bird, Sitting Bull began to sing the eagle's song, which he interpreted as a message from Wakan Tanka:

*My father has given me this nation;*
*In protecting them I have a hard time.*

Believing himself to be divinely appointed, the young warrior grew to become a powerful chief at the forefront of the struggle to protect Indian lands against the encroaching white men. By a treaty of 1868 the sacred Black Hills fell within a huge reservation that was guaranteed to the Sioux for ever.

However, in the summer of 1874, Lieutenant-Colonel George Armstrong Custer led an expedition into the sacred hills in violation of the treaty, and his reports of gold there prompted a flood of miners to the area. In the hostilities that followed, Custer and his forces were massacred by warriors under Sitting Bull and Crazy Horse at the battle of Little Bighorn in 1876.

Nevertheless, the white men won in the end. Today the sacred mountains are a major tourist attraction: the Black Hills National Forest consists of more than a million acres (0.4 million ha) in which the highlights for visitors include the goldrush town of Deadwood and the giant Mount Rushmore carvings of US presidents. But the sheer rugged beauty of the terrain still possesses the power to inspire wonder in all who visit it – these remain places special to the Great Spirit.

## BODHGAYA, INDIA

*A SACRED PILGRIM CENTRE WHERE THE BUDDHA FOUND ENLIGHTENMENT.*

With its single main street, Bodhgaya is similar in many ways to other small villages in the state of Bihar. What distinguishes it, however, are the pilgrims who arrive here in their hundreds every day, for this is the cradle of Buddhism – one of the world's greatest religions. It was to this secluded spot on the banks of the River Niranjana that Prince Siddhartha came some 2500

**PLACE OF AWAKENING** *A stone Buddha contemplates infinity at Bodhgaya. The holy tree (below) was grown from the original beneath which the Buddha found ultimate truth.*

years ago after giving up his royal wealth and family to become a seeker after the ultimate truth. After six years of patient searching, he finally attained enlightenment here under the sacred *bodhi* tree; from then on, he was the Buddha (Sanskrit for the 'Awakened One').

The original tree was to die, but a sapling grown from it was carefully tended and was the 'ancestor' of the *bodhi* tree that still spreads its leafy branches at Bodhgaya. It is surrounded by a decorative metal wall and is always gaily adorned with prayer flags and streamers. The *bodhi* tree is a focus of faith

not only for millions of Buddhists worldwide but for Hindus too, who regard Buddha as an *avatar*, or incarnation, of their god Vishnu. The tree grows in the walled precincts of the large Mahabodhi Temple, a shrine dating from the 1st century AD.

Much renovated since, the temple contains ancient carved railings adorned with images of lotus, birds and animals as well as scenes from the so-called Jakata tales illustrating the Buddha's previous incarnations. In addition, the temple complex is graced by many sculptures and *stupas*, or domed shrines, and a Lotus Pond reflecting

## FENG-SHUI — COSMIC CURRENTS IN THE LANDSCAPE

If Chinese landscape painting exhibits a miraculous harmony of forms, it owes much to the ancient art of Feng-shui. In Taoist belief, all things have a dual nature – drawn from the male breath of Heaven (*yang*) and the female breath of Earth (*yin*). The flow of these energies along hills and mountains, rivers and valleys, determines the particular character of a place. Feng-shui ('wind and water') is a sensitivity to these forces, as well as the ability to balance them harmoniously. In ancient times, Feng-shui was always critically important when siting a sacred building, for correct placing would enhance its spiritual power, while insensitivity to the cosmic flow of energies courted disaster.

Imperial China was landscaped in accordance with the concerns of Feng-shui. Pagodas, in particular, were often erected to offset the effect of, for example, ill-favoured hills. To assist the concentration of power in the imperial capital, Beijing, the natural sinuous streams of earth energy were diverted into long straight channels focused on the seat of government. These channels were *lung mei* – dragon paths – which ran from hilltop to hilltop and were said to be the routes of dragons flying between their nests. No buildings or tombs other than those of the emperor's family were allowed to be sited on the imperial dragon paths.

Practitioners of Feng-shui were consulted on anything that involved altering the landscape. An English missionary described in 1873 how 'when purchasing a site, when building a house, when pulling down a wall, or raising a flagstaff, residents of the Treaty Ports have encountered innumerable difficulties, and all on account of Feng-shui. When it was proposed to erect a few telegraph poles, when the construction of a railway was urged upon the Chinese Government, when a mere tramway was suggested to utilise the coal-mines of the interior, Chinese officials would invariably make a polite bow and declare the thing impossible on account of Feng-shui.'

Though frowned on in communist China, the ancient art of Feng-shui is still practised abroad by people known as geomancers. In the United States it is common for members of the Chinese community to consult a geomancer before buying or building a home. Feng-shui does not submit easily to scientific analysis; for Westerners, the art is as much an enigma as acupuncture. Nonetheless, it has its adherents among those interested in the phenomena of ley lines and dowsing. Geomancers regard nature in all its forms as a magnetic field, and it is often argued that the megalith-builders of prehistoric Europe shared similar beliefs, raising great stones to harmonise earth with heaven, as if regulating the flow of a magnetic force from a conductor.

---

a life-sized statue of the Lord Buddha. The famous Jewel Walk is a raised platform, lined with pillars, where the Buddha is said to have paced back and forth, deliberating on whether he should reveal his new-found wisdom to the world. His decision was positive, and from that time he devoted himself to the good of humanity.

At Bodhgaya every May, the annual Buddha Jayanti festival celebrates that decision as thousands of devout visitors crowd the little village. They sleep on the rooftops to participate in festivities amid the vivid colours of saffron-robed monks, the ringing of bells and the murmured chants of the Buddhist mantra – '*Om Mani Padme Hum*'.

### TONGARIRO, NEW ZEALAND

*MIST-SHROUDED VOLCANIC PEAKS*
*VENERATED BY THE MAORI.*

The thunder that booms around the summit of Tongariro is said by local tribes to be laden with ancestral voices. This massive mountain, which rises from the heart of New Zealand's North Island, was for a long time a place of burial for the Maori, who laid their chiefs to rest in caves on its slopes. Three active volcanoes lend drama to the heights, and their peaks are what the Maori call *tapu* (taboo) – one of the strongest forces of law in their communities. By tradition, all who tried to ascend the mountain would find it growing taller, so that the summit was always out of reach.

Tongariro has three peaks: at 9176 ft (2797 m) Mount Ruapehu is the highest, boasting snow on its ragged crown all the year round. Mount Tongariro itself has a crater-strewn top, flanked by sulphurous volcanic lakes and hot springs. But its taller sister peak, Mount Ngauruhoe, is a classic cone formed as an off-shoot from the main mass of the volcano. This is definitely the most spectacular of the trio: steam and gas issue almost continuously

**VOLCANO'S MOUTH** *Legend tells that spirits inhabit the crater of New Zealand's Mount Ngauruhoe.*

from Ngauruhoe's hellish crater, and it has occasionally detonated with spectacular violence. The fires at the summit were said to have been lit by the local tribe's ancestor, a *tohunga* (holy man) called Ngatoro-i-rangi, and many spirits were believed to haunt the heights in a house called The Roaring of the Sky. When the volcano began to spit fire, the people of the local tribe thought that the spirits were commanding them to make war. By the same token, their neighbours knew they could expect an attack.

Ngauruhoe was regarded with the utmost awe and dread, and the strict *tapu*

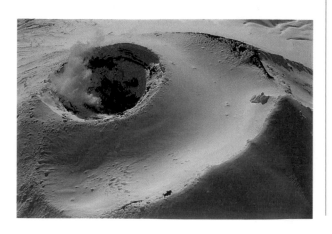

protecting it survived unbroken for many centuries. However, in 1839 J.C. Bidwell, an English botanist, braved the wrath of the ancient shades said to inhabit the mountain to reach its 7516 ft (2291 m) summit. Although the spirits did not punish him for his desecration, he did flee the peak as, with a mighty roar, the volcano came to life. Intrigued though he was, Bidwell 'did not wish to see an eruption near enough to be either boiled or steamed to death'.

To the Maori, the mountains possessed personalities, and argued with and married one another, assuming the motives and passions of human beings. In their lore the Tongariro group is missing one of its original peaks. This mountain, called Taranaki, began flirting with a beautiful, forest-clad wife of Tongariro. The two male mountains quarrelled, hurling fireballs at one another, and in the end Taranaki rushed off westwards. In the mountain's flight, his mighty form carved out the gorge of the Wanganui River, and he at last made his home at the tip of Cape Egmont. There Taranaki remains to this day – also known as Mt Egmont. Tales like these explained the existence of many dramatic topographical features to the native peoples of New Zealand. Theirs was a landscape that was shaped not by geological abstractions but by the dream energies of imagination.

## TAI SHAN, CHINA

*THE THRONE OF THE JADE EMPEROR IS*
*ONE OF CHINA'S SACRED MOUNTAINS.*

It is said that those who climb Tai Shan will live to 100. If this is true, the mountain must be a machine for turning out centenarians, for hosts of visitors regularly make the six-hour ascent, toiling up the 6000-odd steps that lead to the summit. Climbing Tai Shan is unlike climbing mounts Olympus or Fuji, in that the main route up is a stairway. It is furnished with temples, shrines, inscribed stones, bridges, guest-houses and even a 'Journey to the Stars Gondola' – in reality, a cable car. The mountain has attracted visitors for millennia, and if its popularity has caused it to lose something in scenic appeal, its fascination unquestionably endures.

Rising to 5100 ft (1550 m) above the plain of the Yellow River, Tai Shan is the highest peak in the Shandong Peninsula and the most revered of the five sacred mountains of China. According to tradition the sun began its westward journey through the heavens at Tai Shan, and the mountain is particularly important in the Taoist system of belief that emerged through the teaching of the ancient sage Lao Zi in the 6th century BC.

This philosophy celebrates a state of harmony with nature and the universe attained through the Tao (the Way), in which *yin* (feminine forces) balance *yang* (masculine forces). Stressing simple and passive

STAIRWAY TO HEAVEN *Tai Shan's ancient granite steps include some of the world's oldest stairs.*

values, Taoism nonetheless acquired a host of gods and magical cults. Supreme among the deities is the Jade Emperor, who presides over the lives of all humans and animals. His abode is Tai Shan, and his temple stands at the very top of the mountain. At Tai Shan, too, the Princess of the Azure Clouds is especially venerated by the local peasant women; aging grandmothers toil regularly to the mountain top, and make offerings at her temple near the summit.

Through long centuries of imperial government, sacrifices to heaven and earth were made on the top of Tai Shan, and it was not uncommon for the most determined of the pilgrims to climb the mountain on their knees. Five Chinese emperors were among those who made the ascent. The sage Confucius (551-479 BC), who was born at Qufu not far to the south, was another celebrated climber, and in more recent times Chairman Mao also scaled Tai Shan, remarking on seeing the sunrise: 'The East is Red'.

Today visitors still come in their daily thousands, and many gather on the summit before dawn to watch the sun rise. In an age of scepticism, this temple-strewn mountain evidently retains its ability to attract people. According to Chinese belief, certain places are centres of the Earth's living energies, detectable through the ancient art of Feng-Shui, or 'wind and water'. Tai

Shan is perhaps the most remarkable of all such sites in China: not especially high, nor especially beautiful – but unquestionably a magic mountain.

## SANTIAGO DE COMPOSTELA, SPAIN

*A MEDIEVAL CENTRE OF PILGRIMAGE, HOME TO THE REMAINS OF AN APOSTLE.*

The city and the saint are one: Santiago owes its name to St James, who is known in Spanish as *Santiago*. In medieval times, the town was Europe's most popular place of pilgrimage, boasting a splendid cathedral

CATHEDRAL TREASURES
*One of Spain's architectural glories, the cathedral of Santiago de Compostela, is also venerated for its statue (left) and relics of St James.*

alleged to contain the bones of Christ's Apostle St James, one of the two sons of Zebedee, also known as Boanerges, the 'sons of thunder', because of their fiery tempers. James was beheaded by Herod Agrippa in Jerusalem in AD 44. It was widely believed that he had made an expedition to Spain at some

time and had preached there, and legend told how, after his execution, his body was shipped back to a site in Spain not far from present-day Santiago on the north-west coast. In AD 813, it is said, his tomb was discovered. King Alphonso II of the Asturias encouraged the devotion that grew up around this supposed discovery, and the first of a series of cathedral buildings was erected to house his tomb.

Alphonso's realm was threatened by Moorish invaders, and as a champion of Christendom, St James was always a favourite with military men in the front-line battle against them. Visions of him on a white charger were often reported by soldiers, including many knights from France, taking part in the Christian campaigns against the Moors in medieval Spain. Perhaps as a consequence, four great pilgrim routes emerged, beginning at the French centres of Tours, Vézelay, Le Puy and Arles, and the wealthy Benedictine abbey at Cluny built wayside hospitals and priories for travellers along the way. Scallop shells, first picked up on the Atlantic beaches near Santiago, came to be emblems of the pilgrimage and were carved on church walls along the route. On the north side of the cathedral, stalls were set up where 12th-century visitors could buy the shells without having to reach the seashore.

At the shrine, it was said, 'the sick are restored to health, the blind receive their sight, many tongues that were dumb are loosed, the deaf hear again, the lame are given the strength to walk, demoniacs are set free, and what is even more, the prayers of the faithful are heard, their vows are fulfilled, and the chains of their sins are unloosed'. Miracles of St James graced stained glass all over Europe, and devotees came to extend far beyond the warrior class. In Chaucer's *Canterbury Tales*, the Wife of Bath tells us that she has been to Compostela. And a 13th-century record exists of two English women sent there as penitents, one for committing adultery and the other for making love with a godson.

Crowds of pilgrims still flock to embrace the cathedral's gilded statue of St James, and to gaze at a silver casket under the high altar containing the alleged bones of the

FACES OF FUJI *Hokusai's celebrated print depicts Mount Fuji as a surf-topped wave in a surging sea. The photograph displays Japan's holy mountain in quieter mood.*

saint. Whether they really are relics of the Apostle is a subject of dispute, but no one could deny the fervour with which the feast of St James is celebrated on July 24-25. This is one of the greatest events in the Spanish religious calendar, when multitudes choke the city's main Plaza, folk dancers perform in traditional costume, and fireworks splash the cathedral's ornate front with explosive colours. Rooted in its medieval past, Santiago de Compostela is a celebration of a vibrant living tradition.

## MOUNT FUJI, JAPAN

*JAPAN'S HOLY MOUNTAIN HAS BEEN CELEBRATED BY ARTISTS AND POETS.*

A view of Mount Fuji by the illustrator, Hokusai (1760-1849) is the world's best known Japanese print. Framed by a great clawing wave in the foreground, the snowy peak resembles a foam-capped roller – an imaginative metaphor by the master landscapist. The picture is just one in Hokusai's collection *Thirty Six Views of Mount Fuji*, which, despite its title, actually includes 46 scenes. And Hokusai did not stop there; no sooner had he finished the group than he embarked on his even more ambitious *Hundred Views of Mount Fuji*.

Revered from early times as home to the gods, Fuji is Japan's highest mountain, and remarkable for the symmetry of a cone that soars from an almost perfect circular base. The mountain is situated in south central Honshu. It rises to 12 388 ft (3776 m) and is a dormant volcano that last erupted in 1707. Five interconnecting lakes lie at its base, and one of these, Kawaguchi, is celebrated for the inverted image of the mountain reflected in its water.

Fuji is famed for its many faces; the Japanese claim that it never appears twice looking the same. Sometimes clouded, sometimes white-crowned, sometimes glowing blood-red, the mountain has inspired many artists and writers. Standing by Lake Kawaguchi the poet Basho wrote:

*On Kawaguchi's shore I muse*
*While Fuji, through the changing mist,*
*Presents all hundred views.*

The local Ainu people first called the mountain Fuchi, after the fire goddess who was believed to be responsible for its eruptions. In Japan's native religion of Shinto, the summit is the home of Sengen-Sama, goddess of blossoms, who is sometimes manifested as a luminous cloud seen floating over the crater. Buddhist tradition, meanwhile, also venerates Fuji as the gateway to another world. In times past, Fuji was officially worshipped as a sacred mountain, and every summer thousands of pilgrims dressed in white tunics, straw hats and sandals would toil up its slopes to the summit as an act of faith. All of the pilgrims

### MARATHON MONKS

The 'marathon monks' from a monastery on Japan's holy Mount Hiei, north-east of Kyoto, perform rigorous exercises in search of enlightenment. Over a seven-year training period, these 'running Buddhas' run so far around the heights that they figuratively circle the globe on foot.

were male; until 1868, Mount Fuji was completely banned to women.

According to some estimates, about a million people still make the ascent every year, many during the brief official climbing season, which begins and ends with solemn ceremonies and lasts from July 1 to August 31. Though few visitors are pilgrims by strict definition, there is still some sense in which the ascent resembles a religious act. People come to see the sun rise at the summit, and to walk the sacred crater rim. Some spend the night at stations on the way up, though many make the ascent in a single overnight assault, beginning around 4 pm. In the dawn light, stupendous views can open up, taking in almost the whole of mainland Japan. Then the vision is withdrawn: by 9 am, mist and cloud have often gathered around the holy mountain, obscuring the great panorama below.

## MOUNT ARARAT, TURKEY

*THE TRADITIONAL LANDING PLACE OF*
*NOAH'S ARK – IS IT STILL THERE?*

'And the ark rested in the seventh month, on the seventeenth day of the month, upon the mountains of Ararat.' So it is written in the Book of Genesis, describing how Noah's giant ship containing two of every living creature survived the Flood. And the story has proved so compelling that, even during the 20th century, attempts have been made to locate the remains of the Biblical vessel on Ararat's snow-covered summit.

At 16 945 ft (5165 m), Mount Ararat is Turkey's highest mountain. The peak rises in the east of the country from a volcanic massif near the borders of Russia and Iran. As early as the 5th century BC, it is said, Chaldean priests climbed to the top in search of the great ship, and they are reported to have come back with bitumen scrapings from its hull. During the 19th century there was considerable interest in ark-hunting, following reports that a shepherd had sighted a huge wooden ship on the mountain. In 1833 a Turkish expedition reported the prow of a wooden vessel

BIBLICAL ENIGMA *Ark-shaped rocks like this may account for persisting beliefs that relics of Noah's Ark survive on Mount Ararat.*

jutting out of the south glacier in summer. In 1892 the Nestorian Archbishop Nourri spoke of the wreckage of a ship in the ice cap. 'The interior was full of snow,' he said. 'The outer wall was of dark red colour.' A First World War Russian aviator, and four Second World War American airmen, made aerial observations, and photographs were reputedly taken in 1953, though they have since been lost.

Despite the claims of believers, many patient investigators have reported no trace of the Ark – nor of any mysterious wreckage on Ararat. The mountain remains an imposing sight, nonetheless, and as a source of the River Euphrates has an authentic pedigree in ancient history, for the waters brought farming riches to some of the world's earliest civilisations in Mesopotamia to the south. Mount Ararat's fascination endures, however. 'Although we found no trace of Noah's Ark,' one enthusiast declared after a fruitless 12-day search, 'my confidence in the Biblical description of the Flood is no whit the less. We shall go back.'

## LINDISFARNE, ENGLAND

*A CRADLE OF CHRISTIANITY IN*
*ENGLAND AND A PILGRIMAGE SITE.*

Looming out of a sea-haze off the coast of Northumberland, the romantic silhouette of Lindisfarne castle seems to signal a land of fairytale enchantment. In reality the castle, built on a dramatic upsurge of volcanic rock, is a fairly recent feature of the landscape. It was built in 1548 as a garrison fort for the Tudors, and has been much renovated in the present century by the architect Sir Edwin Lutyens.

Lindisfarne possesses a more ancient appeal, however. For Christians, its significance goes back to AD 635 when St Aidan, a Celtic monk, was summoned from Iona by King Oswald of Northumbria to bring Christianity to his kingdom. Oswald appointed Aidan first bishop of Northumbria, and Aidan was based at Lindisfarne, where he founded a mission centre. For well over 200 years Lindisfarne was to serve as a beacon of the Christian light shining among Dark Age kingdoms, and from this

**HALLOWED ARCHES**
*Lindisfarne's ruined*
*monastery has attracted*
*pilgrims for hundreds of years.*

Holy Island some of England's warring northern realms were converted.

St Cuthbert, Aidan's successor as bishop, came to Lindisfarne in 664, but after 12 years he retired to the Farne Islands (to the south-east of Lindisfarne) where he lived as a hermit with only a small stone cell and chapel for shelter. Towards the end of his life he returned to Lindisfarne as bishop, and at his death he was buried in a coffin beside the altar of the Abbey church. It is said that when the coffin was opened 11 years later the saint's body was found to be incorrupt. Examined again in 1104, it still had not perished.

Hobthrush Island, where Cuthbert had a retreat, is cut off from Lindisfarne at high tide but is still accessible to visitors. St Aidan's original monastery was destroyed by the Vikings in 793. The monks rebuilt it, but the Danes returned in 875, and this time the monks decided to remove St Cuthbert's remains for safe keeping, starting on a journey that would take them over much of northern England and south-western Scotland. It ended when they found a spectacular resting place high above the River Wear. Here they built a shrine for the saint's precious remains, and a cathedral, replaced in Norman times with today's great cathedral of Durham.

The monastery was dissolved with other monasteries throughout Britain by Henry VIII, but the ruins remain evocative, with the roofless shell of the church and a graceful arch of vaulting framing the sea and the sky. Pilgrims have been coming to visit this hallowed place for centuries, originally finding paths across the sands at low tide. Today a metalled causeway connects the island with the mainland, although it is completely submerged by the racing tides twice a day. In bad weather, according to Sir Walter Scott, Whitby fisherman used to see the ghost of St Cuthbert hammering on an anvil on the shore:

> And hear his anvil sound;
> A deafening clang — a huge, dim form,
> Seen but, and heard, when gathering storm
> And night were closing round.

## LOURDES, FRANCE

*A RELIGIOUS CITY HAS GROWN UP*
*WHERE A YOUNG GIRL SAW VISIONS.*

The world's largest underground church is the Basilica of Pope Pius X at Lourdes. Built in 1958, it is often said to look more like a car park than a church, but it can accommodate 20 000 people – more than the population of the entire town. And even this great congregation is dwarfed by Lourdes' annual flood of visitors. More than 3 million pilgrims, many of them sick or handicapped, come every year to the small town that lies on the fringe of the

Pyrenees, about 80 miles (130 km) south-west of Toulouse. More pilgrims go to Lourdes than to any other pilgrim centre in the world – including Mecca and Rome.

The vast basilica was built to celebrate a chain of events that had occurred a century earlier. In February 1858 a 14-year-old peasant girl named Bernadette Soubirous claimed that the Virgin Mary had appeared to her in a soft glow above a rose bush in the Massabielle grotto near the Gave de Pau river. More visions followed, and during

*MODERN MIRACLES* *The church of St Bernadette at Lourdes commemorates a peasant girl's visions.*

the ninth episode Bernadette, acting under the direction of the 'beautiful Lady', un-earthed a small spring in the grotto. Water gushed from a spot where none had been known before. From then on crowds num-bering over a thousand people followed Bernadette on every trip she made to the place, and they have flocked there in in-creasing numbers ever since in response to the water's supposed healing powers. Church authorities, at first sceptical, au-thenticated the girl's experiences after a four-year investigation, and a sanctuary was erected over the grotto.

Bernadette witnessed her last vision in July 1858; two years later she entered a convent, where she remained until she died

at the early age of 35. But the reputation of Lourdes increased to the extent that it became known as the greatest shrine in Europe. The first pilgrims arrived indi-vidually, or in small, unofficial groups, but in 1864 the Bishop of Tarbes led a diocesan pilgrimage of 8000 people to the town. Foreign contingents followed in the 1870s, with special trains laid on by the railway companies. By the turn of the century, Lourdes was attracting up to 400 000 people annually. Today there are six official annual pilgrimages every year, the high season being between August 15 and September 8. During that period the town's vast process-ional esplanade teems with thousands of visitors, and provides the setting for im-posing torchlit processions at night.

Besides the underground church, Lourdes boasts two basilicas, the Supérieure (1871) and the Rosaire (1889), several hospitals catering to the hosts of ailing visit-ors, and a multitude of hotels, restaurants and souvenir shops. The grotto, which lies between the basilicas and the river, remains the chief focus of pilgrimage, but it is often barely visible behind the forests of be-lievers' candles. Lourdes today is a major pilgrimage and tourist centre. Yet all the postcards, rosaries, plastic Virgins and other evidence of commercialisation cannot mask the immense expression of faith and hope embodied here.

## MECCA, SAUDI ARABIA

*A SACRED BLACK STONE IS SET INTO THE KAABA SHRINE IN ISLAM'S HOLY CITY.*

More than 970 million people, about a fifth of all humanity, regard Mecca as the world's most sacred place. The dusty desert city is the birthplace of Muhammad, the founder of Islam, and all Muslims must try to make the *haj*, or pilgrimage, to it at least once in their lifetimes. More than a million pil-grims go there every year, and five times each day millions more believers all over the Earth prostrate themselves towards Mecca in communal prayer.

The focus of this vast spiritual energy is the Kaaba, a stark, almost square shrine of granite blocks that owes its name to the

Arabic word for cube. Its grey masonry is covered today with a black cloth known as the *kiswa*, embroidered in golden calligraphy, but before Muhammad's time the Kaaba was hung with the pelts of sacrificed animals. For this was a pagan shrine in origin, at one time crammed with idols and tribal totems. Muhammad rededicated it to Allah in 632, and it has been destroyed and rebuilt several times since.

All the old relics disappeared after the rededication except for the famous Black Stone that Muhammad saluted in the course of his Pilgrimage of Farewell. In pagan times pilgrims had come to touch the stone in the hope of absorbing its mystic power. Muhammad allowed the custom to continue, after sanctifying it in Allah's name.

Legends cling to the Black Stone. Geologists believe it to be meteoric in origin, but tradition holds that it was given to the prophet Abraham by the archangel Gabriel. Set into the south-east corner of the Kaaba, the Black Stone is venerated today by the streams of pilgrims who (if they are able to get close enough) kiss it before passing

**HOLY OF HOLIES** *Muslims gather for evening prayers around the cube-shaped Kaaba in Mecca, Islam's most sacred place. Pilgrims worship at the Kaaba shrine (right).*

counterclockwise around the shrine seven times, chanting devotions – a ritual known as the *tawaf*.

The pilgrims come each year during the holy month of Dhul-Hijja. Discarding their multitude of national costumes, the faithful dress with austere simplicity to enter Mecca's Great Mosque and the immense courtyard in which the Kaaba is situated. A few yards from the shrine is the Zemzem Well, to which Mecca owes its existence. Once the city's only source of water, the Zemzem permitted settlement in an otherwise arid landscape and is now reached down a sloping marble stairway.

Non-Muslims are forbidden to enter Mecca, though several have done so in disguise, including the English explorer Sir Richard Burton. He came in 1853 and

HOME OF THE GODS *For the ancient Greeks, Mount Olympus (left) was the home of the gods. A vase shows the birth of the goddess Athena, said to have emerged fully fledged from the head of her father Zeus after he had been struck with an axe by Hephaestus, the blacksmith god.*

wrote of the old law governing discovery as 'a choice thrice offered between circumcision and death'. Those caught within the walls today still face heavy penalties and deportation. Mecca guards its traditions, and after 13 centuries of pilgrimage remains off-limits to all but the faithful.

## MOUNT OLYMPUS, GREECE

*THE THRONE OF ZEUS AND FABLED HOME OF GREECE'S ANCIENT GODS.*

Gigantic in appearance, many-ridged Olympus is a massif more than a single mountain. Its great bulk extends along the borders of Thessaly and Macedonia for 25 miles (40 km), rising in precipices broken by thickly wooded ravines to a summit of naked rock that is snow-capped for much of the year. At 9570 ft (2917 m) the peak of Mytikas – 'the needle' – is the highest point in Greece.

For the Greeks, Olympus was the roof of the world. According to Homer's *Odyssey* there were never storms at the summit, and the gods dwelt there in the ether, or pure air, high above the clouds. Sometimes they would quarrel and fight, making the heavens ring to the thunder of their combat. Zeus, the father of the gods, held court here, and the heroes of Greek mythology would sometimes go to Olympus to seek guidance or assistance.

In the same way, the Greek gods sometimes came down from the mountain to participate in earthly affairs, and they shared all the human passions. Lusty Zeus, for example, assumed various disguises to approach the mortal women of whom he was enamoured, visiting Leda as a swan, Europa as a bull, Hera as a cuckoo and Danaë in a shower of gold.

The Spring of Daphne, at the foot of the mountain, recalls the tragic love of the sun god Apollo for the forest nymph Daphne. Eros, the god of love, had made Daphne immune to Apollo's advances, and fleeing from him she sought help from the gods, who turned her into a laurel tree. Daphne means laurel in Greek, and henceforward, the story goes, it was always the favourite tree of Apollo. It still grows wild on the banks of the beautiful Vale of Tempe, a glen running between Olympus and Ossa, which was an ancient centre for Apollo worship.

Around 400 BC a temple to Zeus was built at Dion, and its remains survive near the market town of Katerini, which commands superb views of Olympus.

The great mountain was a notorious haunt of bandits in the 19th century, and as late as 1910 the climber Edward Richter was caught and held to ransom by them while attempting the conquest of the summit. Three years later a successful ascent was made, but Olympus was not fully mapped until 1921. Today the Greek army maintains a ski school on the slopes, and there are refuge huts for climbers. Often shrouded in mist, the rugged heights are, however, only recommended for experienced mountaineers. Cloud-gathering Zeus still guards his realm.

## CROAGH PATRICK, IRELAND

*MIRACULOUS MOUNTAIN PEAK WHERE ST PATRICK RID IRELAND OF SNAKES.*

Before dawn on the last Sunday in July, several thousand pilgrims congregate above the greystone ruin of Murrisk Abbey to begin the ascent of Croagh Patrick. Some bear hand-held lights and many go barefoot, cutting their feet as they clamber over the loose rocks and shale that cloak the flanks of the holy mountain.

Croagh Patrick is the focus of one of Ireland's most important pilgrimages, and rich in the lore of its patron saint. There is something of a penitential ordeal about the

## SEEKING THE CENTRE — THE SACRED MAZE

The image of the maze recurs as a religious symbol in cultures all around the world. For mystics it represents the wandering of the spirit in its quest for the still, central point of eternal truth. It can also be seen as symbolic of death: a journeying of the soul into the heart of darkness and then a coming back, or rebirth. The ancient labyrinth of King Minos in Crete is just one example; sacred mazes were also known to the Egyptians, to the Hopi Indians of North America, and to islanders in the Pacific Ocean. From the 11th century onwards, mazes were often depicted on the floors of Christian churches in Europe – the great Gothic cathedral of Chartres possesses a famous example. In the Crusader age, believers would tread the path of a church maze on their knees as penance for not making the pilgrimage to the Holy City; the centre was known as heaven (*ciel*), or Jerusalem.

Among Christians, as among pagans, the maze was also associated with dance rituals. In the labyrinth in the medieval cathedral at Auxerre, in France, a dance was performed annually on Easter Day. To the rhythmic chant of the Easter service the dean and canons capered in a long chain along the path of the maze, while a ball was passed in a woven pattern down the line. For the faithful, Easter dance rites symbolised the joy of the Resurrection.

**DEAD CENTRE** *The tortuous route to eternity is displayed on a tombstone maze from the east of England.*

ascent. On their way up some stop at a pilgrim station at the base of the summit to make seven praying circuits, and on reaching the top they kneel in prayer before making 15 praying circuits at the summit.

The quartzite peak rises to a height of 2510 ft (765 m) above the Mayo coastlands. Once sacred to the pagan god Crom, it was reputed to be the scene of a great supernatural encounter around AD 441. Here, it is said, Saint Patrick battled for 40 days and 40 nights against the forces of darkness, represented by a multitude of evil spirits. According to one version of the legend, when he rang his bell at the edge of a cliff all of Ireland's toads and snakes leapt off the cliff to their deaths (except the natterjack toad).

In another version, St Patrick beat a drum to accomplish his mission, striking it with such fervour that he knocked a hole in it; however, an angel swiftly appeared and mended it – the patched instrument was long exhibited as a holy relic. Whether bell or drum was employed, Ireland has no snakes. And having won the land for Christendom, the saint earned the right to sit at the Lord's side on Judgment Day, to judge the Irish people.

The precipice where the reptiles are said to have plunged to their doom is on the south side of the mountain. At the summit is a tiny chapel where Mass is celebrated, and pilgrims say a series of

**SAINTLY FIGURE** *A statue of St Patrick stands at the foot of Croagh Patrick.*

**HAUNTED SNOWS** *Supernatural beings are said to inhabit the white-crowned summit of Mount Kilimanjaro.*

prayers while walking around it, kneeling from time to time on the sharp stones.

However, not all visitors come in a spirit of penitence, or on the main day of pilgrimage. People toil up Croagh Patrick throughout the year, some of them to admire the sweeping views. To the north, at the foot of the mountain, lies Clew Bay with its scattered islands; and on a clear day the views extend to the blue line of the Kerry mountains far to the south.

## MOUNT KILIMANJARO, TANZANIA

*GLITTERING SNOWCAP ON THE EQUATOR IMBUED WITH LEGEND AND MYSTERY.*

Africa's highest mountain is a white-mantled giant that surges from its surrounding plains to a height of 19 340 ft (5895 m) above sea level. Volcanic in origin, Mount Kilimanjaro combines three peaks in one: Shira, Mawenzi, and Kibo, the highest, whose summit takes the form of an almost perfect circular crater adorned by ice fields hung with steep glaciers. The ancient Greeks had written of a 'great snow mountain' in Africa, but as late as the 19th century European geographers still doubted its existence, since Mount Kilimanjaro lies only 3 degrees south of the equator, and snow at this latitude seemed an impossibility. When Victorian explorers began to report its existence, sceptics suggested that the whiteness of the summit might be an optical illusion created by sunshine striking quartz cliffs.

The tribes around the mountain's base regarded Kilimanjaro as sacred, and discouraged attempts on its summit. Though the meaning of the word Kilimanjaro has often been traced to the Swahili 'mountains of greatness', an alternative hypothesis suggests 'mountain of the demon Njaro'. In 1848 the German missionary Johannes Rebmann was told that the mountain bristled with death-dealing *jinn* and evil spirits. Gunpowder, it was said, mysteriously failed to fire on the flanks of Kilimanjaro, and Rebmann was told of a king who once sent a great expedition to examine the white substance at the mountain top. All members of it perished, except for one man named Sabaya who saw a huge, iron-spiked door open near the summit. Too fearful and exhausted to enter, Sabaya came back crippled for life.

In 1871 an English missionary named Charles New, who became the first man to reach the snowcap, reported: 'We were told all manner of fabulous stories about the supernatural occupants of the mountain's summit, who were watching over immense hoards of gold, silver, and precious stones, and who would treat in the most summary manner any mortal daring to enter upon their sacred domains.'

Eventually conquered in 1889, the wintry peak of Kilimanjaro today attracts hundreds of climbers, who have nine main routes to the summit to choose between. The spirits, it seems, have lost their powers to frighten off visitors.

# A TOUCH 3 OF MAGIC

**GUARDIAN** *The goddess Serket protects a shrine containing Tutankhamun's organs.*

DO MONSTERS HAUNT THE WATERS OF LOCH NESS OR TREAD THE SNOWS OF THE HIMALAYAS? DOES A CURSE HANG OVER TUTANKHAMUN'S TOMB OR THREATEN SHIPS ENTERING THE BERMUDA TRIANGLE? FOR ALL THAT HAS BEEN LEARNED THROUGH SCIENCE ABOUT THE EARTH AND THE COSMOS, REPORTS OF PARANORMAL PHENOMENA STILL EXCITE FASCINATION. EVEN FOR THE SCEPTIC A STATELY HOME'S APPEAL MAY BE ENHANCED BY STORIES OF ITS GHOSTS, A SCENIC LAKE'S BY TALES OF A FABLED WATER CREATURE. NO SURVEY OF THE MYSTERIOUS PLACES WOULD BE COMPLETE WITHOUT TOUCHING ON SITES THAT HAVE SPARKED INTEREST BECAUSE OF THEIR SUPERNATURAL ASSOCIATIONS.

**NEUSCHWANSTEIN** *Ludwig II of Bavaria built this extravaganza.*

# STRANGE PHENOMENA

*'While yet a boy I sought for ghosts,' wrote the poet Shelley, recalling how he sped through caves, ruins and starlit woods in the hope of communicating with the dead. Do uncanny forces reveal themselves at favourable sites?*

Reports of phantoms, prophecies, fabulous animals and inexplicable disappearances all challenge conventional ideas about the laws of nature, opening doorways into the unknown. For believers in strange phenomena, the material realm is merely a veil for uncanny energies – psychic, spiritual or divine – that defy analysis by orthodox science. And the mysterious places of the world have been interpreted over the centuries as focal points for extraordinary energy currents, attracting paranormal events to themselves like magnets.

For the sceptic there are simpler explanations. Any atmospheric ruin, secluded lake or stone circle of unknown purpose might inspire people of past times to weave imaginative tales that became part of local tradition, handed down and further embellished over the generations. Deliberate fakery and charlatanism have been exposed on occasion among occultists. And besides, people are fallible; guilt, fear and the repression of basic human impulses can all cause the unconscious mind to generate hallucinations. Religious dread and a natural awe of death, so the argument runs, are two particularly obvious triggers for such delusions. Small wonder, then, that the phantom monk is reported at the ivy-strewn abbey, or the headless spectre at a place of execution.

Still, many great thinkers have been cautious about rationalising the unknown too glibly. 'The most beautiful thing we can experience is the mysterious,' wrote Albert Einstein. 'It is the source of all true art and science.' Modern laboratories have discovered astonishing facts about the way in which genetic information is invisibly communicated by DNA — the nucleic acid present in every living cell that determines the physical characteristics we inherit. Astronomers scanning the heavens have revealed the existence of black holes – exploded stars where matter vanishes and space and time are distorted.

IMMORTAL MONARCH *This gold mask preserves the features of Egypt's boy pharaoh, Tutankhamun.*

In a universe that is imbued with such an astonishing variety of wonders, it would be extremely unwise to dismiss all strange phenomena out of hand.

## TUTANKHAMUN'S TOMB, EGYPT

*TALES OF A MUMMY'S CURSE HANG OVER THE BOY KING'S BURIAL CHAMBER.*

'Death comes on wings to him who enters the tomb of a pharaoh,' says an Arabic proverb. But the warning has been ignored for centuries by the hordes of travellers, archaeologists and tomb robbers who have searched out the burial places of Egypt's kings. In 1922, the British archaeologist Howard Carter located one of the richest hauls when he burst into the now famous tomb of the boy pharaoh Tutankhamun in the Valley of the Kings, and beheld in the ancient darkness 'wonderful things . . . strange animals, statues, and gold – everywhere the glint of gold'. Following the discovery, some 5000 precious objects were removed to the Cairo Museum: alabaster vases, priceless jewellery, a solid gold coffin

FATEFUL DISCOVERY  *Amid ancient darkness, Howard Carter examines the tomb.*

and an ornamented throne. But what gripped the public imagination even more was the fact that, only a few months after entering Tutankhamun's tomb, Carter's partner, Lord Carnarvon, died from an infected mosquito bite.

Had a pharaoh's curse fallen upon him? Rumours began to circulate. It was said that the mummified body of the pharaoh had a blemish on the left cheek in exactly the same spot as Carnarvon's mosquito bite; back in Britain, Carnarvon's dog howled and died at the time that his master passed away. Within ten years about 20 other people involved in the opening of the tomb had died, some of unnatural causes, including madness and suicide. The stories continued when treasures from Tutankhamun's tomb were sent abroad for display. In 1966, Egypt's Director of Antiquities, Mohammed Ibraham, was ordered to arrange a Tutankhamun exhibition in Paris. He argued strongly against the decision and dreamt that something terrible would happen to him if he let the treasures go. After one last meeting, where his objections were finally dismissed, the director walked out into the street and was knocked down by a car and killed.

Though other tombs in the Valley of the Kings are open to visitors, Tutankhamun's is closed more or less permanently for restoration work so it is not easy to form an opinion of the aura of the place. Sceptics argue that, simply through the law of averages, a measure of misfortune is bound to attend witnesses at any event.

## BIMINI, BAHAMAS

*DO THE DROWNED WALLS OF ATLANTIS LIE OFF THESE HOLIDAY ISLANDS?*

A 'fountain of eternal youth' was said by Caribbean Indians to gush magical waters from the island group of Bimini in the Bahamas. In 1512, fired by the legends, the Spanish explorer Juan Ponce de León, the founder of the first Spanish colony on

SEAFLOOR MYSTERY  *The so-called Walls of Atlantis lie off Bimini in the Bahamas.*

Puerto Rico, set out determined to discover its whereabouts. He missed Bimini but instead happened upon Florida, thus ensuring his place in the history books as one of the discoverers of mainland America.

Bimini's mystical associations do not end with its alleged magic fountain, however. The tiny grouping of islands lies some 50 miles (80 km) off the Florida coast and caused considerable interest in 1968 when aircraft pilots began to report glimpses of what seemed to be walls or building foundations in the waters off the north island. Divers exploring the phenomenon 35 ft (11 m) down spoke of huge white blocks, as square-cut and smoothly fitted as those produced by any ancient civilisation. This was all the more extraordinary because in 1940 the clairvoyant Edgar Cayce had predicted that the lost continent of Atlantis would start to rise again in 1968 or 1969, somewhere in the Bahamas.

The Bimini find caused a worldwide stir among aficionados of the paranormal, and the mystery only deepened when closer studies of the formations revealed them to resemble not so much walls as a huge, man-made roadway marching along the seabed. It appeared to be made up of hundreds of large blocks, extending in regular patterns for several hundred yards. Most experts are now satisfied that the roadway is, in reality, an entirely natural formation. But the phenomenon continues to excite interest among those who believe that lost Atlantis will one day rise again.

## GLAMIS CASTLE, SCOTLAND

*BRITAIN'S MOST HAUNTED CASTLE, BOASTING A PAGEANT OF GHOSTS.*

Ancestral home of the Earls of Strathmore – the family of Britain's Queen Mother – Glamis Castle is a beautiful, brooding fantasy of battlements and towers. Much of what visitors see today dates from the late 17th century, but the original building is much older. It was known to Shakespeare, who made his Macbeth the Thane, or ruler, of Glamis. Macbeth's ghost is just one phantom said to frequent the castle – though the real Macbeth was nothing like the bloodthirsty monster portrayed by Shakespeare.

There are many more ghosts: a spectral thin man known as 'Jack the Runner' has been reported sprinting up the castle drive, and a grey lady kneels among the pews in the chapel. The ghost of a black page boy . . . a tongueless woman . . . a mad earl who paces the roof on stormy nights . . . these are just a few more of the unquiet spirits. Should the visitor hear an eerie rattling emanating from one of the towers, it could well be the ghost of Alexander, the fourth earl of Strathmore. Better known as wicked 'Earl Beardie', he is said to have lost a wager with the Devil, and so been condemned to play dice in the tower until

MONSTER'S LAIR *Was a misshapen heir once concealed in Glamis Castle? Below: the castle crypt.*

the Day of Judgment. Should the visitor see the spectre of a woman glowing with fiery light in the clock tower, it will be the wraith of Janet Douglas, the wife of the sixth earl. Accused in 1537 of an attempt on the life of King James V, she was burnt at the stake in Edinburgh.

Glamis's most famous legend, though, concerns a horribly deformed heir to the family estate allegedly born in the 1800s. Having no neck and only tiny arms and legs, he was kept in a secret chamber in the

# THE LEY LINE ENIGMA

In 1925, an antiquarian named Alfred Watkins published a book called *The Old Straight Track*. His theory was that the landscape of Britain had once been imprinted with a pattern of straight lines that criss-crossed each other in an immense web. The lines he called 'leys', because many of the place names on the tracks ended in 'ley' or 'leigh'. Dictionaries defined the word as an enclosed field, but Watkins proposed that it meant instead a grassy track across the country. He made no occult claims for his leys, taking the view that they were simply straight paths marked by standing stones, crosses and man-made mounds.

Enthusiasts for the theory have, however, taken it much further, claiming that the entire face of Britain is marked with a mystical geometry where paranormal forces are at work. For ley buffs, the sacred sites of early man were carefully placed in a developing pattern. For example, a ley line hundreds of miles long is said to connect the ancient sites of St Michael's Mount, Cadbury Castle, Glastonbury, Avebury and Bury St Edmunds – all along the path of the May Day sunrise. A right-angled triangle, meanwhile, connects Avebury and Glastonbury with Stonehenge.

Archaeologists remain dubious. Statistical probability dictates that a virtually limitless number of patterns can be drawn on maps by connecting ancient sites in straight lines. The patterns may be striking – but entirely meaningless.

**STRAIGHT WAY** *Todmorden church and Studley Pike allegedly lie on a ley.*

---

castle in the expectation that he would die young. However, the Monster of Glamis (as he is referred to) proved to be exceptionally long lived. For a number of generations, so the story goes, the earls of Strathmore were initiated into the grim secret on their 21st birthdays, when they were taken to see the monster in his castle fastness. Thereafter, all became withdrawn and prone to fits of melancholy.

The Monster of Glamis is said to have died in the 1920s. But the castle's supernatural pedigree is maintained by continued reports of spectres and poltergeist phenomena. Even a sceptic may sympathise with Sir Walter Scott's feelings. He once spent a night there and saw no ghost but afterwards confided: 'I must own that when the door was shut I began to consider myself as too far from the living and somewhat too near the dead.'

## BERMUDA TRIANGLE, ATLANTIC OCEAN

*DOES SOME INEXPLICABLE FORCE CAUSE SHIPS AND PLANES TO VANISH HERE?*

Early in June 1991, newspapers worldwide reported the discovery of Flight 19, the legendary Lost Squadron that had disappeared over the Atlantic nearly half a century earlier. The five United States Navy aircraft had set out on a routine training flight from Fort Lauderdale, Florida, at 2 pm on December 5, 1945, and vanished two hours later after losing radio contact with their base. An intensive air-sea rescue operation revealed no trace of the missing planes, and this episode, more than any other, was to be quoted by writers in later decades when stories of a mysterious 'Bermuda Triangle' began to circulate.

Also known as the Devil's Graveyard, the triangle is an area of the sea bounded by Bermuda, Miami and Puerto Rico. At least 50 ships and 20 planes are said to have vanished inexplicably in the region; radio failures and wildly swinging compasses have been reported there too. Triangle buffs have proposed a variety of explanations, from a flaw in the Earth's magnetic field to timewarps and malevolent space aliens. Sceptics, on the other hand, insist that the Bermuda Triangle is no more disaster-prone than any other busy seaway.

During the 1970s, when Triangle fever was at its height, the US Coastguard service declared that, given the volume of traffic and the volatile climatic conditions, they were pleased so few vessels disappeared. Their reports showed that in 1975, 21 vessels were lost without trace off the US coast as a whole; only four of these were in the Bermuda Triangle.

The reported discovery of Flight 19 in June 1991 was greeted with obvious interest by both sides in the debate. The five aircraft were located on the ocean floor by a high-technology vessel from the Scientific Search project, which was looking for sunken Spanish galleons. Clear television pictures were broadcast of the five aircraft, which lay at a depth of 500 ft (150 m) in a tight

**DEVIL'S GRAVEYARD** *Grumann Avenger planes of the type lost over the Bermuda Triangle.*

*MURDEROUS INTENT* *The assassin, John Wilkes Booth, approaches the unsuspecting Lincoln as he sits with his wife in a Washington theatre box.*

formation that indicated they had been ditched under control. The planes were identified as Grumman Avengers, as anticipated – but they lay only 10 miles (16 km) off Fort Lauderdale, which was much closer to base than Flight 19 had been when radio contact was lost. And further doubts about their identity were raised when the search team examined the planes more closely. The Avengers were of an earlier model than those of Flight 19.

After all the ballyhoo that accompanied the discovery, the director of salvage operations had to inform reporters: 'We are in the unenviable position of telling you that we are now certain this is not Flight 19.' The mystery only deepened. Scientific Search had come upon a cluster of bombers that no one had ever reported missing. The location of Flight 19, meanwhile, remains unknown.

## THE WHITE HOUSE, UNITED STATES

*IS THIS OFFICIAL RESIDENCE HAUNTED BY THE GHOST OF PRESIDENT LINCOLN?*

Shortly before his assassination in 1865, the 16th President had a premonition of his own death. Lincoln recounted a dream to a close friend, Ward Hill Lamon, describing how it seemed that the White House was full of mourners and he came before a catafalque on which rested a funeral-wrapped corpse. '"Who is dead in the White House?" I demanded of one of the soldiers. "The President," was his answer. "He was killed by an assassin." Then came a loud burst of grief from the crowd, which awoke me from my dream.' On April 14, a

few days after he had recounted this dream to his friend, Abraham Lincoln was shot by John Wilkes Booth as he sat in his box at Ford's Theatre in Washington, DC, and died early the next morning.

It is said that Lincoln's ghost still haunts the White House. Grace Coolidge, the wife of the 30th president, was the first person to report the spectre, which she saw at a window in the Oval Office. Lincoln's bedroom, known as the Lincoln Room, is a particularly favoured place for sightings, which have even been witnessed there by various visiting heads of state. Queen Wilhelmina of the Netherlands, for instance, once heard a knock on the door, and on opening it found herself face to face with Abraham Lincoln in a frock coat and top hat. The Queen fainted.

President Harry S Truman used to think he heard Lincoln's footsteps, and in the more recent presidency of Ronald Reagan, the president's daughter Maureen reported seeing Lincoln's ghost in the Lincoln Room.

## FIJI, PACIFIC OCEAN

*FIRE-WALKERS PASS BAREFOOT OVER RED-HOT COALS.*

Can an ecstatic state of mind induced by magic ritual suppress both pain and physical damage? The ceremony of walking across fiery stones or hot coals has been reported in many places around the world; Plato and Virgil made reference to it in ancient times, and it is still practised among peoples as different as Hindu worshippers in India and the fire-dancing Navajo people of North America.

Even in the Western world, there are Greek Christians who dance on burning coals, clutching icons of the saints. But if one place is famous for its fire-walking rituals, it is Fiji in the Pacific. Once known as a haunt of cannibals, the coral-fringed

*HOT STUFF* *Almost nonchalantly, Fiji islanders perform the fire-walking ceremony.*

NESSIE'S REALM  *The real-life Urquhart Castle contrasts with the controversial 'surgeon's photograph'.*

islands also attracted world-wide interest long ago for their astonishing tribal rites.

In a typical ceremony the fire-walkers are all male, ranging in age from young boys to old men, and they avoid the company of women for days beforehand. On the night before the ordeal they offer prayers to Tui Namoliwai, the water god. A long pit is filled up with stones to a depth of 6 ft (1.8 m) and layered with logs and brushwood to make a fire that burns all night long. By morning the stones are shimmering with heat and, after assembling in a hut to say final prayers, the fire-walkers enter the pit. The temperature there may be as much as 650°C (1200°F), yet they

---

### FIRE DANCE

Every year on May 21, villagers at Lankadas, Greece, perform a ritual fire dance on a glowing pit some 12 ft (3.6 m) square. The dancers clutch sacred pictures and tread the fiery logs and embers until all flames are extinguished. Temperatures as high as 454°C (850°F) have been measured. 'I would have expected third degree burns in all cases,' said a doctor from Athens General Hospital.

---

walk barefoot across the stones amid the applause of the spectators.

Very occasionally a fire-walker has been badly injured by the ordeal, but the majority

emerge wholly unharmed. For believers it is a triumph of mind over matter, and sceptics have been baffled by the ritual's evident authenticity. The writer George Sandwith recalled a banker who very grudgingly 'admitted the fire-walking was genuine, for he had thrown something on the pit and it had caught fire at once, but he was strongly of the opinion that the Government ought to stop it! When asked why, he became very annoyed, replying that it does not conform with modern scientific discoveries. When I suggested that something of value might be learnt from the fire-walkers, he was so furious he turned on his heel and left me.'

Science is not entirely at a loss to explain the phenomenon, however. Many investigators believe that the stones give off their heat at a sufficiently slow rate for them not to scorch on contact. The principle is the same as that which allows a person to pass a finger rapidly through a candle flame. Additionally, some fire-walkers moisten their feet in damp grass before the ordeal, which may provide brief insulation.

## LOCH NESS, SCOTLAND

*SONAR RESEARCH INTO THE MYSTERIOUS WATERS OF THE SCOTTISH LOCH.*

On May 2, 1933, the *Inverness Courier* carried the following account, based on a description given by a couple called Mr and Mrs Mackey: 'The creature disported itself,

rolling and plunging for fully a minute, its body resembling that of a whale, and the water cascading and churning like a simmering cauldron.'

The first reported sighting of a water monster living in Loch Ness was made by St Columba, the 6th-century Irish-born missionary who brought Christianity to western Scotland. It was the Mackays' spectacular description, however, that launched the modern mania for 'Nessie' stories. More reports flooded in during the months that followed, and they were given credence by a blurred picture, the so-called 'surgeon's photograph' taken in 1934, which appeared to show a long-necked creature moving among the ripples.

It has recently emerged that the surgeon's photograph showed, in reality, a piece of shaped wood driven by clockwork. And though many more photographs have been published and thousands of sightings filed, no convincing evidence of a monstrous inhabitant has ever come to light. Are there subterranean caves and tunnels to the sea in the black depths, perhaps sheltering a colony of prehistoric creatures? Are the genuine reports caused by nothing more than floating logs, outsize eels or schools of otters at play?

Loch Ness certainly presents formidable problems to the investigator. The largest body of fresh water in Britain, it contains more water than all the lakes and reservoirs in England and Wales put together. Until recently, the only serious attempt to survey its underwater topography had been made in 1903 by an early oceanographer, Sir John Murray, who worked from a rowing boat with an assistant, using a lead weight fixed to a long piece of piano wire.

It was only in 1992 that the immense underwater environment was subjected to full-scale scientific investigation. Project Urquhart, as the operation was called, used a 69 ft (21 m) sonar research ship to cruise the entire water, taking some 7 million depth readings in a fan-shaped sweep of the loch bed. The lowest spot was found to lie at an impressive 786 ft (240 m) down, at a point north-east of Invermoriston. By feeding sonar data into a computer, it proved possible to produce 'virtual reality' images of the underwater landscape. Loch Ness, it seems, has steep, sometimes almost perpendicular sides that drop to a flat floor. Though the bed is slightly pitted, there are no caves or tunnels. Sadly for Nessie fans, no animals larger than salmon, pike and Arctic charr have been located. If a monster does lurk in the shadowy waters, it must possess powers of evasion even more awesome than were previously thought.

## TOWER OF LONDON, ENGLAND

*HISTORIC SITE OF EXECUTION AND*
*MURDER, HAUNTED BY ROYAL SHADES.*

In 1674, when restoration work was being carried out at the Tower of London, workmen came upon a wooden box under a staircase with the bones of two boys. They were assumed to be the remains of the two princes believed to have been murdered in the Tower in 1483. According to Shakespeare and others, the young Edward V and his brother Richard were killed on the orders of their hunchbacked uncle, so that he could take the throne as Richard III; more recently, historians have suggested that Henry VII was another candidate for villain. Either way, the find strengthened the view that the princes had been murdered, for in 1933 the remains were examined by an expert in anatomy. He concluded that they were of two brothers, one of 12 or 13, the other 'about midway between nine and eleven' – the ages of the two princes.

**HAUNTED FORTRESS** *Whilst imprisoned in the Tower of London (below), Sir Walter Raleigh lodged in these rooms (left) in the Bloody Tower. An engraving (right) gives an imaginary depiction of the murder of the princes.*

The Tower of London, a royal fortress on the Thames, has a bloodstained history, and more than its normal share of ghost lore to go with it. Two spectral children have been reported wandering its precincts hand in hand, interpreted – inevitably – as the murdered princes. Other ghosts, however, are associated with the Tower's long history as a jail for high-ranking prisoners destined for the executioner's block. The Earl of Northumberland is said to haunt Martin Tower, while Sir Walter Raleigh walks the environs of the Bloody Tower. It took the executioner five blows to behead Catherine Howard, the luckless fifth wife of Henry VIII, and her screams are still heard, they say, on the anniversary of her death on February 13, 1542.

The ghost most often reported, however, is that of Anne Boleyn, executed for adultery in 1536. In 1864, a sentry of the 60th Rifles faced court martial for being asleep on watch at the Tower; his defence was that he had lost consciousness after seeing her shade. He twice challenged the ghost, 'Then, as it still did not stop, I charged at it with my bayonet. But I went slap through the figure, striking my head so badly against the wall that I fell down unconscious, and remembered nothing till I found myself under arrest in the guard room.' Two Beefeaters also testified to seeing the mysterious figure, and the court found the soldier not guilty.

Anne Boleyn was seen by another sentry in 1933. The headless spectre floated towards him at dead of night, and he immediately fled his post. However, because of the Tower's reputation, he got off with no more than a reprimand.

## CAPE OF GOOD HOPE, SOUTH AFRICA

*THE SPECTRAL FLYING DUTCHMAN HAUNTS THE TIP OF AFRICA.*

According to the most common account, the 'Flying Dutchman' ghost ship is a 17th-century Dutch East Indiaman under the command of a Captain Hendrik van der Decken. In the waters off the Cape of Good Hope, the vessel met a violent south-

easterly gale and battled against it for weeks without making any headway. Legend asserts that as the captain grew ever more enraged, he swore a blasphemous oath defying God to stop him from completing his destined course. As punishment, he was condemned to sail round the cape for ever without making a port.

The tale inspired Richard Wagner to compose his opera *Der Fliegende Holländer* (*The Flying Dutchman*), first produced in 1843. And it has at least some basis in fact, in that the waters off the Cape of Good Hope are notoriously dangerous to navigators. The headland was discovered in 1488 by the Portuguese sailor Bartolomeu Dias, who called it the Cape of Storms in reference to its frequent tropical gales. It

**GHOST SHIP** *Moonlight flickers around the Flying Dutchman, depicted in an illustration of 1900.*

was the Portuguese sovereign John II who later renamed it Good Hope, 'for the promise it gave of finding India'.

Although all can agree on the perils of rounding the Cape, Flying Dutchman sightings are more controversial. Since the 17th century countless reports of a spectral sailing ship have been made by seamen travelling in these waters. In sailors' lore, any vessel that sights the doomed phantom will meet misfortune. England's King George V reported an episode from the time when he served as a midshipman on

HMS *Bacchante*. He had seen the ghost ship with a figure in historical costume at the stern. On the following day, a crewman fell from the rigging and died.

Rationalists argue that phantom ships seen at sea are probably mirages, and that imagination may supply a witness with the period detail. Group sightings are not, however, so easy to explain. In March 1939 a mysterious sailing vessel was seen by some 60 people who were idling on Glencairn beach on the Cape at the time. It appeared to have the high poop and rigging of a 17th-century merchantman. 'Let the sceptics say what they will,' said a witness named Mrs Helene Tydell, 'that ship was none other than the Flying Dutchman.'

## LAKE OKANAGAN, CANADA

*'THE CANADIAN LOCH NESS' – REPUTED HAUNT OF THE MONSTROUS OGOPOGO.*

A music hall ditty current in the 1920s celebrated the giant serpent that is said to inhabit Lake Okanagan in the Canadian province of British Columbia:

> *His mother was an earwig,*
> *His father was a whale.*
> *A little bit of head*
> *And hardly any tail,*
> *And Ogopogo was his name.*

Like 'Nessie' in Scotland, Canada's famous water spirit has been granted a comforting, childish name – perhaps to exorcise the very real fear it must once have struck in the hearts of people who lived near the lake. Ogopogo is a term coined by a newspaper in 1872, but its origins stretch back much further in time. The shores of Lake Okanagan, on mountain slopes near Canada's Pacific seaboard, were once home only to native American Indians who lived in dread of a creature called Naitaka, 'the monster spirit of the lake'. They believed that it lived on a small island in the 69 mile (111 km) long expanse of water, and used to leave offerings for it in the form of sacrificed animals. When white men arrived and settled the land, sightings of the monster persisted. In 1854 the creature was said to have devoured a team of horses. It was, an eyewitness said, 'at least 20 ft [6 m] long, and had a heavy snake-like body, a horse's head, and was well-bearded'.

Interest has continued into the 20th century, when the area's scenic attractions have made it popular with tourists. In 1959 a boating party on the lake reported a large, blunt-nosed, serpentine creature following their motor cruiser. In 1968 a water-skier named Sheri Campbell claimed to have got within 5 ft (1.5 m) of the beast and noted that its skin glittered with 'blue-green-grey scales' before it swam off at speed, leaving V-shaped waves in its wake. In 1977, a Mrs Lillian Vogelgesang screamed

NASTY SURPRISE *A Victorian engraving shows boatmen startled by a wild-eyed Canadian lake monster.*

at the sight of a many-humped creature some 50 ft (15 m) long near the dock at Sarsons Beach. 'If I hadn't had the children,' she said, 'I would have run down to the edge of the dock, for I could actually have touched it, it was so close in.' The fact that sceptics remain unimpressed does not trouble the local tourist industry – the lore of Ogopogo is as much an asset as the beauty of the mountains around.

## VERSAILLES, FRANCE

*A HOTLY DEBATED GHOST STORY CENTRES ON LOUIS XIV'S PALACE.*

If one spirit can be said to haunt the glorious precincts of Versailles, it is surely that of Louis XIV. The French sovereign's taste for splendour earned him the title of the Sun King and at Versailles between 1676 and 1708, he built a palace that became the envy of all Europe. A thousand courtiers and 4000 servants inhabited its gilded chambers and galleries, while the gardens sprawled over 250 acres (100 ha).

For ghost-hunters, however, the chief focus of interest is a house at Versailles known as the Petit Trianon, which the king built for his mistress, the Marquise of Pompadour. On August 10, 1901, two English academics, Eleanor Jourdain and Annie Moberly, were walking towards the Petit Trianon when both felt an eerie and oppressive sensation. Then they came upon two men in historical costumes of grey-green coats with small three-cornered hats. When they asked for directions, the men guided them towards a kiosk and bridge where a man sat slouched in hat and cloak.

They saw other mysterious figures besides: a running man wrapped in a cloak (though it was a warm summer's day); a woman in a pale green fichu (a lightweight scarf tied around the shoulders) sitting on a seat on the lawn. The two women afterwards concluded that the Petit Trianon was haunted, and returned the next year to investigate further. On their second visit, in January 1902, they again encountered figures in period costume.

Historical research suggested to the women that they had seen visions from the

PARANORMAL EXPERIENCES
*Mysterious figures in period
costume were sighted in 1901
around the Petit Trianon
area of Versailles. Psychic
researchers believed them to
be courtiers from the time of
Marie Antoinette (above).*

time of Marie Antoinette, the wife of Louis XVI. The woman in a green fichu was the queen herself; the two men in grey-green coats were her attendants, the brothers Bercy; the figure in a slouch hat could have been a well-known courtier, the Comte de Vaudreuil. The kiosk and bridge they had seen did not exist in 1901 – but corresponded to 18th-century examples. The two Englishwomen published their story in 1911, under the title *An Adventure*. Their experiences had not been spectacular, nor was their evidence especially compelling, but the book sparked widespread interest. Miss Moberly and Miss Jourdain were women of good reputation – both daughters of churchmen – and soon similar experiences were being reported from other visitors to the Petit Trianon.

These have persisted to recent times, despite a rational explanation furnished in 1965 by the writer Philippe Jullian. In a biography of the French aristocrat and poet, Robert de Montesquiou, the author pointed out that during the 1900s Montesquiou and his circle used often to visit the area around the Trianon – some of them dressed in period costume. The entire controversy surrounding the ghosts haunting Versailles may simply have been triggered by their whimsical activities.

## LAKE IKEDA, JAPAN

*A TWO-HUMPED MONSTER IS SAID
TO INHABIT THESE JAPANESE WATERS.*

In 1978 a shopkeeper named Matsubara, from Kagoshima city, was awarded a prize of 100 000 yen for the first photograph of 'Issie' – an unidentified creature said to frequent Lake Ikeda. Like the photographs

of Nessie in Scotland, it is a blurred image offering nothing that science would regard as evidence, but enough of a ripple pattern for monster buffs to puzzle over. 'Something huge came up from the water and disappeared again in 15 to 20 seconds,' said Mr Matsubara.

The lake lies at the southern tip of Japan's Kyushu Island and is well known for the creature said to haunt its depths. Tradition holds that a Samurai lord once stole the foal of an immaculate white mare that lived near the lake. Heartbroken, the mare jumped into the water and plunged to the bottom. The creature that bursts to the surface at irregular intervals is said to be the forlorn mare searching for her lost foal.

Touching as the tale may be, however, it does not tally with 20th-century reports that have described a creature or

'SOMETHING HUGE CAME UP'
*Japan's Lake Ikeda is the
home of the elusive 'Issie'.*

YETI'S DOMAIN **Key sightings of the Abominable Snowman have been made on Mount Everest. Left: mountaineer Eric Shipton examines footprints said to have been left by the monster.**

*Below: Sir Edmund Hillary and Sherpa Khumbo Chumbi display a 'yeti scalp'.*

creatures with two large humps and a complexion that is far from white. 'The skin was very dark,' reported Yutaka Kawaji, a local builder. To form their own opinion of the monster, Issie-spotters can scan the lake today from a purpose-built observatory that was opened in 1978.

## MOUNT EVEREST, HIMALAYAS

*THE WORLD'S HIGHEST MOUNTAIN IS A HAUNT OF THE ABOMINABLE SNOWMAN.*

Curious footprints were reported by Westerners in the Himalayas as far back as 1887, but the Abominable Snowman became a world story in 1921. The first British Mount Everest Expedition that year was headed by Colonel C.K. Howard-Bury, who led an attempt on the northern face.

At about 17 000 ft (5180 m) on the Lhapka-La Pass, the team noticed through their binoculars a number of dark figures moving upright on a snowfield high above. On reaching the spot, they found huge footprints 'three times the size [those of] of normal humans', as Howard-Bury reported. The Sherpas identified the tracks as those of the *yeti* or *mehteh kangmi* (man creature, snow creature). The latter term, mistranslated as 'Abominable Snowman', gave pressmen a sensational news story.

In the decades that have followed, photographs of giant footprints, exhibits of yeti scalps and sporadic sightings have regaled newspaper readers worldwide. Sir Edmund Hillary, the conqueror of Everest, concluded that some alleged yeti scalps he examined were made from the hide of the rare Tibetan blue bear, a creature that sometimes travels above the snowline. Its paw marks, enlarged by sunshine on melting snow, may also account for some outsize footprints. The langur monkey, too, is known to live at considerable heights.

More adventurous researchers have proposed that the reports are caused by hominid creatures not yet known to naturalists: living ape-men or Neanderthal survivals. There is some general agreement among believers that the yeti is not itself a creature of the Himalayan snows, but a secretive denizen of the mountains' vast forested flanks that strays only rarely onto the higher ground. For many yeti-buffs, the favourite candidate is *Gigantopithecus*, a prehistoric giant ape of which fossil relics have survived in various parts of Asia.

The sightings, meanwhile, continue. Yetis are said to make frequent visits to the garden of Thyangboche Buddhist monastery in the shadow of Everest. In July 1973 it was reported that a young Sherpa girl in the Khoner area, near Everest, had been knocked unconscious by a yeti, which killed five of the yaks she was minding. Four to five feet (1.2-1.5 m) tall, the creature had 'thick black hair below the waist and brownish hair above'.

## MAUNA LOA, HAWAII

*A GHOST GODDESS OF THE VOLCANO WALKS HAWAII'S NIGHT ROADS.*

At 13 667 ft (4166 m), Mauna Loa rises impressively from the heart of the coral island of Hawaii in the Pacific. One of its craters, Kilauea, is volcanically active – and active in folklore too. For Kilauea Crater is said to be the home of a ghost goddess named Madame Pele, who governs a family of fire gods within the molten core of the mountain. According to one legend, the Queen of Eruptions fled to Hawaii from the island of Tahiti to escape the fury of a sister whose husband she had seduced. The memory of the episode causes her to send lava streaming down the mountainside, and to assuage her wrath islanders leave roast chickens as offerings on the crater's edge.

Bad luck is supposed to follow anyone taking stones away from the volcano. Naturalists at the Volcanoes National Park in Hawaii at one time received up to 40 packages of rock a day from tourists who had ignored all warnings and were later afflicted by everything from sprained ankles, broken arms and fractured wrists to lightning strikes and head-on car crashes. No sooner did they return the stones than, it is said, the disasters ceased.

Madame Pele is wrathful, but not essentially malign; should the volcano threaten a serious eruption, she comes down to warn people of the impending destruction, appearing in the form of a beautiful young woman dressed in red, with a little white dog at her heels. Motorists who encounter the ghost are supposed to stop and offer her a lift – to fail to do so is to court disaster when the volcano erupts.

FIERY SPIRIT *The spectre of volatile Madame Pele is said to frequent Mauna Loa.*

# HAITI – ISLAND OF VOODOO

For those with Western notions of religious faith, the world of voodoo seems a nightmarish one, haunted by images of sacrificial magic, spirit possession and the walking dead. Its sinister mystique is only enhanced by the fact that Haiti, its home, is the poorest country in the Caribbean and has endured brutal dictatorships that have long caused tourists to stay away. Ruled by strange beliefs and reverberating to the rhythms of African drums, the country does not seem wholly one of the Americas – it is a mystery land, a place apart.

Haiti forms one half of the island of Hispaniola (the other is the Dominican Republic), discovered by Christopher Columbus in 1492. It was colonised in the 17th century by French sugar planters, who imported slaves in large numbers from Africa. Following mass revolt they declared their independence in 1804, forming the first black republic in the world. To this day, more than 90 per cent of the people are of African descent, and the rest are mostly of mixed race. Voodoo played its part in the rebellion, for the first revolt was initiated by a man named Boukman, a *houngan* (or voodoo priest), who, with conch-shell trumpet and drums, called the rebels to torch Haiti's northern plains.

**CALLING DOWN THE SPIRITS**
*Haitians dance themselves into a trance-like state during a Voodoo ceremony.*

Voodoo itself is a blend of beliefs that were derived initially from the tribal cults of West Africa, where most of the slaves originated. The word comes from the African *vodun*, meaning sacred object or supernatural being, but the belief system soaked up many elements of Catholicism as well as bits of ceremonial taken from textbooks of ritual magic current in 18th-century France. Out of this rich mix comes

ACT OF POSSESSION *A Voodoo worshipper falls to the ground, 'possessed' by a* loa *(spirit).*

a world inhabited by *loas*, or spirits, such as the spectacular black-clad, top-hatted Baron Samedi who is lord of the underworld and watches over cemeteries with rod and skull. Other *loas* include Papa Legba, guardian of doors, roads and crossroads; Ogun, spirit of war; and Erzulie, a female spirit who has much in common with the Virgin Mary.

Ceremonies usually take place on a Tuesday or Saturday night, when Haitians assemble at the local *hounfort*, a sanctuary with an altar and an earthen floor, and dance to the frenzied, relentless beating of skin and mahogany drums. The purpose of this is to encourage trance-states in which the spirits may descend and 'mount' a

MUD FOR A GOD *Bathing in mud that is believed to have magic properties is part of the rituals in honour of the Voodoo* loa *(spirit)* Ogun, *patron of war.*

dancer so that he or she whirls around, arms flailing, eyes glazed with excitement, sometimes screaming and sometimes uttering predictions. A variety of different rhythms are played on the voodoo drums to encourage the various *loas* to come down, and the ground is marked with symbols in cornmeal flour or ash to appease the spirits in question.

Comparable rites are known in Brazil, Cuba and Jamaica, but in Haiti voodoo is the popular religion. It is by no means entirely sinister; ceremonial dances and songs serve as social recreation, as in many other faiths around the world. Nonetheless, voodoo certainly does possess its darker side. Dolls stuck with pins to harm enemies and chickens beheaded to propitiate the spirits are both forms of magic associated with it, and a more disquieting aspect is the belief in zombies.

The term 'zombie' probably comes from the Congo word *nzambi* (spirit of a dead person); it is said that voodoo sorcerers can steal the soul from a corpse and then direct it as if it were a mindless automaton – generally for use as slave labour. According to a more scientific view, the sorcerer administers a potion to a living victim that causes the metabolic rate to drop so low that he or she merely appears to be dead – the zombie may then be buried, dug up again and revived with other drugs.

In 1930, on a trip in Haiti, the French anthropologist Georges de Rouquet came across four cotton pickers his guide assured him were zombies. While the other workers were lithe and fit, these men seemed almost fleshless; their gait was curiously shambling,

DRESSED FOR THE JOB
*A Candomblé priest is attired in full regalia. Like Voodoo, Candomblé in Brazil mixes African and Catholic influences.*

and their arms hung lifelessly at their sides. 'The most arresting feature about them was their gaze. They all stared straight ahead, their eyes dull and unfocused as if blind. They did not show a spark of awareness of my presence, even when I approached them closely. To test the reflexes of one I made a stabbing gesture toward his eyes with my pointed fingers. He did not blink or shrink back. But when I attempted to touch his hand the overseer prevented me, saying that this was not permitted.'

Brain-damaged, drugged or dehumanised by ill-treatment, the pitiful figures can be explained by means other than sorcery. But fear of zombification remains very real in Haiti where, it has been said, people are not as scared of being harmed by a zombie as they are of becoming one.

# FOLKLORE, FICTION AND FAIRYTALES

*'Every time a child says "I don't believe in fairies" there is a little fairy somewhere that falls down dead.' J.M. Barrie's words from* Peter Pan *enshrine a human truth: wherever magical belief dies, imaginative riches are put in jeopardy.*

When the Pied Piper led the children of the German town of Hameln (or Hamelin) into a hill from which they never returned, he was participating in a widespread European myth that associated fairy music with grassy mounds. In England, William Brockie, the folklorist of County Durham, wrote: 'The fairies usually took up their abode during the day underground in the bosom of isolated round green hills. I have met with people who knew this to be a fact, because sometimes on a fine, still summer evening, when they had lain down on these hills with their ear close to the ground, they were astonished to hear piping, fiddling, singing, and dancing going on far down in the interior.'

Dragons that slumber over fantastic stores of treasure . . . evil witches . . . wishing wells where dreams come true . . . fairytale themes like these seem merely picturesque today, but belief in them was common among country folk in the not-so-distant past. Tales of fairies are associated with Celtic Europe, where they were traditionally propitiated with offerings left for them at holy wells, lakes and groves of trees.

A belief in the 'little people' has never entirely died out. The novelist Sir Arthur Conan Doyle, who created the shrewd detective Sherlock Holmes, in 1920 astonished his admirers by proclaiming his belief in the authenticity of some 'fairy photographs' taken by two girls aged 16 and 10 at the

ENCHANTMENT *Bavaria's Neuschwanstein Castle belongs to the landscape of fairytale.*

Yorkshire village of Cottingley. (The photographs turned out to be fakes, made from cut-outs of illustrations from *Princess Mary's Gift Book* of 1915.)

## FAIRYTALE ROAD, GERMANY

*AN ENCHANTED LANDSCAPE THAT*
*INSPIRED THE BROTHERS GRIMM.*

Cinderella, Snow White, Rumpelstiltskin and Sleeping Beauty . . . they have entered the folk consciousness of the entire world. The original stories were collected by two brothers, Jakob (1785-1863) and Wilhelm (1786-1859) Grimm, from the area of Germany where they lived. From early childhood they had been captivated by the make-believe world of the peasant imagination, with its princely heroes, golden-haired princesses, goblins, witches and wicked stepmothers. Their great collection of folk tales was published in 1812-14 as *Kinder und Hausmärchen* (*Children's and Household Tales*). In introducing to the world the likes of Rapunzel and Hansel and Gretel, they also immortalised the landscape of the German heartland, with its ancient forests, picturesque castles and half-timbered houses.

The Fairytale Road, or *Märchenstrasse*, is a 370 mile (600 km) route that meanders

STORYBOOK IMAGES *Little Red Riding Hood supposedly lived in Alsfeld in Germany.*

WITCH WATERS *Objects are hung out to petrify in the Dropping Well at Knaresborough.*

northwards from the brothers' birthplace at the little town of Hanau near Frankfurt-am-Main to the port of Bremenin the northwest of the country. On the way it takes in the town of Steinau, where their father was a magistrate and the brothers spent much of their boyhood. The road then winds on towards medieval Alsfeld, which claims Little Red Riding Hood as one of its former inhabitants, and Sababurg, whose turreted hunting lodge is thought to be Sleeping Beauty's castle. The road continues along the banks of the fast-flowing River Weser before it reaches Hameln (or Hamelin), celebrated for its legend of the Pied Piper.

Tradition holds that in 1284 the town was infested by rats, and that a wandering piper offered to lure them into the river – for a fee. Though the ratcatcher accomplished his task the citizens refused to pay him, accusing him of sorcery. The next Sunday he came back and played a tune that enticed all the youngsters (except one lame boy) into a door in a hill, from which they never returned.

The tale inspired the Grimm brothers, and is reckoned to have some basis in historical fact. According to one account it alludes to the conscription of young men to fight in an unpopular war during the 13th century, when so many youths vanished that

people spoke of their being spirited away by the Devil playing his flute. Others believe that the story refers to the time when thousands of children joined the Children's Crusade in the early 13th century, many never returning .

The image of the brightly clad ratcatcher survives. His story is re-enacted every summer Sunday on the terrace of the *Hochzeithaus* (Wedding House) in Hameln. Rat-shaped pastries are sold in the shops, and the *Rattenfängerhaus* (Ratcatcher's House) has frescoes illustrating the legend. To this day no music is played in the adjacent street, down which, according to legend, the children were led by the ratcatcher piping his spellbinding tune.

## KNARESBOROUGH, ENGLAND

*CAVE AND WELL OF THE WITCH AND*
*PROPHETESS MOTHER SHIPTON.*

Damp and eerie, the Dropping Well at Knaresborough, North Yorkshire, has the property of turning to stone any object placed in it. Science has a ready explanation: the phenomenon results from the quantity of lime in the water, which solidifies over a period of time. Close by is a cave with more enigmatic associations, for this is the alleged home of Mother Shipton, a witch who is said to have lived in the woods and made prophecies of uncanny accuracy.

Tradition holds that she lived in early Tudor times, and that her maiden name was Ursula Southill. She is said to have been born around 1488, the daughter of a witch named Agatha, and was so dwarfish and ugly that people called her the Devil's Child. Notwithstanding these disadvantages, at the age of 24 she reputedly married a builder from York, Tobias Shipton, and died in 1561, aged 73.

Her most remarkable prophecies concerned prominent figures at the court of Henry VIII, including Lord Percy and Cardinal Wolsey (whose arrest for treason she foretold). She is also credited with anticipating the reign of a virgin queen (Elizabeth I), the execution of Charles I, and the Great Fire of London. Lines attributed to her even foretell the coming of motor cars and metal ships:

*Carriages without horses shall go*
*And accidents fill the world with woe,*
*In water, iron shall float*
*As easily as a wooden boat.*

Historians doubt whether the doggerel was really penned in the 16th century – and even whether Mother Shipton existed. Nonetheless, Britain's most famous seer retained a grip on the popular imagination.

## DRACHENFELS, GERMANY

*A DRAGON'S ROCK AND A CASTLE LINKED WITH THE LEGEND OF SIEGFRIED.*

The picturesque Siebengebirge (seven mountains) is a group of wooded hills that – though not especially high – are visible from far across the Rhine plain. Geologists may describe them as volcanic in origin,

HEROIC ENCOUNTER *Siegfried's battle with the dragon supposedly took place at Drachenfels.*

but tradition holds that they were created by seven giants who, while digging out a channel for the Rhine, heaped up seven

### DRAGON-SLAYING SITES

Researchers have often noted the number of early Christian churches dedicated to a dragon-killing saint. St Michael, in particular, was venerated: for example, in the strikingly similar offshore island monasteries of Mont St Michel in France and St Michael's Mount in England. Both sites have long pre-Christian traditions, and it is thought that the dragon-slaying motif symbolised the struggle for control over vital life forces in order to preserve the cosmic balance.

great mounds of earth. At 1053 ft (321 m) high, the Drachenfels or 'Dragon Rock' is the most famous of the hills, occupying a magnificent position overlooking the river near Königswinter. The valorous medieval hero Roland, nephew of Charlemagne, is said to have spent some time in the ruined 12th-century castle that crowns the summit, and there to have fallen in love with the

lord's charming daughter. But the hill is better known for its legends of dragon-slaying and of Siegfried, the hero of the *Nibelungenlied* saga.

The saga is a medieval epic that incorporates older and more primitive myths of the Dark Age German tribes. Half way up the Drachenfels is a shadowy cavern which is said to have been the home of a ferocious dragon. In the *Nibelungenlied*, Siegfried slew the monster and bathed in its blood so that his skin became invulnerable to wounds (except in one place, where a linden leaf fell on him as he stooped to bathe). Today vines are cultivated on the slopes of the Siebengebirge and yield a red wine called *Drachenblut* – dragon's blood.

According to another legend (perhaps adapted by Christian monks to advance their faith), the dragon's cave was occupied by a loathsome creature that fed on human sacrifices supplied by local pagan priests. A Christian maiden of great beauty was once offered to the dragon; as the monster dragged its coils from the cavern, fire gushing from mouth and nostrils, she astonished the crowd by showing no fear. Instead, she met its onslaught with a hymn of praise.

When she held out her crucifix the dragon flinched and plunged to its death in the Rhine. Awestruck, the people converted to Christianity, one of the first to

HELL'S MOUTH *Flames burst from Hekla's crater during the eruption of 1970. According to medieval legend, the Icelandic volcano was a fiery gateway to hell.*

adopt the new faith being the maiden's pagan captor, a warrior named Rinbod. Having seen the crucifix's power he renounced his barbarian ways, married his beautiful captive and (so the story goes) built a castle for her on the Drachenfels, whose ruins survive to this day.

## HEKLA, ICELAND

*A VOLCANO KNOWN IN MEDIEVAL EUROPE AS THE HOME OF THE DAMNED.*

When people in the Middle Ages imagined Hell, they pictured a subterranean realm that included scalding fires and sulphurous smoke, echoing to the screams of tormented souls. And they located the mouth of hell at Iceland's Mount Hekla, a squat volcano that has erupted more than 20 times in recorded history – it is just one of some 200 volcanoes in Iceland, many of which are active, with one erupting, on average, every five years.

Hekla's name means 'hooded', a menacing term that alludes to the thick bank of clouds in which the 4892 ft (1491 m) summit is often hidden. It is not, in reality, Iceland's most active volcano, but it is its most conspicuous – seamen in medieval times on board ships passing south along the coast could not help being aware of its brooding presence.

Here was a place of terror: one gigantic eruption, in 1104, covered more than half of Iceland under an immense tonnage of volcanic ash – fields around Hekla, which rises from the edge of one of Iceland's richest agricultural regions, were buried under 3 ft (1 m) of it, and all farms around the mountain were destroyed, never to be rebuilt. In 1300, large rocks were seen moving about in the fire 'like charcoal in a blacksmith's hearth', and the ashfall was so great that people could not tell whether it was day or night.

It may have been this terrifying episode that first prompted people to write of Hekla as the gateway to Hell. The mountain had certainly earned this reputation by the 16th century, when a German writer spoke of it resounding to lamentable and miserable yellings, while sinister swarms of

ugly black ravens and vultures hovered about. Local people, he reported, believed there was a descent to hell in it, and that whenever battles or bloody slaughter were committed anywhere around the world 'monstrous screeches are heard about this mountain'. Another German traveller of the same period noted icebergs in the sea and asserted: 'The damned souls are tormented in the flame in the mountain, and after in the ice.'

Superstition may have lost its grip in the 20th century, but Hekla's powers are undiminished. An eruption in 1766 caused considerable loss of life; in a more recent one, in 1970, 45 million tons of debris were lofted into the air, scattering fallout over every part of Iceland.

## CALLANISH, SCOTLAND

*STANDING STONES LOOM LIKE GIANTS OVER A HEBRIDEAN ISLAND.*

Throughout Europe, the huge megalithic monuments that had been raised by prehistoric communities survived to baffle succeeding generations of villagers. They were explained in mythological terms – often as the work of wizards or giants – by

SOLEMN GATHERING
*Legend holds that the Callanish Stones are a group of petrified giants who rejected Christian teaching.*

local people, who felt instinctively drawn to them as places of significance, and they prompted numerous curious legends. Maen Llia, a monolith on the Brecon Beacons in Wales, for example, is said to go down to the River Neath to drink when it hears the cock crow.

Apart from Stonehenge in England and Carnac in Brittany, however, no site is more impressive than that of Callanish on the Isle of Lewis in the Outer Hebrides. In this wild moorland setting looms a circle of tall, lichen-covered monoliths, approached by a 270 ft (82 m) long avenue of guardian stones. At the centre of it is a chambered mound in the form of a cross. The site dates back to around 3400 BC, and probably served a purpose connected with observation of the lunar cycle.

Seen from a distance, however, the stones look like a great and solemn gathering of human figures – and this is how local legend interprets them. According to

# LEGENDS OF THE ROCK HURLER

Huge, isolated boulders or monoliths raised by prehistoric men were often explained in the past as missiles hurled by a giant, or the devil. There is a remarkable consistency in tales from around Europe. In Rudston churchyard, in the north-east of England, is the tallest standing stone in the country, a monolith over 25 ft (7.6 m) high. It is said to have been hurled by the Devil in the hope of smashing the church (he only just missed). The same story is told of a large stone near the cathedral at Cologne. According to the Brothers Grimm, 'It is called the Devil's Rock because imprints of the claws of the Evil One became embedded in it when he threw it at the chapel of the Three Holy Kings. The Devil was trying to destroy it, but the attempt failed.'

**DEVIL'S WORK** *The monolith in Rudston churchyard was allegedly hurled by Satan.*

tradition, the Callanish Stones are giants who were turned to stone by St Kieran. The 6th-century saint was one of the founders of monasticism in Ireland, establishing Clonmacnoise Abbey, which developed into the most famous of Irish monastic cities, attracting scholars from all over the island. He was also supposed to have visited the western parts of Scotland. The giants apparently met at Callanish to reject the Christian faith that St Kieran was preaching and were turned to stone as a punishment for their unbelief.

## REED FLUTE CAVE, CHINA

*SITE OF THE LEGENDARY*
*MONKEY KING'S VICTORY.*

In the limestone wonderland of China's Guilin Hills are spectacular caverns visited by thousands of tourists every year. The most famous of them is known as the Reed Flute Cave, taking its name from the reeds that once grew thick around the entrance, and were used to make musical instruments. More than 825 ft (250 m) long, the cave was first discovered during the Tang dynasty (618-907). It was then generally forgotten about for a long time, although it often served the locals as a refuge from bandits and the ravages of war. The vast inner grotto is known as the Crystal Palace. Divided into two parts by a pool, it is filled with stalactites and stalagmites and holds up to 1000 people.

Illuminated today by multi-coloured electric lights, the cave's weird rock formations resemble gnarled trees, dense shrubs, animals such as horses, lions and a number of other ferocious beasts, and even musical instruments, all glittering in the hues of coral, agate, amber and jade. Among the human figures shaped here by nature is one known as the Old Scholar. He turned to stone, so the legend goes, after making fruitless attempts to evoke the beauties of the setting in verse.

The cave is best known, however, as the treasure-crammed palace of the Dragon

**FABLED CAVERN** *A Dragon King supposedly inhabited China's Reed Flute Cave. His army of sea creatures was petrified into the floor.*

King in the centuries-old tale called *Journey to the West*. This hugely popular narrative describes the adventures of a Chinese pilgrim who goes to India in order to obtain the true texts of the Buddha's teaching,

## DRAGON POWER

In ancient mythologies, the snake or dragon often symbolised the principle of evil. In China and Japan, however, dragons have greater prestige as beneficient creatures. They are imperial symbols and represent forces of nature. Even in Europe, dragons sometimes have kingly attributes: King Arthur's father, Uther Pendragon, carried a dragon standard in battle. Dragons were often perceived as magical rather than evil creatures. They were dwellers in the inner parts of the earth, the guardians of its secrets.

travelling in the company of the highly mischievous Monkey King. In Reed Flute Cave, the Monkey King destroyed the Dragon King's army of crab generals, shrimp soldiers, snails and jellyfish, leaving them petrified on the floor of the cave. A limestone pillar in the grotto was supposedly the Dragon King's magic needle.

## SNAEFELLSJOKULL, ICELAND

*GLACIER-CAPPED VOLCANIC MOUNTAIN*
*IMMORTALISED BY JULES VERNE.*

The ice-cap shines atop a peak at the western end of Iceland's Snaefellsness peninsula. At 4743 ft (1446 m) it dominates the surrounding country and can be seen on a clear day from Reykjavik 60 miles (100 km) to the south. The glistening peak is formed by a glacier covering the crater of a long-extinct volcano; with such natural attributes it is no small wonder that Snaefellsjokull has attracted the attention of myth-makers.

Most famously, the mountain features in the Frenchman Jules Verne's novel *Journey to the Centre of the Earth* (1864) as the place where the explorers enter the depths of the planet. 'The crater of Sneffels was in the shape of an inverted cone with an opening about a mile [1.6 km] across,' writes the author. 'I was involuntarily reminded of a

huge, funnel-shaped blunderbuss, and the comparison alarmed me. "To go down into a blunderbuss," I thought, "when it may be loaded, and may go off at the slightest touch, is sheer lunacy . . . "'

There follows a 3000 mile (4800 km) journey deep below the Earth's surface, where the explorers meet terrible hardships in dark forests of giant vegetation, witness battles between fearsome prehistoric

'SHEER LUNACY' *In* Journey to the Centre of the Earth *the explorers descend by way of Snaefellsjokull's volcanic crater.*

monsters and suffer the torments of a violent electrical storm.

The glacier also plays a mystical role in *Christianity at Glacier*, by the Nobel prize-winning novelist Halldor Laxness. In recent years, New Age pilgrims have taken to gathering beneath the glacier every summer in search of cosmic experiences. To reach the magic mountain they must cross a raven-haunted peninsula steeped in the ancient lore of the Icelandic sagas.

At Froda, overlooked by the mountain, is the ghost-ridden locale of the Eyrbyggja Saga. Here a greedy farmer's wife called Thurid sparked a series of evil happenings through her refusal to honour the deathbed wish of a mysterious visitor from the Hebrides. A shower of blood from the sky warned the visitor of her forthcoming death, and she insisted that her bedclothes and scarlet cloak be burnt, or disaster would

strike the entire household. When Thurid refused to burn them, the visitor came back, first as the ghost of a naked woman, and later as a seal. The farmer, the family and many servants all perished and returned to haunt the farm; once-buried corpses paced the house, shaking earth from their garments; drowned men dripped seawater on the floor. The house was only finally rid of its plague of phantoms after a Christian ghost-banishing ceremony presided over by the elder Snorri the Wise.

## TRANSYLVANIA, ROMANIA

*HOMELAND OF VAMPIRES AND OF THE FICTIONAL COUNT DRACULA.*

The story of the bloodsucking count was told in dramatic diary form by Bram Stoker in his novel *Dracula* (1897). Events begin and end in the mountains of Transylvania, a region of Romania rich in superstitions, from which travellers returned as early as the 16th century with horrifying tales of creatures neither living nor dead who feasted on human blood. Stoker himself never visited Transylvania, but researched his novel in the British Museum and received additional folkloric information from a man named Arminius Vambery. Nonetheless, in choosing this beautiful, mountainous land as the setting for his supernatural tale he created a dreamscape that is now wholly associated with the vampire myth.

Transylvania (which means 'Land Beyond the Forest') is one of the three main regions of Romania, the others being Wallachia and Moldavia. Though creatures similar to vampires are referred to in folklore all around the world, the tradition is especially fertile in Transylvania. Villagers speak of a multitude of species, each of which has its own characteristics, but underlying them all is the notion that they are 'undead'. They are corpses that have fallen

DRACULA COUNTRY

*Transylvania's Bran Castle and (inset) the real life villain, Vlad the Impaler, who partially inspired the Dracula story.*

under the influence of an evil spirit and that are used by it for malevolent purposes.

Stoker seems to have based his villainous count on a historical character, Vlad Tepes (1431-1476), ruler of Wallachia, who was known as Vlad the Impaler from his reputed habit of impaling enemies on

stakes. Dracul (meaning 'devil' or 'dragon') was the title given to his father; Vlad Tepes was Draculea, or Dracula, which means 'Son of Dracul'. The novelist may also have been inspired by another bloodthirsty ruler, the Hungarian Countess Elizabeth Barthory (1560-1614), who lived in a castle in the Carpathian mountains and used to bathe in the blood of murdered girls in the hope of preserving her beauty.

Today the Romanian government cashes in on Transylvania's gruesome fame, organising trips through Dracula country. The most photographed sight is Bran Castle, rising in grim majesty from its rocky crags 74 miles (119 km) north of the the country's capital Bucharest. Built in 1377, the castle was once owned by Vlad Tepes' grandfather, and the Impaler himself is said to have been imprisoned there by a 15th-century owner, King Matthias I Corvinus of Hungary.

These are tenuous connections, perhaps – but enough to earn the fortress the title of 'Dracula's Castle'.

## CHANCTONBURY RING, ENGLAND

*LORE OF GHOSTS AND OF THE DEVIL CLING TO THIS HILLTOP TREE-CLUMP.*

The Celts knew this downland hill 2000 years ago and built a hillfort on its 779 ft (237 m) summit. The earthwork bank and ditch can still be seen on the South Downs north of Worthing, and aged trees now rise tall and thin in a clump within the encircling defences. In the centre are traces of a

HAUNTED HILLTOP *Does the ghost of an ancient Druid wander about Chanctonbury Ring on England's South Downs?*

Romano-British temple. The dark silhouette of the trees and the sound of the wind gusting in their branches combine to create a haunted atmosphere, enhanced by the

### PUMPKIN HEAD

The Hallowe'en tradition of making pumpkin heads originated in the Celtic festival of Samain. The spirits of the dead were believed to return to the land of the living on the night of October 31. But the Celts venerated severed heads, and in their Hallowe'en human skulls were on view.

hill's historic pedigree. Here, if anywhere, the visitor may feel, there must be ghosts.

And so there are, say some. The spectre of a white-bearded Druid is alleged to haunt Chanctonbury Ring, searching for treasure buried within the hill. It is also said to be impossible to count the number of trees accurately, but anyone who happens upon the right number will raise the ghosts of Julius Caesar and his invading legionaries. Episodes of levitation have been reported at Chanctonbury Ring, and tradition asserts that if you run backwards round the trees seven times at midnight on Midsummer Eve, the Devil will appear.

A downland path leads south towards Cissbury Ring. The larger Iron Age fort here is poorer in supernatural lore but boasts a minor historical mystery. The flanks of the hill were intensively mined for flints by New Stone Age men, and in one

deep shaft investigators found the skeleton of a woman who had met her death at the bottom. Was it an accident, or was she pushed? No one will ever know.

## BLARNEY, IRELAND

*A STONE SAID TO CONFER THE GIFT OF ELOQUENCE ON ALL WHO KISS IT.*

Ireland's most visited castle, Blarney is a magnificent building set in gracious parkland 5 miles (8 km) north of Cork. It was erected in 1446 by the local lord, Cormac MacCarthy, and was built to last: the main walls rise to more than 85 ft (26 m) and are more than 11 ft (3.5 m) thick at the base – the length of two men placed end to end. But it is not the grandeur of the building that attracts tourists. The lure is the famous Blarney Stone set high in the battlements of the keep. Kissing the stone is said to give people smooth-talking powers of cajolery, and thousands try its efficacy every year. It is not as easy as might be imagined: to kiss the awkwardly placed stone the visitor has to hold on to an iron rail and lean over the battlements.

The tradition is thought to have originated in a comment made by Elizabeth I of England. She was overwhelmed by the non-stop chatter of Dermot MacCarthy, a 16th-century lord, who streamed with verbosity in order to prevent her from taking his estate. 'It's all Blarney, what he says, he never means,' the queen is said to have despaired. By the time of Francis Grose's 18th-century *Dictionary of the Vulgar Tongue,* 'to lick the Blarney' was already a current expression for fibbing, flattering or 'telling a marvellous story'.

CELEBRATED STONE *Blarney's most famous relic is set high in the castle battlements.*

# STRANGE
# LANDSCAPES
# 4

STEPPING STONES *The columns of the Giant's Causeway are shaped with curious symmetry.*

VIOLENT EARTH UPHEAVALS AND PATIENT FORCES OF EROSION HAVE SHAPED SOME MYSTERIOUS SCENERY AROUND THE WORLD. THE HEXAGONAL BASALT COLUMNS OF THE GIANT'S CAUSEWAY IN IRELAND, THE DREAMLIKE LIMESTONE SPIRES OF CHINA'S GUILIN HILLS, AND THE AIRY SPLENDOUR OF UTAH'S DESERT ARCHES ALL PROVOKE THOUGHTS THAT A COSMIC ARCHITECT MUST HAVE CONCEIVED THEIR DESIGN. YET THESE ARE NATURAL STRUCTURES FORMED BY THE RESTLESS ENERGIES OF A LIVING PLANET. AND TO MATCH ITS STRANGER HABITATS, THE EARTH HAS ALSO SPAWNED BIZARRE LIFE-FORMS — FROM BLIND, CAVE-DWELLING SALAMANDERS TO DESERT BEETLES THAT FEED ON FOG.

CONE HOUSES *Cave dwellings survive in Cappadocia.*

# EXTRAORDINARY FORMATIONS

*Tricks of nature have conjured up cathedrals of ice, rock ridges in the desert and geyser explosions at sea. Is it any wonder, then, that human witnesses have often discerned in such marvels the handiwork of gods, giants or sorcerers?*

In the Sahara and the other great deserts of the world, crescent-shaped creeping dunes known as *barchans* can be seen. These beautiful forms are created where the wind blows constantly from the same direction and the pattern of the dunes alters from day to day.

Change in the landscape is universal. Even granite mountains have a finite existence on a planet whose continents are adrift, whose oceans are opening and closing and whose air is in ceaseless circulation. According to scholars, the Earth has existed for 4.6 billion years, and during that time the entire mosaic of lands and seas has been shaped, destroyed and then reshaped repeatedly under the influence of cosmic gravitational and electromagnetic forces. On a day-to-day basis, meanwhile, the erosive forces of wind and weather continually resculpt the scenery so that even the most familiar

landmarks may change dramatically during an individual's lifetime.

Rock pinnacles that look like hooded men . . . caves hung with stalactite draperies . . . stone trees and surreal arches flung across arid plains . . . the most puzzling landforms can be explained in terms of natural forces acting on a changing planet. Yet it is not hard to see how they once inspired stories that mythologised their creation in supernatural terms. According to the ancients, a giant lies writhing under the grumbling mass of Mount Etna in Sicily; according to the Cheyenne, a malevolent god beats thunder drums on Devil's Tower, Wyoming. Imaginative realities helped to give shape to people's lives in past times, and they still have the power to lead us into the realm of dreams.

## EISRIESENWELT, AUSTRIA

*A MAGICAL LABYRINTH OF ICE CAVERNS, GALLERIES AND FROZEN WATERFALLS.*

Half-hidden among cliffs in the Austrian Alps south of Salzburg lie the fairytale caves of the Eisriesenwelt – the World of the Ice Giants. The full complex of galleries forms one of the most extensive cave systems in the world: exploration has revealed some 30 miles (50 km) of passageways, caverns and underground halls, and there may yet be more to be charted. The caves open at a height of 5459 ft (1664 m) in the Tennen massif, and nothing quite prepares the visitor for the frozen splendours that are revealed on arrival at the entrance.

Illuminated by the magnesium flares of the guides and the carbide lamps of the visitors is a fantastic construction of ice architecture, curtained with translucent draperies and jewelled with crystal droplets. Its frozen waterfalls, domes, pillars and other formations are up to 65 ft (20 m) thick in places, and many features have been named after characters from Norse legend, such as the Hymir Hall and the Frigg Veil. Here, too,

ICE WORLD *The interior of the Eisriesenwelt caves presents a glittering scene at the frozen heart of the Austrian Alps.*

THE BUBBLE BURSTS *The jet of boiling water at Strokkur first wells up, then explodes in an astonishing upthrusting cascade.*

are an Ice Organ, an Ice Door and an Ice Palace as well as a wall of ice layered in different strata of blue and white.

The ice adorns the cave walls for about 1/2 mile (0.8 km) from the entrance to the system, and its total volume has been estimated at more than 1 million cu ft (30 000 m³). The depth of the cave system behind the entrance is instrumental in shaping its frozen wonders. In summer, cool air from the darkest recesses is sucked out towards the entrance, but in winter the reverse occurs. The mountains' height above sea level results in very low temperatures, and wintry gusts sweep into the cave from outside. Temperatures remain well below zero even as the spring sunshine warms the snowfields outside. Melting snows then seep into the cave system, where they freeze almost instantly – whether dripping from the roof or falling in waterfalls over ledges.

## GEYSIR AND STROKKUR, ICELAND

*SEETHING JETS OF SCALDING WATER THAT BURST FROM THE EARTH'S CRUST.*

When the 19th-century English artist and craftsman William Morris visited Iceland, he made a pilgrimage to Geysir (the Gusher), the legendary site of a boiling

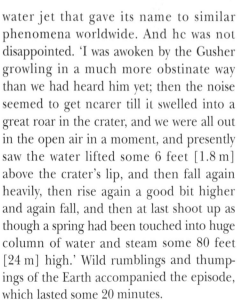

water jet that gave its name to similar phenomena worldwide. And he was not disappointed. 'I was awoken by the Gusher growling in a much more obstinate way than we had heard him yet; then the noise seemed to get nearer till it swelled into a great roar in the crater, and we were all out in the open air in a moment, and presently saw the water lifted some 6 feet [1.8 m] above the crater's lip, and then fall again heavily, then rise again a good bit higher and again fall, and then at last shoot up as though a spring had been touched into huge column of water and steam some 80 feet [24 m] high.' Wild rumblings and thumpings of the Earth accompanied the episode, which lasted some 20 minutes.

Iceland's great Geysir, a round pool 60 ft (18 m) in diameter and 4 ft (1.2 m) deep, seems to have started gushing in 1294. It could in times past be relied on to erupt several times a day, and has been known to hurl a seething jet 180 ft (55 m) into the air. However, visitors today are unlikely to be granted such a spectacle. Since 1907 the

Gusher has spouted only sporadically of its own accord, though it has been induced to perform by soap thown into the crater. This produces lighter bubbles that are more easily lofted into the air than the heavier water below. The basic problems, however, are that the heat source under the geyser seems to have diminished, and its pipe has become plugged. Nothing today is guaranteed to trigger an eruption.

Other water jets in the area are, however, obligingly active. In Iceland, super-heating of the Earth's crust as a result of volcanic action has furnished more hot springs, geysers, steam vents and mudbaths than anywhere else in the world, and although the great Geysir itself has become unreliable, it lies in a valley that grumbles with dozens of hot springs still boiling underground and staining the rocks yellow with sulphur.

Only 100 ft (30 m) away from the old Gusher is a neighbouring geyser that – though smaller – is far from exhausted.

This is Strokkur (the Churn), which boils over every 10 minutes or so in spellbinding displays of power that send a 70 ft (21 m) column of water rocketing up to the sky.

## PINNACLES DESERT, AUSTRALIA

*A PANORAMA OF FANGED ROCKS RISING SHEER FROM THE DESERT FLOOR.*

Just inland from the coast of Western Australia, in remote country lying approximately 150 miles (250 km) north of Perth, stand thousands of eroded limestone piers. The strange assembly covers an area of $1\frac{1}{2}$ sq miles (4 km²) of desert and looms so improbably from the fine yellow sand that it is hard to conceive of its being shaped by nature alone. Rising to head-height and much taller, the limestone pillars seem grouped with a solemn purpose that is emphasised by their long shadows at sunset. They recall temple ruins, or sacred megaliths like those of prehistoric Europe.

These are, however, geological formations shaped between 80 000 and 15 000 years ago by rainwater that leached lime from the upper layers of sand dunes, cementing their lower layers into soft limestone. At the time the climate was more benevolent in this part of Australia, and the dunes were cloaked with green plants whose roots insinuated themselves into an underlying layer of limestone, accelerating the leaching process. Later, drifting sands covered the vegetation and the roots decayed, leaving channels in the rock. As rainwater seeped down, these gradually widened and filled with sand. But although the softer areas of limestone eroded, the harder remnants formed pillars that were exposed to the sky when the wind blew the sand away.

PIN PRICKS *The limestone pillars of the Pinnacles Desert create an improbable, spiky landscape.*

Precisely when the sand veil was stripped off the pinnacles remains something of a mystery. The pillars do not feature in any known tradition of the Aborigines. This has led scholars to speculate that the unveiling was very recent, especially since a Dutch seaman named Abraham Leeman, who was stranded in the area in 1658, makes no reference to them in his diary. Nor were they mentioned in the chronicles of any of the region's 19th-century explorers or settlers. In fact there is no certain record of the pillars' discovery until 1956, when a local historian, Harry Turner, brought them to the world's attention. The wind still scours the area and the dunes continue to shift. One day, perhaps, the pinnacles will vanish again under the desert's yellow blanket.

## MOUNT ETNA, ITALY

*ONE OF THE WORLD'S MOST ACTIVE VOLCANOES – NICKNAMED 'I BURN'.*

'I do not think I shall ever forget the sight of Etna at sunset,' wrote the English novelist Evelyn Waugh, 'the mountain almost invisible in a blur of pastel grey, glowing on the top and then repeating its shape, as though reflected, in a wisp of grey smoke, with the whole horizon behind radiant with pink light, fading gently into a pastel grey sky. Nothing I have ever seen in Art or Nature was quite so revolting.'

The novelist's mischievous intention was to satirise the rhapsodic style of those travel writers who had written glowingly about Mediterranean landscapes in general and Mount Etna in particular. Seen from a distance at sunset, this, Europe's largest active volcano, is certainly a thing of beauty. But Etna is also a beast and at close quarters reveals its monstrous character. According to one estimate, the mountain has been active for 66 000 years, and in exploring its enormous lava dunes, strewn with slag and pockmarked with over 200 craters, the traveller might be wandering another planet.

Etna rises in east Sicily to a height of 10 902 ft (3323 m). Its name derives from the Greek *aitho* ('I burn'), and from ancient times the fiery mountain has inspired

legends. The Greeks explained Etna's mysterious rumblings by saying that Zeus had crushed the giant Typhon beneath it, and that his turning made the Earth tremble; or that the workshop of Hephaestus (the god of fire) and the Cyclops, forgers of thunderbolts, lay underneath. The Athenian dramatist Aeschylus referred to an eruption of 475 BC, while a detonation in 396 BC stopped a Carthaginian army in its tracks. Throughout the Middle Ages the mountain continued to belch out fire. The ferocious activity has continued into the 20th century, with eruptions of particular severity in 1910-11, 1928, 1950-51, and 1983.

With such a record of violence it may seem surprising that human settlements still cling to the mountainside. However, the volcanic soil on the lower slopes is so fertile that farmers continue to tend vines, orchards and olive groves here, and Catania flourishes as the second city of

LAVA FLOWS *Fiery streams of molten rock descend the slopes of Mount Etna.*

Sicily after the capital, Palermo. The moods of the volcano nonetheless dominate city life, and in the streets and squares are many monuments made from its black lava.

## THE UTAH ARCHES, UNITED STATES

*STONE ARCHES CARVED BY THE DESERT WINDS DEFY LOGIC AND GRAVITY.*

Little in the landscape mystifies the eye more than a great rock arch curving out from sea cliff or desert floor through the miracle of natural engineering. Isolated

DESERT ARCHES *Sandstone ribbons loop the parched wastes of Utah (overleaf).*

examples can be found all around the world, but more can be found in the Arches National Park, Utah, than anywhere else on Earth. Over 200 are on display here, including the world's longest rock arch, the Landscape Arch, which runs through the air like a sandstone ribbon for a breathtaking 291 ft (89 m). Each of the park's formations, moreover, has its own character, and for many visitors the show stopper is the free-standing Delicate Arch, looping up to a height of 65 ft (20 m) from the rim of a deep rock bowl, solitary and wildly improbable. Here, too, are twin arches known as The Spectacles; the Turret Arch with its natural rock tower; and the Eye of the Whale – a long slit peering out beneath a great hump of sandstone.

Freakish, fantastic, the Arches are sculpted from pale red sandstone, a grainy rock consisting of particles of quartz cemented by silica or calcium carbonate. In this part of Utah it overlies an unstable bed of salt that, over tens of millions of years, has shifted under the weight of the sandstone, causing some layers to bulge up in domes and fracture as narrow 'fins' of rock. Rain and melting snow have seeped into joints, dissolving the cement that binds the sandstone, eroding weaker patches of rock. Where the base of a fin has been worn away at the centre, a crude arch appears, and it is left to the sand-laden winds to smooth off jagged contours.

The erosion never ceases: before November 1940 a formation called Arch in the Making had an opening that was partially blocked by a huge chunk of sandstone. One cold night the sandstone block fell and shattered, vastly increasing the aperture. No longer 'in the making', the formation was renamed Skyline Arch.

## FINGAL'S CAVE, SCOTLAND

*THE ARCHITECTURE OF A SEA GROTTO IMMORTALISED BY MENDELSSOHN.*

When waves surge into this dark, pillared cavern they cause a resonant booming that can be heard outside. In Gaelic, Fingal's Cave is called Uamh Binn (Melodious Cave) – a tribute to its tuneful acoustics.

And the grotto's musical associations do not end there. In 1829 the German composer Felix Mendelssohn came to the island of Staffa by rowing boat. Approaching the famous cave, he was inspired by the tide's descending roar to jot down a melody. The brief tune appeared as the theme of his overture *The Hebrides* – better known as *Fingal's Cave.*

The island of Staffa in the Inner Hebrides is a basalt wonderland that forms part of the same geological feature as the Giant's Causeway in Ireland. Here, as on the Antrim coast, visitors can marvel at hexagonal columns and stepping stones shaped by the cooling of ancient lava flows. The whole island is basaltic and displays many bizarre formations of splayed, sagging and bending columns. The prize exhibit is Fingal's Cave, situated at the southern end of Staffa. Here the mighty fist of the tide has smashed into a forest of basalt columns, plucking out uprights to penetrate 227 ft (69 m) into the cliffs. The cave is roofed by a crust of volcanic slag that cooled more quickly than the pillars, giving it the look of a monstrous canopy flung over the uprights. On one side of the cave the stumps of shattered pillars form a natural causeway, allowing visitors access to a shadowy interior where yellow stalactites glisten against the fluted walls.

The ancient myth-makers were clearly impressed by the cave, asserting that it was created by the giant Fingal (or Fion-na-Gael). It has long been admired by scientists, too: in 1772 the great botanist and explorer, Sir Joseph Banks was staggered by its vaulted grandeur. 'Compared to this,' he wrote, 'what are all the cathedrals and the palaces built by men!' And the 19th-century

MELODIOUS GROTTO
*Basalt columns, looking like organ-pipes, flank the mouth of Fingal's Cave.*

Romantics, above all, were entranced by the cave's Gothic effect. The poets Scott, Keats, Wordsworth and Tennyson all made pilgrimages to the site; Turner did sketches of the cave. Here, supremely, was a place to stir the soul with awe of nature's mysteries. Even the Victorian statesman Sir Robert Peel, founder of the Metropolitan Police, became a poet on approaching Fingal's Cave. He was moved to write of his visit that he 'had seen the temple not made with hands, had felt the majestic swell of the ocean – the pulsation of the great Atlantic – beating in its inmost sanctuary'.

## THE DEAD SEA, ISRAEL/JORDAN

*THE WORLD'S SALTIEST BODY OF WATER, BUOYANT AND LIFELESS.*

'Then the Lord rained upon Sodom and Gomorrah brimstone and fire from the Lord out of heaven; And he overthrew those cities, and all the plain, and all the inhabitants of the cities, and that which grew upon the ground.'

In the Old Testament story of Lot, the cities of the plain were destroyed by the Lord for their sinfulness, and when Lot's wife looked back at the devastation she was turned into a pillar of salt. The Biblical cities are believed to lie today somewhere below the waters of the Dead Sea, and present-day Sedom, 4 miles (6 km) south of the Sea, takes its name from Sodom. Modern Sedom is the headquarters of a giant chemical and fertiliser industry exploiting salts and minerals from this remarkable body of water.

Lying on the Israeli-Jordanian border, the Dead Sea is renowned for its supersaltiness. Visitors who come here for health cures delight in having themselves photographed in its mysteriously buoyant waters, comfortably reading newspapers as if supported from below by unseen deckchairs. The high salinity is what permits such easy floating; the Dead Sea is some seven to eight times saltier than the world's oceans. Almost a third of its volume consists of salt and other minerals such as potash, magnesium and bromine. No fish can survive in

UPPER CRUST SALT *Salt columns stack up around the shores of Israel's Dead Sea.*

so salty a soup, which discourages waterbirds. This lifelessness accounts for the Dead Sea's name: only certain salt-loving micro-organisms can survive in it, including *Halobacterium halobium*, which flourishes through photosynthesis, absorbing light to convert water and carbon dioxide into energy-giving carbohydrates.

Covering an area of about 400 sq miles (1050 km²), the Dead Sea is not in fact a true sea but a lake, lying in an extension of East Africa's Rift Valley. At 1299 ft (396 m) below sea level it is the lowest place on the Earth's land surface and swelters during the summer at temperatures of more than 50°C (122°F). This annihilating heat has played a crucial role in shaping the Sea's bizarre characteristics. Water from the River Jordan feeds into the lake from the north, but there is no outlet for it. Instead the huge volumes of water that pour in during the wet season are lost through summertime evaporation and leave their salt-rich sediments in the lake.

The deposits are particularly conspicuous as salt cakes and crusts in the shallow southern part of the Dead Sea. Here, in centuries past, gradually rising water levels buried the Biblical Sodom. But

white salt pillars of the type that inspired the story of Lot's wife can still be seen looming up in forests underwater, forming tiny, crusty islands on the surface.

## MAMMOTH CAVE, UNITED STATES

*EERIE, AWESOME FORMATIONS OF THE LONGEST CAVE IN THE WORLD.*

In 1972 a young caver named Patricia Crowther managed to inch her way through a narrow passage in Kentucky's extensive Flint Ridge cave complex and enter another system, which turned out to be that of Mammoth Cave. By discovering the connection between the two systems, she

FROZEN NIAGARA *Stalactite draperies curtain off corners of Mammoth Cave.*

increased Mammoth's dimensions: already celebrated for its colossal size, it could now boast 144 miles (232 km) of tunnels. And more links kept on being found. In 1979 explorers found a link with neighbouring Proctor Cave, and in 1983 with Roppel Cave. By 1994 the total mapped length was 348 miles (560 km), making it by far the longest cave system in the world.

The cave owes its name to its gigantic scale rather than to the extinct elephant. It lies in a great bed of limestone laid down about 300 million years ago, and was formed by the action of water erosion. Rain filtering down through decaying vegetation became sufficiently acidic to dissolve solid limestone. Seeping down through sink-holes, it ate away at cracks and fissures, enlarging them into a labyrinth of vertical shafts, horizontal galleries and chambers, one of which – the Rotunda – is as big as the main hall of New York's Grand Central Station. When the water sank to deeper levels, the upper passages were left as dry corridors. The process is continuing to this day as the Echo River flows through Mammoth's profoundest depths, cutting out new channels.

The river, which is frequented by pale, eyeless fish, flows at a depth of about 360 ft (110 m) and owes its name to the resonance of its passages. And Mammoth Cave holds many other wonders: stalactites, stalagmites and translucent draperies fashioned by the action of mineralised water dripping from fissures in the cave roof. Where water flows across a surface, it forms flowstone instead of dripping. One result is a spectacular formation known as the Frozen Niagara, created by the water flowing across a chaos of rocks.

For contrast, there are marvels in miniature too, in the sparkling formations of gypsum, a white mineral that encrusts cave walls with snow-like deposits and sometimes crystallises as fragile formations resembling petalled flowers.

White settlers entered the cave in 1799, but they were by no means the first people to discover it. Local Indians had already explored Mammoth Cave 4000 years ago using bundles of giant cane for torches, remnants of which have survived. They mined the gypsum, which they used for ceremonial and perhaps trading purposes. In 1935, about 2 miles (3 km) in from the cave's entrance, the corpse of an Indian gypsum miner dubbed 'Lost John' was discovered; he had died about 420 BC, crushed by a 5 ton boulder that his own excavations had dislodged.

## METEOR CRATER, UNITED STATES

*A MIGHTY HOLE BLASTED FROM THE ARIZONA PLAINS BY A METEORITE.*

When the Apollo astronauts were looking for somewhere to try out their lunar roving vehicles, they came to Meteor Crater, south-west of Winslow, Arizona. For here, on the floor of the Earth's largest meteorite crater, was terrain which was very much like that of the Moon's surface, making it an ideal testing ground. The crater, which is almost circular, measures 4150 ft (1265 m) across and about 575 ft (175 m) deep, and has a rim that stands 130-155 ft (40-47 m) above the level plane of limestone and sandstone. Seen from the surrounding area it resembles a low hill, and after its discovery in 1891 it was widely mistaken for an extinct volcano. However, the man who found it, Daniel Moreau Barringer, a mining engineer and geologist from Philadelphia, correctly identified it as a meteorite crater and staked a claim to it with the intention of mining it for nickel and iron. His hopes proved fruitless as there were no minerals worth mining, but the crater is still owned by his family and is often referred to as Barringer Crater.

Scientists believe that the hole was smashed into our planet around 50 000 years ago when a 300 000 ton iron-nickel meteorite hit the ground at a speed of perhaps 45 000 mph (72 000 km/h). The explosion was titanic, having a force 1000

**LUNAR LANDSCAPE** *Moon buggies were tested in the desolate hollow of Meteor Crater in Arizona.*

times greater than that of the atomic bomb dropped on Hiroshima in 1945. While the sky blackened with the colossal tonnage of rock and Earth lofted heavenwards, iron from the shattered meteorite was strewn over an area of 6 miles (10 km) from the point of impact, in fragments ranging from pebbles to large blocks weighing hundreds of pounds.

Comparable events happen every year on Earth – though not recently on such an apocalyptic scale. A meteorite is any hunk of interplanetary debris, usually composed of iron, stone, or a mixture of the two, and often originating from a disintegrating comet or asteroid. Often no bigger than stones, they fall to Earth on average 150 times per year. On November 30, 1954, a 9 lb (4 kg) meteorite crashed through the roof of a house in Sylacauga, Alabama, bruising the occupant, a Mrs Ann Hodges, on the arm and hip. She entered the record books as the only person to have been injured by a meteorite.

## LAKE VANDA, ANTARCTICA

*A NATURAL SOLAR HEATER IN*
*THE DRY VALLEYS OF A POLAR WASTE.*

Almost everything about Lake Vanda seems wrong. For one thing, it is fed by a river that flows inland from the sea, not towards it as most of the world's rivers do. For another, the lake has fresh water in its upper layers and salty water below them. Lastly – and most remarkably – it is frozen at the surface but gets increasingly warmer lower down, attaining a luxurious 25°C (77°F) at the bottom.

ANTARCTIC PUZZLE  *A*
*surveyor investigates Lake*
*Vanda in the Dry Valleys.*

---

## SITES OF COSMIC COLLISION

When a meteorite falls towards the Earth, it often arrives as a fiery mass due to the increasing resistance that it meets as it encounters the denser levels of the Earth's atmosphere. While kinetic energy is transformed into heat, eddies of air behind the meteorite produce a terrifying thundering sound, and the meteorite will often disintegrate with a loud explosion. These startling phenomena did not go unnoticed by ancient man. Awestruck peoples worldwide were convinced that meteors – trails of light in the sky – and the burning meteorites that caused them came from the gods, and stones from the sky were venerated in many ancient cults. The Black Stone of the Kaaba in Mecca is just one example; a meteorite was honoured by the Greeks at Delphi;

others were cherished in Rome and ancient Mexico.

Supernatural associations, however, long caused scientists to be sceptical of meteorites' heavenly origins. The great 18th-century French chemist Antoine Lavoisier was one doubter. 'There are no stones in the sky,' he told the Academy of Sciences, 'therefore stones cannot fall from the sky.' Even when investigating a 7 lb (3 kg) meteorite that dropped with a loud explosion on Luce in Maine, France, he remained sceptical, suggesting that the stone was probably unearthed by lightning.

It was only after 1803, when a shower of stones fell from the sky at l'Aigle, not far from the French capital, that the Paris academy began to give credence to meteorites – the rest of the scientific world

gradually followed suit. Meteor Crater in Arizona is the largest crater definitely known to have been formed by a meteorite. Other notable examples survive in Australia, where the Henbury Craters comprise a cluster of 12 saucer-shaped depressions formed by a meteorite that broke up on approaching the Earth's surface. The impact occurred some 4700 years ago, and the Aboriginal name 'sun walk fire devil rock' suggests the event may have had human witnesses. Earlier in prehistory the planet was scarred by mightier collisions. Gosse Bluff in Australia is a rock-rimmed crater over 2 1/2 miles (4 km) across, formed by the impact of a comet – a mass of cosmic ice and dust – but the collision happened 130 million years ago when there were only dinosaurs for witnesses.

---

The lake lies in Antarctica's Dry Valleys, strange glacier-gouged troughs in the McMurdo Sound region where no rain has fallen in 2 million years. The rockscape left after the glaciers departed remains bare because its sun-warmed surface evaporates much of the winter snow, and cold, dry winds blow away any residue, resulting in the largest continuous areas of ice-free land in Antarctica. Caught in its stony embrace, Lake Vanda is fed by the Onyx River, the only sizable watercourse in Antarctica. Its

source is a coastal glacier where melting ice in summer causes the river to flow inland and replenish the 250 ft (75 m) deep lake.

For much of the rest of the year an ice layer some 13 ft (4 m) thick covers the surface of the lake. When water evaporates from the top, the dissolved salts are forced to the bottom, which explains why the depths are saline but the surface waters are drinkable. The warmer temperatures at the lower depths result from an extraordinary effect of the ice, which acts like a greenhouse under the Antarctic sun. As the ice freezes underneath and evaporates from the top, the ice crystals become vertically aligned. They act like tubes transmitting sunlight to the water below, and Lake Vanda becomes a huge solar heater.

## GUILIN HILLS, CHINA

*A DREAMSCAPE OF STEEPLY RISING*
*HILLS, INSPIRATION FOR MANY ARTISTS.*

'I often did paintings of the Guilin hills and sent them to my friends, but few believed what they saw. There is no point arguing with them,' wrote Fan Chengda, a Chinese author of the Song Dynasty (AD 960-1279).

The scenery around the town of Guilin in southern China has qualities of strangeness and beauty that belong more to the world of romance than to that of reality. From the green paddy fields along the Li Jiang River, the limestone hills rise in abrupt, fantastic cones and domes that float in misty silhouette against the skyline, some rearing up almost vertically 330 ft (100 m) from the flat plain.

The extraordinary scenery has been celebrated for centuries by Chinese poets, one of whom, Han Yu (AD 768-834), likened the Guilin hills to 'blue jade hairpins'. Painters have loved them too, and the hills were so often depicted on scrolls that they have come to furnish many Westerners with a stereotypical image of the wonders of the Chinese landscape.

Inevitably, folklore has an explanation for the scenery. Long ago, legend tells, the people of this province were threatened by flooding from the South Sea. To save them, one of the Immortals decided to move all the hills from the north of the province to the south to form a sea wall. He did this by turning the hills into goats, which he allowed to wander seawards. However, as the creatures flocked over the Guilin plain a strange gust of wind swept over them, and the goats turned back into hills, remaining immobilised to this day en route for a destination they never reached.

It is a pleasing tale that reflects how out of place the tall hills appear in their flat landscape. Geology has a different explanation, however. About 300 million years ago the Guilin region, consisting of a bed of limestone formed by layers of sediment, lay under the ocean. An upheaval in the Earth's crust caused the bed to buckle upwards, emerging above sea level where it formed hilly terrain exposed to the elements. Rainwater seeped into the limestone, carving out subterranean channels and caves whose eventual collapse helps to explain the almost vertical slopes of the Guilin landscape.

Stunted trees cloak the hills today, clutching precariously at all but the steepest rock faces. Many of the peaks have such strong personalities as landforms that they have acquired names to match, such as Solitary Beauty Peak, Hill of Folded Colours, Camel Hill and Climbing Tortoise. The arrangement of the Seven Star Crags resembles the pattern of the constellation of the Great Bear, and the Seven Star Cave is famous for its stalagmites and stalactites. The hills are, in fact, riddled with caves and grottoes that hold considerable fascination in their own right. Here, for example, is the Reed Flute Cave, fabled through the exploits of the mythical Monkey King. And here, too, is the famous Dragon Refuge Cave containing hundreds of carved inscriptions, some over 1600 years old.

**DREAMLIKE BEAUTY** *China's Guilin Hills have captivated countless poets and painters over the centuries.*

On the gently flowing river, further interest is provided by the bamboo boats, whose fishermen use trained cormorants to make their catch. And with such attractions it is no wonder that the visitors come to Guilin in great numbers: 350 000 foreigners every year, and far more Chinese (among whom it is especially popular with honeymoon couples). Nevertheless, the hills are big enough to soak up the influx. The limestone towers cover a 75 mile (120 km) stretch of the Li Jung River, and in their brooding silence they continue to convey a sense of mystery unmatched by many other landscapes on Earth.

## ROTORUA, NEW ZEALAND

*A HUGE BED OF PRESSURISED STEAM*
*WITH MUD POOLS AND BOILING GEYSERS.*

Hissing acid gases cause strange mists to swirl over the waters of Lake Rotorua on New Zealand's North Island. The whole area steams with hot springs, geysers and

STEAM UP *A geyser spouts at Rotorua. Maori tap the heat to warm their homes.*

pools of heaving, plopping mud, for Rotorua lies in an extremely unstable volcanic zone where the water underground is heated by molten rock.

The subterranean bed of steam and hot water has created a mysterious landscape where the earth often rumbles disquietingly underfoot. Yet it is also beneficial to humans: local Maori have long heated their homes using the hot pools as well as washing and even cooking in them. Since 1940 water from them has been used to heat Rotorua's public buildings as well as some private homes. The North Island's geothermal resources have also been used to generate electricity. But the hot pools also have traditional ritual and social importance. Here in times past people would bathe to purify themselves before any important ceremony – or simply meet to pass the time of day. In 1847, when John Johnson, an English doctor, visited Rotorua, he found about 150 people of every age and both sexes enjoying the waters, including old men smoking their morning pipes and young mothers suckling children at the breast. 'But the strangest scene of all was a row of young men sitting up to

their necks in water, in front of whom was squatted a man who was asking questions, which were answered by the posse in full chorus. I found on enquiry that these were a set of young novitiates aspiring to an entrance into the Christian field, who were repeating the ten commandments to their teacher as an initiatory rite.'

The stench of hydrogen sulphide – the odour of rotten eggs – everywhere loads Rotorua's air, and savage eruptions have sometimes afflicted the region. In 1886, for example, nearby Mount Tarawera suddenly detonated in an explosion that buried three villages and caused 153 deaths. Yet Rotorua is also a place of wonder and beauty, with the exotic colours of volcanic mineral pools and the drama of geysers such as Pohutu, which is capable of throwing a column of scalding water some 100 ft (30 m) up into the air.

## THE GIANT'S CAUSEWAY, NORTHERN IRELAND

*ASTONISHING BASALT PILLARS THAT*
*MARCH FROM SHORE CLIFFS TO THE SEA.*

'A remnant of chaos' is how the English Victorian novelist William Makepeace Thackeray described this extraordinary coastland, suggesting that it must be left

STEPPING STONES *The Giant's Causeway resembles a raised footpath built in ancient times by monstrous hands.*

# LIMESTONE — THE MYSTERY MAKER

Eerie stalactite caverns, improbable sinkholes, subterranean passages and rivers that flow underground . . . these are just a few of the oddities associated with limestone country worldwide. And the varied wonderlands all derive

**LIMESTONE PAVEMENT** *One of many bizarre formations in Malham Cove, Yorkshire.*

their existence from the simple fact that the rock dissolves in water. Limestone derives from the shells and skeletons of numberless millions of sea creatures, which sank and formed beds on the seafloor aeons ago. The Earth's upheavals brought the beds up above sea level, where they were vulnerable to erosion by the elements. Water, in particular, is the culprit: issuing from rain and streams it filters down into the bed, following the natural joints. And because it becomes acidic after absorbing carbon dioxide gas from the air and soil, it eats away at the fabric of the rock.

In limestone country a stream may disappear down a vertically eroded

fissure to run for miles along a horizontal fault as an underground river. When it sinks to a still deeper level, dry galleries, caves and shafts are left. Stalagmites appear as lime (calcium carbonate) from dripping water accumulates on a cave floor. Lime left on the roof, meanwhile, accumulates as stalactites, and sometimes a hanging stalactite may extend downwards to meet an upgrowing stalagmite so that a pillar appears, extending from floor to ceiling.

Limestone areas typified by sink holes and underground drainage are known as karst regions, after the Karst region of Yugoslavia where these features are well developed. But they are seen all around the world; wherever water runs into limestone, curiosities are likely to occur, and they are never so

**CAVE HANGINGS** *Stalactites hang from the ceiling of a Tasmanian cave.*

mystifying as when the eroding streams vanish, leaving their handiwork to baffle the eye.

---

over from the time of the Creation. Ireland's only World Heritage Site, the Giant's Causeway is among the planet's most remarkable rock formations, consisting of some 37 000 dark basalt columns stacked beneath the dizzying cliffs of northern Antrim.

It is their geometry that most surprises. The columns are polygons – symmetrical figures with equal sides and interior angles – that appear to have been laid out by some supernatural architect. Indeed, folklore asserts that these are stepping stones put here by the giant Finn MacCool to make a walkway to Scotland. (Similar columns emerge from the sea on the Scottish island of Staffa, and Fingal's Cave there owes its name to the giant Fingal, who is the Scots' Finn.) A touching version of the tale describes how Finn wrought the wonder so that the woman of his dreams – a giantess on Staffa – could reach him without getting her feet wet.

Hard-headed science offers a different explanation. According to geologists, the fabric of the Causeway issued from the bowels of the Earth some 60 million years ago in repeated outpourings of volcanic lava. As the molten basalt cooled, it

contracted at such an even rate that the solidifying rock cracked according to a strict geometry. The basalt columns average 18 in (46 cm) across and are mostly hexagonal (six-sided), though figures with four, five, seven and eight sides can also be seen.

The compact body was later eroded by Ice Age glaciers, and by the hammering Atlantic surf. Segments were ripped from the mass to create a generally stepped appearance, but in some places towering columns can still be seen. Elongated pipe-like pillars rise sheer from the sea in a formation known as the Giant's Organ, for example. Elsewhere along the cliffs the basalt has produced weird structures that have been given names such as the Giant's Pot Lid, the Wishing Chair, the Key Stone, the Harp and the Coffin.

In 1588 a formation known as the Chimney Tops was mistaken for Dunluce Castle, farther to the west, by seamen of the Spanish Armada, who consequently fired upon it. W.M. Thackeray, who visited the Causeway in 1842, was told that another Armada ship had been wrecked off the Causeway coast. He took the story for 'a parcel of legends', but it turned out to be

perfectly true: in 1967 an underwater search revealed the wreck of the *Girona* – the largest vessel in the entire Armada. The ship was carrying a large amount of treasure, which has been recovered from the seabed and is now on display at the Ulster Museum in Belfast.

## ULURU (AYERS ROCK), AUSTRALIA

*MYSTICAL SANDSTONE MONOLITH, SYMBOL OF AUSTRALIA'S RED CENTRE.*

At the heart of Australia is a vast desert region, scoured by dust storms, where daytime temperatures can soar to more than 40°C (104°F). It is called the Red Centre after the characteristic colour conferred on the landscape by iron in the rock, which oxidises when exposed to the air. And here, looming massively from an arid plain in the Northern Territory, stands Uluru (formerly known as Ayers Rock). No other geological formation on Earth has a more strange and compelling personality than Uluru. Rising abruptly to 1142 ft (348 m) above the flat scrubland, it is more than 5½ miles (9 km) around the base.

This is reckoned to be one of the world's biggest monoliths, or single rocks, but size alone does not account for its powerful presence. It is a mystical thing which, like a gigantic sandstone chameleon, changes colour with its environment through the day. Shading between beige, amber and terracotta in daylight, it becomes at sunset a glowing crimson ember, deepening to darkest purple with the gathering dusk.

The rock began to form some 600 million years ago. Subsequent movements of the Earth tilted this sandy conglomerate through more than 70 degrees, and today

**SACRED HEART** *Looming up from the surrounding desert, Uluru in central Australia is venerated by the Aborigines.*

the greater body of the formation lies underground; like an iceberg it offers only a small proportion of its full volume to the eye. Sand-blasting by desert winds helped to smooth its contours, and the rock has also been eroded by occasional bursts of heavy rainfall, which cause water to hurtle with an awesome roar down gullies in its flanks. Sandstone debris from the main mass litters the ground around, and the run-off nourishes scrubby vegetation such as eucalyptus, acacia and desert oak. The rains also feed more than eight waterholes, one of which is reliable for most of the year. Called Mutitjulu (formerly Maggie Springs), it is shaded by walls of rock on three sides so that evaporation occurs slowly.

The rock takes its name from the Yankunytjatjara Aboriginal word *Uluru*, the name of a waterhole on the rock's summit.

It was formerly named after Sir Henry Ayers, a 19th-century premier of South Australia. For the local Anangu people, who were here long before the Europeans, it is a place of great sanctity, shaped in far distant times when beings of immense power wandered the land.

Caves within the rock are decorated with rock paintings, and every cliff and boulder is imbued with significance. So, for example, an upthrust of sandstone on the north-eastern side is thought to be the devil dingo Kurpany, who has also left his footprints in the form of cavities in the rock below. A stone slab leaning against the north-eastern flank is Ngaltawaia, the ceremonial pole of the mythological Mala (Hare-Wallaby) men who were in conflict with Kurpany's makers, the Wintalka or Mulga Seed men; a neighbouring boulder

is Lunpa, a Kingfisher woman who was travelling with the Mala woman. The waters of Mutitjulu are refilled when Wanampi, another totemic being, regurgitates what he has swallowed.

Aboriginal beliefs concerning the rock's significance are contained in the concept called Tjukurpa, a complex system of thought that incorporates ancient tribal religion and law. And although a tourist complex with hotels, lodges and campsites has been constructed only 14 miles (23 km) from the monolith, the maintenance of the rock remains a sacred duty of the local Aborigines, to whom its ownership was restored in 1985. They have run the surrounding National Park jointly with the Australian Nature Conservation Agency since then. The National Park was recognised as part of the World Heritage in 1989.

## DEATH VALLEY, UNITED STATES

*A DESERT REALM WHERE STONES SEEM TO MOVE OF THEIR OWN ACCORD.*

Among enthusiasts for paranormal phenomena, California's Death Valley is well known as the site of a dry lakebed called the Racetrack Playa. At 3 miles (5 km) long, it has long mystified visitors because of the rocks scattered across it that appear to have moved, leaving shallow trails behind them in the parched clay. No one has seen them move, but there is ample photographic evidence of the trails. Explanations for this have ranged from the effect of the Earth's magnetism, sun-spots and lunar influence to intervention by extraterrestrials.

HOT SPOT *Extreme temperatures in Death Valley have created a forsaken landscape of desiccated canyons, salt flats and dunes. The desert floor cracks in the shattering heat.*

Most geologists believe that high winds cause the stones to slide when rainstorms lubricate the Racetrack's concrete-hard surface with slippery mud. However, rocks

### VAMPIRE FANGS

Vampire Peak in South Dakota, United States, owes its name to the fang-like twin spires of hardened volcanic ash that provided pioneering settlers travelling across the continent with a distinctive landmark. However, on November 22, 1950, one of the fangs fell away during a thunderstorm, and the natural processes of erosion are stripping the other fang down by an average of 6 in (15 cm) per year.

sometimes zigzag or even angle back on themselves; moreover, the force of the wind must be exceptional, for although some of the stones are mere pebbles, others are large boulders weighing several hundred pounds.

A combination of gale-force winds, rain – and possibly winter ice – remains the most plausible explanation, but a favourable set of circumstances must be relatively rare. Death Valley is so dry that in some years not a drop of rain falls; too much rain, on the other hand, would bog the stones down instead of propelling them across the *playa* (evaporated lake).

The hottest, driest and lowest region in North America, Death Valley is a place where the visitor may expect uncanny phenomena. The desert takes the form of a geological depression of salt flats and sand dunes in eastern California. Baking temperatures are routine during the summer months, and an awesome 55°C (134°F) was once recorded at Furnace Creek. With such harsh extremes of temperature it is not surprising that the region had a bad reputation among early settlers.

Death Valley was given its name by a party of gold prospectors who narrowly escaped dying there of thirst in 1849. Place names within the Valley suggest sinister associations, too. The lowest point, for example, is called Badwater; it lies 282 ft (86 m) below sea level and was given its name by a surveyor whose mule refused to

STONE TREES *Tree trunks strew the Petrified Forest as if tumbled from a giant log pile.*

drink there. Deadman Pass and Dry Bone Canyon are no more welcoming, while an area of salt towers and brine pools at the salt-caked heart of the Valley goes by the name of the Devil's Golf Course.

## ARIZONA'S PETRIFIED FOREST, UNITED STATES

*TERRAIN STREWN WITH REMNANTS OF FALLEN CONIFERS TURNED TO STONE.*

In the lore of the Navajos who frequent this dry wilderness, the stone tree trunks are the bones of the giant Yietso. To the Paiute Indians they are the arrow shafts of the thunder god Shinauv. The Petrified Forest National Park in the United States contains the world's largest collection of petrified timbers, and even in a sceptical age that has lost faith in tribal gods and giants there can be no denying the marvellous strangeness of the natural forces that shaped them.

The Petrified Forest lies in a region of north-eastern Arizona known as the Painted Desert after the bands of brilliantly coloured rock that adorn the contorted landscape. About 225 million years ago this was a lush

### EARTH PILLARS

For sheer comedy no geological formations rival the earth pillars seen at various sites around the world, and particularly in the Tyrol, where boulders are balanced like hats atop slender pinnacles. Rain falling on boulder clay has shaped these creations. While downpours wash much of the earth away, stray rocks in the bed act like umbrellas to screen off the rain's eroding force and the pillar survives with its protective capping.

swampland threaded by rivers winding northwards towards a now-vanished sea.

Dinosaurs moved among the tree ferns and cycads of the marshes, while the drier uplands around were stacked with large conifers. The tallest among these was a 100 ft (30 m) pine known as *Araucarioxylon arizonicum*, which grew to 8 ft (2.5 m) or more in trunk diameter. This was the species that accounted for most of the present-day park's petrified wonders.

When the great trees fell, titanic floods sometimes carried them down from the hills to the marshes, where they accumulated at river bends and sandbars. Before long the log jams were covered by layers of sediment that arrested decay by cutting off oxygen. Thus embalmed, the trees underwent a metamorphosis. Water leached silica from volcanic ash in the sediment, and it soaked in turn into the trees, crystallising in the form of quartz inside the cell walls and reproducing both the external shape and the internal structure of the original trees. Over the course of time the organic matter was entirely replaced by invasive minerals; in this way the pines became stone trees. Earth tremors later snapped their brittle trunks, accounting for the log-like look of many pieces today.

It only remained for the natural processes of erosion to wear away their soft rock covering and reveal them to the Arizona sky. They litter the landscape today, from a distance resembling tumbled stacks of firewood. Closer inspection, however, reveals that the logs are rock hard and

MONSTROUS GROTTO *These strange formations at Lang's Cave come from the vast Gunung Mulu complex.*

glisten with the rainbow colours of the quartz. In some cases the invasive minerals have crystallised to stud the trees with semi-precious stones.

## GUNUNG MULU CAVES, MALAYSIA

*THE WORLD'S LARGEST CAVERN*
*REACHES INTO REMOTE HILLS.*

Bats in clouds of hundreds of thousands burst at dusk from the mouth of Deer Cave deep in the Malaysian jungle, the foul stench of guano, their accumulated excrement, loading the cave's humid air. Yet there are wonders too: three tremendous waterfalls drop from a height of 623 ft (190 m) to the floor at the cave's entrance.

The setting is a remote, rain-drenched limestone ridge adjoining the mountain of Gunung Mulu in north Sarawak, on the island of Borneo. From a summit of 7795 ft (2376 m), rivers hurtle down among huge trees and gorges and have, over millennia, eroded caves of gigantic proportions in the porous limestone. The Clearwater Cave, for example, meanders for 32 miles (51 km) into the hills; that places it among the world's longest cave passages. Threaded through by a river, festooned with stalagmites and stalactites, it is an eerie domain of blind snakes and translucent crabs that

### UNDERGROUND LIFE

One of the modern world's more startling statistics is that 40 million Chinese people still live in caves. In addition, Stone Age troglodytes survive in Sri Lanka, Sulawesi and the Philippines. To escape the heat of southern Tunisia, Berbers of the Matmata area have cut out houses from the soft local rock. Former leper caves on Crete were colonised by hippies in the 1960s; Guadix in Spain has a population of 10-20 000 gipsy cave-dwellers.

have adapted to the lightless environment. A mile or so from the entrance, sunlight suddenly pours through a hole in the roof, but beyond this lies nothing but miles of pitch-black corridor.

DANCING PEAKS *Patagonia's Paine Horns surge like waves in a restless sea.*

Lost under the jungle canopy, the Gunung Mulu caves were not seen by Western eyes until 1978, when the area was designated a national park and a party of British explorers was sent in to investigate. In 1981, while investigating Good Luck Cave, they discovered the astonishing Sarawak Chamber. Some 230 ft (70 m) high, it covers a ground area the size of 16 soccer pitches and is strewn with boulders as big as houses. This proved to be the largest cave chamber known to the world, its area being six times that of the previous record-holder: Carlsbad Cavern, New Mexico.

## PATAGONIA, ARGENTINA/CHILE

*A COLD, HIGH DESERT AT ONE*
*OF THE ENDS OF THE EARTH.*

'One day, without anyone expecting it, we saw a giant, who was on the shore of the sea, quite naked, and was dancing and leaping, and singing, and whilst singing he put

the sand and dust on his head . . . He was so tall that the tallest of us only came up to his waist.' So wrote a member of an expedition headed by the Portuguese navigator Ferdinand Magellan. In 1520, during the first circumnavigation of the world, he and his men skirted the coast of Patagonia in southern South America and recorded a description of colossal inhabitants. The area owes its name to the Spanish term for the occupants, *patagones*, meaning 'big feet', and the notion that Patagonia was a place of giants became lodged in the Western mind. Charles Darwin, exploring the region in 1834, met a group of the fabled Patagonians and reported a cordial reception from them. 'Their height appears greater than it really is, from their large guanaco (llama) mantles, their long flowing hair, and general figure.' They were tall, certainly, averaging about 6 ft (1.8 m), but by no means superhuman in stature.

Yet, although the myth of giants has been dispelled, an air of strangeness still lingers about this chill tableland at the southern tip of mainland South America. As remote in its way as Timbuktu, and remembered as the place to which the outlaws Butch Cassidy and the Sundance Kid fled with Etta, Patagonia has long exerted a unique appeal for travel writers.

The cold desert plateau occupies the four southernmost provinces of Argentina, with part of southern Chile besides, covering 300 000 sq miles (770 000 km²) south of the Negro and Limay Rivers. Much of this is bleak, sheep-nibbled pampas, forest, rock and ice. The inhospitable terrain peaks at Andean heights where icebergs are hatched in mountain waters by glaciers descending from a perpetual ice cap. Gale-torn seas at the Strait of Magellan divide the continent from the archipelago of Tierra del Fuego,

COLOUR CODING  *Tinted lakes at Keli Mutu are believed to contain the souls of sinners and innocents.*

and at the mainland's southernmost extremity the shore is riven by deep ravines. Here Darwin found scenes of extreme desolation. Despite the gales, not a breath of wind stirred in the hollows: 'So gloomy, cold and wet was every part, that not even the fungi, mosses or ferns could flourish. In the valleys it was scarcely possible to crawl along, they were so completely barricaded by great mouldering trunks, which had fallen down in every direction.'

Patagonia remains one of the Earth's last frontiers, though its spectacular mountain scenery draws increasing numbers of hardier travellers. The sharply twisted spurs of rock known as the Paine Horns, in particular, are a magnet, forming a citadel of swirling granite spires at the tail end of the Andes. They are among the most striking examples of a glacier-carved landscape to

be found anywhere in the world. Wind-battered and remote as it is, Patagonia nonetheless contains landscapes of exhilarating beauty.

## KELI MUTU, INDONESIA

*A TRIO OF LAKES – EACH A DIFFERENT COLOUR – IN ADJACENT CRATERS.*

Indonesia's tropical isles boast a fantastic diversity of landscapes, from coral reefs to dense jungles, verdant paddy fields to lowering volcanoes. It is appropriate, then, that a leading tourist attraction should be a multicoloured trio of crater lakes. Separated by low ridges, the three tinted waters lie on the island of Flores and are cupped in three craters of Keli Mutu, an extinct volcano rising to some 5200 ft (1600 m) above sea level.

The lakes are quite distinct in colour – black, green and pale turquoise lying alongside one another so that, seen from the air, they might be children's paint pots. The islanders believe that the black lake contains the souls of sorcerers, the green is the home of sinners and the palest holds the souls of virgins and infants.

It has been suggested that the waters are tinted by minerals dissolved from the crater basins. The lakes change colour from time to time – not long ago they were black, maroon and blue – which presumably results from the water dissolving different mineral layers at varying rates, or from changes in acidity. Whatever the cause, it is fair to assume that Keli Mutu's present tints are only temporary; through the bizarre chemistry of the craters, a new colour scheme will be on view before long.

## DEVIL'S TOWER, UNITED STATES

*A TREE-STUMP OF A MOUNTAIN, WHERE CLOSE ENCOUNTERS WAS FILMED.*

One of the most exciting moments in recent cinema history was the climactic landing of the alien mothership in Steven Spielberg's *Close Encounters of the Third Kind*

FILM SET *The mysterious Devil's Tower was immortalised by Hollywood's Steven Spielberg.*

### ROBOT MONSTER

If the stony wilderness of Bronson Canyon in California has a mysteriously familiar look, it is because innumerable Hollywood movies were filmed there. The makers of low-budget science fiction offerings had a particular fondness for this setting. Bronson Canyon is the location of *Robot Monster* (1953), widely rated as one of the worst films of all time, in which the monstrous extraterrestrial was played by a man in a gorilla suit, wearing a deep-sea diver's helmet.

(1977). An intricately detailed model spacecraft lit by 160 000 volts of electricity was used to create extraterrestrial effects.

The landing site, however, is real enough – a weird, sawn-off rock pillar that looms to 869 ft (265 m) over the Belle Fourche River in the plains country of Wyoming. This is the Devil's Tower, a freak mountain so fantastic in appearance that it was always destined to spawn legends.

Geological evidence indicates that the Tower's formation began about 50 million years ago, when immensities of molten rock surged up through the sedimentary bed of an ancient inland sea. The mass of volcanic material gradually cooled, hardened and contracted within the sedimentary bed, and in the process it also cracked to form a bundled stack of columns.

Over the millions of years that followed, the softer sedimentary rock surrounding the volcanic core was gradually worn away by weather and the swirling waters of the Belle Fourche River, and the volcanic upthrust was exposed to the sky.

Plants such as grasses and moss grow on top of the tower, and it has become home to birds and chipmunks, while parts of it have become covered in lichens. It was the first natural feature in the US to be designated a national monument, in 1906.

# GREAT RIFT VALLEY, EAST AFRICA

The scar of the Great Rift Valley so marks the planet that on a clear day it is visible from the Moon. Running for some 4000 miles (6400 km) from the Dead Sea south as far as Mozambique, the Rift is a geological depression caused by continental drift. Two plates in the planet's crust are moving apart, splitting with such force that gaps 25-35 miles (40-56 km) wide have appeared. These are the rift valleys, floored by terrain that has dropped below the level of the land on either side.

The entire length of the Great Rift Valley is prone to earthquakes and volcanoes, and in some places the troughs are hard to discern because the sunken land has been filled with lava flows. In southern

**DEEP RIFT** *The Great Rift Valley, created by the movement of two of the Earth's plates, cuts a swathe many miles wide across Kenya from north to south. A succession of shallow lakes and extinct volcanoes occupies the valley floor.*

Kenya, however, the effects are dramatic, with cliffs rising thousands of feet above the arid basins. Shallow soda lakes dot the valley floors like unstrung necklace beads, providing some of the strangest animal habitats in the world. The soda comes from volcanic ash that has been spewed out by eruptions, and it stains some waters white. Others are tinted pea-green or pink by the algae (microscopic water plants) and tiny shrimp-like creatures that thrive in the alkaline soup.

These species in turn attract millions of flamingos, who carpet the surface with their own dazzling colours. The birds feed on algae or insect larvae, which they scoop up and filter through their beaks, held upside down, and they owe their pink plumage to the pigments in their foodstuff.

Edged by hot springs, steaming geysers and scorching soda sludge, the bizarre East African lakes are overlooked by some equally remarkable volcanoes. One of these, Ol Doinyo Lengai, spits out washing soda (sodium carbonate) when it erupts. Known to the Masai tribespeople as the 'Mountain of God', the rumbling colossus often appears snow-capped at the summit. In reality, though, the whiteness comes from the pale ash of its eruptions.

The curious landscape of the Great Rift Valley, however, forms only a part of its mystique, for the great land-rip is also regarded as the cradle of humankind – the place where scientists have uncovered the earliest clues to the mystery of human evolution. Some 5 million years ago, it is thought, there was little difference in development between our ape-like ancestors and the gorilla or chimpanzee. In a bed of volcanic ash at Laetoli in Tanzania, however, anthropologists have found a trail of footprints belonging, perhaps, to two adults and a child. These are the oldest hominid footprints known, and they prove that our ancestors were walking upright nearly 4 million years ago.

From Hadar in Ethiopia comes the partial skeleton of what was probably a female, whom scholars have nicknamed 'Lucy'. Her remains provide some corroborating evidence, for her hip and thigh bones suggest that she must have walked upright, like a human being. Skulls of the first tool user, *Homo habilis*, which are nearly 2 million years old, were found on the east side of Lake Turkana and at Olduvai Gorge in Tanzania. These and many other finds from the Rift are much earlier than any yielded by Europe, Asia or the Americas.

**ENCRUSTED LAKE** *Soda and algae form on the surface of Lake Natron.*

**DEEP ESCARPMENT** *In places the valley is several thousand feet deep, and vegetation on the valley floor is barely discernible.*

Why should the East African Rift have triggered developments found nowhere else on Earth? Although scholars are reluctant to commit themselves, a popular theory focuses on the effects of the continental drift. The Rift started to form some 20-15 million years ago as a portion of East Africa began to tug away from the main body of the continent. The mountains of the Kenyan and Ethiopian highlands were thrown up in the process, forming a watershed that robbed the valley of rainfall and created dry grasslands there. Separated from the apestock of the damp, equatorial forests, our ancestors had to adapt to life in the open savannah. It has even been suggested that they first learned to rear on their hind legs in order to see over the long grasses (as other prairie creatures such as South Africa's meerkat do). In all events, it seems less likely that our ancestors 'came down from the trees' than that the Rift caused the trees to desert them.

# SCENERY OF THE BIZARRE

*The mystery of some bizarre places depends as much on its inhabitants as on its landscape features. How, for example, can living things exist in the sand sea of the Namib Desert, or the pitch blackness of the Postonja caves?*

A blind salamander whose skin is so pale that it dies in sunlight might seem poorly adapted to the remorseless struggle for existence on Earth. Yet creatures like the olm, as it is known, have flourished and reproduced themselves in the caves of Postonja, in the Julian Alps of Slovenia, for millions of years. Adapted to living in a pitch-black, subterranean environment, they prey on small worms and can survive for long periods without feeding. The olm does not experience sunlight and so needs no protection from it. Eyes are superfluous (though they were present at some stage of the creature's evolution – in the adult olm they are hidden by a covering of skin, but they are clearly visible in the young larvae).

The olm is just one of some 3 to 10 million different kinds of plants and animals in the world. Religion and myth have

long tended to explain them as if they were produced, ready-made, by divine hands. But most scientists now believe that they evolved very gradually from primitive organic ingredients in the thick, soupy fog of gases that surrounded the primeval Earth 3.5 billion years ago.

Following different evolutionary paths, organisms colonised the sea, the land and the air, becoming amazingly varied and specialised as they developed. It was about 350 million years ago that our own lungfish-like ancestors emerged from the Earth's fecund waters, using their bony front fins to clamber onto beaches and seek their fortunes on dry land.

Life flourishes today in almost every corner of the world, including some of its most remote and inaccessible places: from lightless caverns to waterless desert dunes, from Antarctic ice packs to volcanic vents in

the ocean floor. Nature acts ruthlessly to eradicate those species that are unable to make use of a habitat's opportunities. But where living things have found a comfortable niche, they will continue to exploit it until new influences are exerted. The principle applies not only to the flora and fauna; it operates just as much in the human world, where cave-dwelling and Stone Age lifestyles survive even in the age of satellite communications.

## NAMIB DESERT, NAMIBIA

*MONSTROUS, MIGRATING SAND DUNES*
*WHERE LIFE IS SUPPORTED BY FOG.*

Some of the world's tallest dunes move incessantly across the Namib Desert, forming a huge, drifting geometry of sand soaring to as high as 1000 ft (300 m) at the desert's heart at Sossusvlei. This is a place of surreal grandeur, reducing human figures to insect proportions against its gigantic hard-edged planes and sweeping angular curves. Shaded with hues of rose-pink and tangerine, the dunes might have been sculpted and tinted by some celestial Picasso. Yet they are nature's work, formed from the coral-coloured sands of the South Atlantic coast, driven ashore by the waves and whipped inland by the wind.

The Namib Desert stretches the length

SEA OF SAND *Tirelessly shaping and reshaping itself under the lashing of the wind, the Namib Desert is in permanent flux. Below: the* Welwitschia *plant has learnt to adapt.*

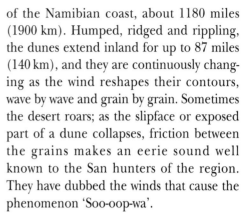

of the Namibian coast, about 1180 miles (1900 km). Humped, ridged and rippling, the dunes extend inland for up to 87 miles (140 km), and they are continuously changing as the wind reshapes their contours, wave by wave and grain by grain. Sometimes the desert roars; as the slipface or exposed part of a dune collapses, friction between the grains makes an eerie sound well known to the San hunters of the region. They have dubbed the winds that cause the phenomenon 'Soo-oop-wa'.

As the groaning dunes advance northwards, one of their strangest encounters is with the Kuiseb River. Here the strong currents of the watercourse flush the sand away. Satellite photography reveals a split landscape where the arc of the river appears to stop the sand dead in its tracks. Scientists studying dune movements have found, however, that the sand is gradually winning a long war with the river. Inching remorselessly forward and spilling into the watercourse, it threatens to choke the Kuiseb, which is retreating northwards. Studying a big dune at Gobabeb, the geologist John Ward has estimated that it would take about 250 years to cross the river: 'In human terms it may not be moving very fast, but in geological time it's galloping!'

Unstable and waterless, the dunes might seem the least promising place on Earth to support living things, yet the Namib Desert has a rich ecosystem. It relies almost exclusively on fog, which rolls in from the South Atlantic and veils the dunes with precious moisture. This nourishes unusual plants such as the fantastically shaped *Welwitschia mirabilis*, whose splayed leaves trap the mist in their myriad pores and feed a carrot-like base. Almost incredibly, a *Welwitschia* can live for 1000 years or more. Other prodigies include the black onymacris beetle, which scales the crest of a dune when fog arrives and stands on its head so that moisture condensing on its back will trickle in droplets into its mouth. The Namib golden mole is a rare, sightless mammal whose eyelids grow together at an early age to keep sand out; burrowing into the dunes, it relies on hearing to locate food such as insect larva. The 'dancing white lady' spider escapes predators by folding its legs and cartwheeling down the dunes; to conceal its burrow it drapes a web camouflaged with sand over the entrance. Snakes, lizards and scorpions also form part of the Namib's community, all testifying to the adaptability of the planet's life forms.

## SURTSEY, ICELAND

*ISLAND THAT BURST FROM THE OCEAN IN 1963 IN A FLOOD OF LIQUID BASALT.*

The island takes its name from Surtr, the Fire Giant, who was venerated by Norse peoples as the forebear of the gods. Invisible and incomprehensible, he was both the First Cause and Destroyer of all things. 'Surtr rides first, and both before and behind him flames burning fire. His sword outshines the sun itself,' a 13th-century text proclaims.

Although Surtsey's name has ancient roots, its origin is very recent. The island astonished the world by bursting from the sea in November 1963 in a storm of volcanic eruptions. The event occurred off

**DEBUT APPEARANCE** *The volcanic isle of Surtsey emerges from the sea.*

the south coast of Iceland, some 12 miles (20 km) from the Westman Islands, where rumbling seas, lava floods and a vast plume of smoke advertised the birth of a new land on Earth. The disturbances lasted several months, during which time an island 490 ft (150 m) high and about 1 sq mile (2.5 km²) came into being. When the smoke cleared and the grumbling died away, scientists discovered a grey-brown monster rising out of the ocean, scoured by wind-blown sand and scattered with pumice and black cinders. Within the main crater was a round hole about 1 ft (30 cm) in diameter; this was the throat of the volcano that coughed Surtsey onto the world map.

Edged by brittle lava cliffs and a beach of volcanic ash, Surtsey is no one's idea of a paradise island. Yet for naturalists it has always had a unique fascination. Only months after the eruptions ceased, living things had begun to colonise Surtsey's forbidding terrain. From seeds carried by wind, water and birds came flowering plants: first to bloom was the sea rocket, *Cakile maritima*, a bushy lover of sand and shingle, bearing smooth, fleshy leaves and white or lilac flowers. Later came the seaside sandwort, *Honkenya peploides*, growing in large patches whose yellowish-

green leaves crowd together on stems that are often almost buried in the sand. Grey mosses began to tuft the very crater of the volcano. Midges appeared and settled in order to reproduce. Stray butterflies graced the bleak island, and fulmars nested here in crevices and on cliff ledges.

Surtsey offers scientists a rare opportunity to watch dead rock come alive, to record the first arrivals, to study what perishes and what endures. A small custodian's hut is about the only sign of human presence; to avoid any possible contamination the island has been declared a sanctuary, and permission to visit is granted to very few people. This, after all, is a place where the mystery of life is unfolding – a single stray footstep could destroy an organism of future importance to the ecology of the Fire Giant's isle.

## BALIEM VALLEY, IRIAN JAYA

*VALLEY OF FARMER-WARRIORS, UNSEEN BY WESTERNERS BEFORE 1938.*

*Terra incognita*, or unknown land, is a term that can be applied to only a few remaining parts of the Earth. But travellers flying across Irian Jaya (Indonesian New Guinea) can still see great patches of territory marked on the flight map 'Relief Data Incomplete'. Here are inaccessible swathes of swamp and mountain containing some of the last outposts of Stone Age peoples. Head-hunting was still practised in many areas until recently; when 23-year-old Michael Rockefeller, the son of the New York Governor, disappeared in 1961 in the territory of the notorious Asmat people, it was widely speculated that he had fallen victim to the gruesome custom.

The coastal Asmats were known to the West as far back as 1770, when Captain Cook's landing party was driven off with volleys of arrows. But until the coming of aviation the home of the Dani people in the interior still existed in secret isolation. Their domain is the Baliem Valley some 5000 ft (1500 m) up in the Central Highlands, and it was on June 23, 1938, that an American adventurer, Richard Archbold, became the first outsider to set eyes on it. Gazing from

the windows of his Catalina flying boat he discovered a beautiful green oasis scattered with huts with rose rising from them and neatly planted with sweet potato vines laid out, as a later flyer would say, 'in chequerboard squares as perfectly formed as farmlands of the Snake Valley in Idaho'.

Exploration revealed an extraordinary lost world of Stone Age farmers who went clad in feathered headdresses, with ivory boars' tusks piercing their nostrils. The men also wore huge penis sheaths – grotesque to European eyes – while the women wore grass skirts. So cut off were the Dani in their mountain fastness that, although they used cowrie shells for currency, they had no concept of the sea. Metal was also unknown to them: stone axes, boar's tusk scrapers, wooden digging sticks and bamboo knives served them for implements. Their diet consisted almost entirely of sweet potatoes, which they farmed with efficient

**LOST WORLD** *Dani villages in the Baliem Valley were still living in the Stone Age until the 1930s. A Dani warrior (right) is clad in traditional garb, with a boar's tusk piercing his nostrils.*

irrigation, leaving plenty of time for the village men to engage in their favourite pastime: ritual warfare with other villages. These were chiefly exhibitionistic encounters that involved much aggressive posturing and trading of insults by warriors smeared with pig grease. Their long spears and bows and arrows rarely caused battlefield deaths.

Over 50 years after contact was made with the outside world, life in the Baliem Valley is modified but not wholly changed. The feathers and penis sheaths, the sweet potato diet – and the occasional ritual battle – are still features of everyday life.

Nor have ancient beliefs died out. The world of the Dani is one haunted by the spirits of the landscape and of ancestors, where the desiccated corpses of important tribesmen are still revered for supernatural reasons. Akima Village in the Baliem Valley has become particularly celebrated for the crumpled, smoke-blackened mummy of Werapak Elosorek, a warrior, which is brought out and displayed for the benefit of visitors' cameras.

## MARIANA TRENCH, PACIFIC OCEAN

*THE DEEPEST SPOT ON EARTH – A COLD RAVINE BEYOND THE REACH OF THE SUN*

'We have reached the abyssal zone, the timeless world of eternal darkness,' the Swiss physicist Auguste Piccard reported to his escort ships. The date was January 23,

1960, and Piccard was sealed up with Donald Walsh of the US Navy inside the steel cabin of his deep-sea submersible, the *Trieste*. The vessel, known as a bathyscaph, had just attained a level of about 3280 ft (1000 m) below the surface, so deep that the Sun's rays cannot penetrate it. The craft grew colder – in the abyssal zone temperatures never rise above 4°C (39°F) – and their journey was only just beginning.

Piccard and Walsh were the first men to descend to the bottom of the Mariana Trench, a curving rift on the sea floor near Guam in the north-western Pacific Ocean that lies at the margin of one of the Earth's plates. Its lowest spot, the Challenger Deep, was discovered by HM Survey Ship *Challenger* in 1951, and marks the deepest spot in the oceans. At 36 198 ft (11 033 m) below the surface of the sea it is a place of unimaginable depth, plunging further towards the bowels of the Earth than Mount Everest rises above it. (If Mount Everest were placed in the Challenger Deep, there would be 1 mile – 1.6 km – of water between the top of the mountain and the ocean's surface.)

Descending at the rate of about 3 ft (1 m) per second, the explorers travelled for almost four hours without reaching the bottom, and twice noticed tiny leaks in their cabin. These were anxious moments, for if the thick steel walls should crack and allow water to rush in, certain death would result. However, the sheer pressure of water on the cabin sealed the leaks, and eventually the echo sounders started to register the ocean floor.

The vessel touched down at 35 823 ft (10 919 m), not far short of the ultimate low point. Here the water was exerting a crushing pressure of 200 000

**STRANGE WORLD** *Underwater exploration has revealed mysterious forms of life.*

tons on their vessel. Outside, through the thick Plexiglas viewport, lay the planet's basement floor, a sludgy bed of sediment lit by the *Trieste*'s headlights. For a place so mysterious and inaccessible it was remark-

### THE OLDEST PLANTS

The Dry Valleys of Antarctica contain some of the oldest living plants known on Earth. Some of the specialised lichens adapted to the bitterly cold, barren rockscape are reckoned to be at least 10 000 years old.

ably nondescript, but the explorers did notice a flatfish gazing back at them with bulging eyes. Almost incredibly, life had adapted to the black depth and extreme pressure of the ultimate abyss.

Claiming the ocean bed for science and humanity, Piccard and Walsh remained on

the floor of the Challenger Deep for some 20 minutes before beginning the ascent. Completing a mission as remarkable in its way as the conquest of Everest, the two men broke surface safely after 8 hours and 35 minutes underwater.

## CAPPADOCIA, TURKEY

*BIZARRE CONES OF VOLCANIC ROCK, HOME TO CAVE-DWELLERS.*

In the region of central Turkey known as Cappadocia are fantastic landscapes of cone-shaped rocks as strange as any geological formations on Earth, and they have been made even more outlandish by the fact that they have human occupants. The tapering rocks are riddled with doors and windows that seem to gaze back at the visitor like the features of hooded giants.

Cappadocia is an area south-east of Ankara where volcanic action some 8 million

**WEIRD HABITAT** *Goreme in Cappadocia boasts some remarkable rock formations. Cone-dwellings like those at Uchisar (right) make them seem even more grotesque.*

years ago produced a vast outpouring of tuff – a soft rock consolidated from the ash thrown out by eruptions. It formed an extensive plateau 4000 ft (1220 m) thick in some places, but was easily eroded by wind, snow and rainwater that streamed over its surface, cutting out mazes of gullies and ravines. As these deepened and widened over the millennia, they left conical hills between their V-shaped incisions. These are the tuff cones seen today, and they range in height from 50 to 300 ft (15-90 m).

Easily weathered, the tuff is also soft enough to be worked with a knife. As far back as 4000 BC people began cutting out

cave-dwellings, and these became warren-like as the excavators tunnelled ever deeper into the hills, also burrowing downwards to make subterranean refuges. Cappadocia was an early retreat of the dispersed Christians – St Peter's first letter was written to the Cappadocians – and in the 4th century AD the cave systems became highly elaborate as the faithful hid here in numbers from their persecutors. Entrances were placed high in the cones and were reached by rope ladders that could be withdrawn for security. Finger and toe-holds were chipped out of perilous rock faces, allowing adepts to reach up to ten storeys.

Meanwhile the underground labyrinths expanded into subterranean cities, with ventilation shafts, communal kitchens, wells, wine vats and stables. For defence there were secret guardrooms, blind passages and trap doors. At Derinkuyu and Kaymakli many thousands of people could withstand siege by rolling large stone discs across tunnel entrances.

In the 13th century, under a tolerant Turkish administration, around 30 000 Christians inhabited the area, worshipping at more than 300 subterranean chapels and monasteries. In the Goreme Valley many of these can still be seen, including one monastic complex decorated with fine 10th-century frescoes. In addition, among the rock cones there are many lonely abodes of hermits, with chimney-like shafts running up the middle (known locally as 'fairy chimneys' from a superstition that they are frequented by spirits). Typically, the shaft led up to a solitary cell and chapel, with a carved stone bed and cupboards, and a ledge for a cooking stove.

Although a fear that the caves may be haunted has dissuaded some from taking up residence, many of Cappadocia's rock-cut homes are still inhabited by the region's farming people, who live much as other Turkish peasants do. Ozkonak is the largest of the underground cities still functioning, while the picturesque village of Urgup, with

cliff houses and cones around a large pumice hummock, attracts many tourists – the redness of its rock only increases the strangeness of its unearthly architecture.

## POSTONJA CAVES, SLOVENIA

*INCREDIBLE LIMESTONE DOMAIN OF A BLIND 'HUMAN FISH'.*

During the 1600s, river flooding washed some unusual creatures out of a limestone mountain range in Slovenia. Eyeless and ghostly white, with broad, flat heads and narrow snouts, the reptilian animals were up to 1 ft (30 cm) long, with limbs that strangely resembled miniature human hands and feet. Taken for baby dragons – or 'human fish' – the mysterious creatures won further attention in 1689 when a dwelling place was discovered in the subterranean lake of the Grotto of the Maddalena, deep among the spectacular caves of Postonja. Scientists were to identify them as a rare species of exclusively aquatic salamander, officially named *Proteus anguinus* and more commonly known as the olm. Adapted to living in pitch-black waters below the Earth's surface, these cave-dwellers were helpless above ground. Those washed from the caverns quickly died in the daylight, for their unpigmented skin could not withstand the sun's rays.

Still a rarity, the olm has since been found in several underground lakes and streams in southern Austria and north-eastern Italy. But Postonja remains the place most closely associated with the dragon children, and its caves provide a fittingly marvellous setting for the grotesques. A miniature train today carries visitors into the vast labyrinth, which forms one of the finest limestone cave systems in Europe. The entrance gallery has walls that are smoke-blackened from World War Two fighting, when Partisans sabotaged a German fuel dump, but beyond it the train swerves

UNDERGROUND LAKE
*Postonja's subterranean waters provide a habitat for the sightless olm.*

through dank, illuminated corridors deep into the mountain, where the caves and the galleries display fantastic stalactite and stalagmite formations. The names evoke something of their appearance – The Tortoises, The Mummies, The Haystacks. Here are billowing curtains and draperies of fine-spun limestone, fluted walls that recall some mighty church organ, and colonnades formed from pillars of rock.

The largest cave in the system is the awesome Concert Hall, 3 miles (5 km) into the mountain and 120 ft (37 m) high, which has accommodated several hundred people for musical events. It houses a restaurant

VOLCANO ISLAND *Tristan da Cunha's inhabitants cannot escape the volcano's shadow.*

and even a special post office where visitors can post cards from the bowels of the mountain. Not far away are pools in the rocks containing living specimens of the extraordinary olm. Silent, primeval, the olm was here aeons before humans penetrated the mountain fastness. In all probability the sightless dragon children have inhabited Postonja for 80 million years.

## TRISTAN DA CUNHA, SOUTH ATLANTIC

*THE MOST REMOTE INHABITED PLACE ON EARTH.*

The world's loneliest people, it has been said, inhabit Tristan. A mere pinprick on the map of the South Atlantic, the tiny island lies 1320 miles (2120 km) from its nearest inhabited neighbour, St Helena. Tristan is one of a group of four islands that together make up the British dependency of Tristan da Cunha, but the other three are uninhabited; Tristan itself boasts no teeming multitude.

Only 40 sq miles (104 km²) in extent, the island is formed almost entirely by one large cone volcano whose peak is often cloud-covered. The cloud can descend to form an umbrella over the whole island, even when the immense ocean skies are blue. But a mild climate, good fishing and farmable land help to explain why Tristan attracted permanent settlement. Discovered in 1506 by the Portuguese, the island acquired the nucleus of a community in 1815 when a temporary garrison was placed on it to prevent any attempt to rescue the French emperor Napoleon, imprisoned on St Helena after Waterloo. Their descendants, later settlers and shipwrecked sailors, all formed the basis of a settled population living in thatched crofters' cottages walled

with volcanic tuff. To this day they take pride in a tranquil lifestyle and a 19th-century form of spoken English. The islanders' quietness was disturbed in 1961, when Tristan's 6760 ft (2060 m) volcano unexpectedly erupted. The population was evacuated to Britain and did not return until two years later.

Lost in the blue vastness of the Atlantic, Tristan's human population has a curious enough story. The island's interest is enhanced, however, by the migration pattern of the great shearwater (*Puffinus gravis*). Known to birdwatchers as a regular autumn visitor to the northerly seas of Europe, this remarkable species breeds only on the Tristan da Cunha group. The evolution of this migration pattern is a mystery, but, as if

VOLCANIC ACTIVITY *The Sierra Negra volcano in the Galápagos Islands is home to thousands of giant tortoises, who mate in the crater.*

to compensate for the tiny human population, 4 million great shearwaters nest on Tristan da Cunha every year.

## GALAPAGOS ISLANDS, PACIFIC OCEAN

*VOLCANIC ISLANDS THAT GAVE UNIQUE INSIGHTS INTO THE MYSTERY OF LIFE.*

In 1994 newspapers carried bizarre headlines that proclaimed 'Galápagos wildfire threatens giant tortoises'. The menace was a forest fire sweeping towards the Sierra

Negra volcano, home to about 6000 tortoises. In the event, disaster was averted, but the threat helped to focus attention once again on one of the world's most remarkable animal habitats.

The Galápagos Islands have been called the strangest islands on Earth. A volcanic group lying on the equator 680 miles (1100 km) west of Ecuador, they possess a lunar landscape of grey lava cliffs, cactus desert and dense mangrove swamps whose oddity is enhanced by a unique wildlife. Most of the reptiles and over half the flora are unique to the islands, which the first Spanish explorers referred to as Las Encantadas – The Bewitched – on account of their curious life forms.

In 1835 the islands were visited by Charles Darwin during the historic voyage of the *Beagle* when the English naturalist collected evidence that influenced his theories on natural selection. Darwin proposed that forces such as competition, climate and disease acting on an animal population resulted in the survival of those best fitted to the environment. On the Galápagos Islands he identified 26 kinds of land-birds, all of which – except one finch – were to be found nowhere else. Here were also flightless cormorants, iguanas of nightmarish appearance and monstrous tortoises, some so heavy that it took eight men to lift them off the ground.

Darwin concluded that the isolated habitat had allowed species on the Galápagos to develop in directions impossible in a normal environment with the usual predators, notably man. Encountering human beings, the Galápagos animals proved astonishingly fearless – too much so for their own good. The docile, gigantic tortoises in particular were at one time butchered in numbers for their meat; now an endangered species, they are protected by the fact that most of the Galápagos has been declared a national park.

It is, above all, the giant tortoise, *Testudo nigra*, that confers a primeval strangeness on the islands. With a lifespan of probably 100 years, males can grow to up to 600 lb (272 kg), and ten different races of the giants forage among the volcanic slopes,

some with low-slung shells that enable them to graze on plants near the ground, others with longer necks and saddle-shaped shells that allow them to reach taller vegetation. In February, when the rains come, the great tortoises start to lumber up to the volcanic summit of Isla Isabela to mate in the muddy wallows of the craters. An infinitely strange, guttural roaring fills the sulphurous air as the males try to mount the females. Huge and cumbersome, however, the giant tortoise is not an adept suitor and often fails to mate successfully – another reason why it is almost extinct.

## THE FLORIDA EVERGLADES, UNITED STATES

*ALLIGATORS HAUNT THE MANGROVE SWAMPS OF THIS WETLAND WILDERNESS.*

A brooding melancholy hangs over the waterlogged marshes and mangrove labyrinths of the Everglades. The largest area of subtropical wilderness in the United States, this mysterious region forms a national park covering some 2188 sq miles (5667 km$^2$) of swamp and forest in southern Florida. The mystery lies partly in its uncanny flatness. The featureless expanses of saw grass – a plant that takes its name from the saw-toothed edges of its blades – are the predominant characteristics of the scenery. Green, yellow or brown according to the season, the grassy seas stretch as far as the eye can see. Jungle-covered islands and forested ridges break the level panorama, but there is a nothingness in the far distance, as if some giant hand had stripped the hills from the horizon to leave the landscape bereft.

The Everglades are fed by an extraordinarily broad, shallow river flowing south from Lake Okeechobee. About 50 miles (80 km) wide, it moves across a porous limestone bed to Florida Bay at a dawdling rate of no more than 1 ft (30 cm) a minute. Ridges in the rock rise just high enough above the water to support pine groves and islands of trees known as hammocks. Closer to the sea, thickets of red mangrove flourish in the brackish swamps, the plants' roots arching weirdly above the water to draw

oxygen from the open air. Tangled and interlocking, the roots form barriers that collect so much silt and plant debris that new islands arise to block the passage of the sluggish water. Here is a steamy otherworld haunted by both exotic and nightmarish creatures. Snowy egrets, great white herons and rare roseate spoonbills grace the swamp with their elegant plumage, while rainbow-coloured fish dart beneath the surface. Yet these delightful denizens share the water with snakes, and with blunt-snouted alligators that grow to an awesome 16 ft (5 m) long. The mangrove swamps are

**LURKING DANGER** *Cypress trees in the Everglades swamps stand up to their ankles in water. Left: an alligator loiters among the reeds and lily pads in Shark Valley.*

also the sole remaining habitat of the American crocodile, distinguished by its longer, thinner snout.

When taken as a whole, the Everglades form a naturalist's paradise, boasting some 900 plant species and more than 600 kinds of animal, from tree frogs, jumping spiders and zebra butterflies to the elusive Florida panther. This, though, is a paradise in jeopardy. For decades now, its waters have been dirtied and diverted by upstream development. The flocks of wading birds – once so vast that they blotted out the sun – have dwindled, and rare animals are losing critical habitats. Under pressure from environmentalists a clean-up has begun, but it remains to be seen whether the Everglades will prove everlasting.

# INDEX

# PICTURE CREDITS

T=top; C=centre; B=bottom; R=right; L=left

**3** Peter Arnold Inc. **6** Sygma. **7** Simon Marsden. **8** Mirror Syndication, BL. **8-9** The Bridgeman Art Library/The British Museum. **10** National Maritime Museum, TL; Hulton Deutsch Collection, BL. **10-11** Peter Arnold Inc/Malcolm Kirk. **11** NHPA/Robert Thompson, TR. **12** Fortean Picture Library, TR, TC, BL. **13** Bruce Coleman Ltd/J. Zwaenepoel, CL; Images Colour Library, BR. **14** DRK Photo/Tom Bean. **15** David Harris/Courtesy Israeli Antique Authority, TR, CR. **16** Porterfield/Chickering/Photo Researchers/OSF, TL; AKG London, CL. **17** Douglas Peebles. **18** Bruce Coleman Ltd/Gerald Cubitt, T; Topham Picture Source, BR. **19** J. Allan Cash. **20** Robert Harding Picture Library/Adam Woolfitt, TR, C. **21** Bruce Coleman Inc/E. Degginger. **22-23** Sienna Artworks Limited, London. **24** Bruce Coleman Ltd/Dr Stephen Coyne. **25** Sienna Artworks Limited, London. **26-27** Bruce Coleman Ltd/Brian Henderson. **27** Bruce Coleman/Roger Coggan. **28-29** Robert Harding Picture Library/Robert Frerck, T. **28** The Mansell Collection, C. **29** Charles Walker/Images Colour Library. **30** Comstock/Dr Georg Gerster, TL; AKG London/Erich Lessing, TC. **31** Comstock. **32-33** Sienna Artworks Limited, London. **33** Robert Harding Picture Library. **34** Robert Harding Picture Library, CR, B. **35** Sienna Artworks Limited, London. **36** Richard Packwood/OSF, T; David Harris/Courtesy Israeli Antique Authority, C. **37** Sienna Artworks Limited, London, T; Sygma, BL. **38** Werner Forman Archive/The Egyptian Museum, Cairo, BL; Werner Forman Archive/Egyptian Museum, Berlin, CL. **39** Hulton Deutsch Collection. **40** Greg Evans International. **41** Charles Walker/Images Colour Library, TL; Sylvia Cordaiy Photo Library/Colin Hoskins, BR. **42-43** DRK Photo. **44** Tom Stack & Associates/Lorran Meares, TL; Royal Geographical Society/Chris Caldicote, BR. **45** Comstock/Dr Georg Gerster. **46** The Hutchison Collection/Christine Pemberton, TC. **46-47** Comstock, B. **47** Charles Walker/Images Colour Library. **48** Comstock, BL; Robert

Harding Picture Library/Adam Woolfitt, CB. **49** Sienna Artworks Limited, London. T; Bruce Coleman Inc/J. Carton, BL. **50** Museum of the Rockies/Bruce Selyem, TL; Comstock/Dr Georg Gerster, BR. **51** Robert Harding Picture Library. **52** Sygma, CL; Robert Harding Picture Library/Explorer, B. **53** Sienna Artworks Limited, London. **54** Novosti Photo Library, TL; Frank Sponer Pictures, BR. **55** Sienna Artworks Limited, London, TR; Rex Features, BL. **56** J. Allan Cash, BL; The Bridgeman Art Library/Giraudon, BR. **57** J. Allan Cash. **58** C. Helliwell/OSF, TL; Topham Picturepoint, BL. **59** Aspect Picture Library/Larry Burrows, TL; Peter Arnold Inc, BR. **60** Aspect Picture Library/Phil Conrad. **61** Peter Arnold Inc. **62** Robert Harding Picture Library/Robert Frerck, BL; Mike Slater/OSF, CR. **63** Robert Harding Picture Library/Gavin Hellier. **64-65** Robert Harding Picture Library/Adina Tovy. **65** Mireille Vautier, TL; AKG London, BR. **66** Robert Harding Picture Library. **67** Aspect Picture Library/Larry Burrows, TR, B. **68** Mireille Vautier, TC. **68-69** Michael Gogden/OSF. **70** Peter Arnold Inc, TR; Pierre Tetrel/Photo Researchers/OSF, BL. **71** Robert Harding Picture Library. **72** Telegraph Colour Library, BL. **72-73** Telegraph Colour Library. **74** Michael Holford, TL; Terry Harris, TR. **75** John Watney. **76-77** Photo Researchers/OSF. **77** Magnum Photos/B.Barbey, TR. **78** Mireille Vautier, BL, BR. **79** Bavaria Bildagentur/Gerd Krauskopf. **80** Comstock, TL; Fortean Picture Library, B. **81** Peter Arnold Inc/Fritz Prenzel, TR; Tom Stack & Associates, BR. **82** Magnum Photos/Don McCullin. **83** Magnum Photos/Raghu Rai, TC; LifeFile/Graham Buchan, BR. **84** Zefa. **85** Royal Geographical Society. **86** Tom & Pat Leeson/Photo Researchers/OSF. **87** The Hutchison Library/J. Pate, BL; J. Allan Cash, BR. **88** Comstock. **89** Lowell Georgia/Photo Researchers/OSF. **90** Nik Wheeler, BL; Photo Researchers/OSF, C. **91** Magnum Photos, TL; The Bridgeman Art Library/Christie's, London, TR. **92** Magnum Photos/Ara Guler. **93** Magnum Photos/Ian Berry. **94** Sonia Halliday/F.Birch. **95** Magnum Photos/Abbas, T; Photo Researchers/OSF, BR. **96** Michael Holford, TL; Terry

Harris, CL. **97** Fortean Picture Library, TR; The Slide File, BL. **98** Zefa. **99** Robert Harding Picture Library, TL; Tony Stone Images, BR. **100** Robert Harding Picture Library. **101** International Stock Photo/Greg Johnson, TR; The Griffith Institute/Ashmolean Museum, BL. **102** Robert Harding Picture Library/Adam Woolfitt, CR, B. **103** Images Colour Library, TR; Malcolm Passingham, BR. **104** Peter Newark's American Pictures, TL; Jack Fields/Photo Researchers/OSF, BR. **105** Spencer Grant/Photo Researchers/OSF, TL; Solo Syndication, TR. **106** Comstock/Simon McBride, CL; Mary Evans Picture Library, CR; Aspect Picture Library, B. **107** Jean Loup Charmet. **108** Fortean Picture Library, TL; The Bridgeman Art Library/Lauros-Giraudon, TR; Zefa, BC. **110** Aspect Picture Library, T; Royal Geographic Society, BL; Popperfoto, BR. **111** Telegraph Colour Library. **112** Katz/Randy Taylor. **113** Katz, TL, BL; Sue Cunningham, TR. **114** Tony Stone Images/Hans Peter Werten. **115** Charles Walker/Images Colour Library, TR; Jean Loup Charmet, BL. **116** Jean Loup Charmet, TC; Mats Wibe Lund/Gardar Palsson, BR. **117** Robert Harding Picture Library/Adam Woolfitt. **118** Robert Estall, TC; Heather Angel, BR. **119** Mats Wibe Lund, CR; Mary Evans Picture Library, BR. **120** Simon Marsden; Charles Walker/Images Colour Library, BR. **121** Images Colour Library. **122** Zefa. **123** Sylvia Cordaiy Photo Library, TL; Tony Stone Images, BR. **124** Austrian Tourist Office. **125** Peter Arnold Inc, TR; Mats Wibe Lund, CR. **126** Comstock. **127** Magnum Photos/Ferdinando Scianna. **128-9** Tom Stack & Associates/Tom Algire. **130** Telegraph Colour Library. **131** Aspect Picture Library/Peter Carmichael, TR; Connie Toops, BR. **132** Photo Researchers/OSF. **133** Mountain Camera/Colin Monteath. **134-5** George Chan/Photo Researchers/OSF, B; Peter Skinner/Photo Researchers/OSF, TC; Robert Estall, BR. **136** Bruce Coleman Ltd/Chris James, TL; Telegraph Colour Library, TR. **137** Jim Steinberg/Photo Researchers/OSF. **138-9** Aspect Picture Library/Gavin Hellier. **139** Tony Stone Images/Gary Yeowell. **140** Tom Stack & Associates/John

Cancalosi, TL; NHPA/B. Jones & M. Shimlock, BR. **141** Bruce Coleman Ltd/Hans Reinhard. **142** Robert Harding Picture Library/C. Tokeley. **143** Comstock. **144** Peter Arnold Inc. **145** Bruce Coleman Ltd/Christer Fredriksson, TR; Gerry Ellis, BL. **146-7** Bruce Coleman Ltd/Gerald Cubitt. **147** Bruce Coleman Ltd/Dr Eckart Pott. **148** Mats Wibe Lund/Garclar Palsson. **149** The Hutchison Library, T; Bruce Coleman Ltd/Alain Compost, BR. **150** Al Giddings Images Unlimited, BL. **150-1** Bruce Coleman Ltd/N. Blake, T; Tony Stone Images/Peter Poulides, CR. **152** Robert Harding Picture Library/A. Waltham, BL; Frances Furlong/OSF, CR. **153** Bruce Coleman Ltd/Hans Reinhard, B; Bruce Coleman Ltd/Dieter & Mary Plage, CR. **154-5** Tony Stone Images/Jon Riley, T. **155** Comstock.

FRONT COVER: Mireille Vautier; Tom Till/DRK Photo, C.

BACK COVER: Telegraph Colour Library.

77-005-3